Eclecticism and Modern Hindu Discourse

Eclecticism and Modern Hindu Discourse

BRIAN A. HATCHER

New York • Oxford
Oxford University Press
1999

Oxford University Press

Oxford New York
Athens Auckland Bangkok Bogotá Buenos Aires Calcutta
Cape Town Chennai Dar es Salaam Delhi Florence Hong Kong Istanbul
Karachi Kuala Lumpur Madrid Melbourne Mexico City Mumbai
Nairobi Paris São Paulo Singapore Taipei Tokyo Toronto Warsaw

and associated companies in
Berlin Ibadan

Published by Oxford University Press, Inc.
198 Madison Avenue, New York, New York 10016

Library of Congress Cataloging-in-Publication Data
Hatcher, Brian A. (Brian Allison)
Eclecticism and modern Hindu discourse / Brian A. Hatcher.
p. cm.
Includes bibliographical references and index.
ISBN 0-19-512538-X
1. Hinduism—Doctrines. 2. Hinduism—Relations. 3. Syncretism (Religion)—India. I. Title.
BL1212.74.H36 1999
294.5'172—dc21 98-27348

1 3 5 7 9 8 6 4 2

Printed in the United States of America
on acid-free paper

To my mother and father—
Martha Allison Hatcher and Graham Stuart Hatcher

What do you expect of a damme *writer* of words, anyway?
Truth? Hell, you will get *contrast*, and no mistake!
—G. V. Desani

ACKNOWLEDGMENTS

When I first contemplated writing this book, I imagined I might get it done rather quickly. I envisioned it less as a magnum opus and more as a somewhat timely and provocative essay into an understudied category in the history of religions. Not surprisingly, the project took longer than I anticipated. Mostly that's to the good, since it turned out there was a great deal I needed to learn. And when I consider the help I've received along the way, I feel certain this is a better book for the time it took. Nevertheless, I fear some of my arguments will not appear as fresh or as provocative—even within the study of the religions of South Asia—as they appeared to me when I first conceived the project. That said, if this book should draw attention to the problem of eclecticism generally, or to the dynamics of Hindu eclecticism more specifically, I will feel my time has been well spent.

The idea for this book took shape over the course of several years devoted to the study of religious change in modern India, especially in nineteenth-century Bengal. Inevitably, as we read, certain words attract our attention more than others; over time, we begin to develop an almost nervous sensitivity to their presence. Eclecticism has been one such word for me. It was only a matter of time until a myriad of random sightings called out for more systematic reflection. Why has this word been applied to the likes of Rammohun Roy, Keshub Chunder Sen, and

Mahatma Gandhi? What distinguishes the valency of the word as used by a Western Indologist or by a Hindu apologist? What, if anything, does the eclecticism of the modern Hindu share with the pastiche of contemporary architects or postmodern theorists?

The first occasion I had to think out loud about such questions came when I agreed to contribute to a panel on religious change in modern India for the annual meeting of the American Academy of Religion in 1992. The paper I gave, on the eclecticism of the Indian renaissance, was built around the exercise in visualization that opens chapter 6. I'm not sure what became of the rest of that essay, but I do know that my fellow panelists—John Cort, Jack Llewellyn, and John Stratton Hawley—subsequently offered me valuable feedback as that paper grew into a long-term project. I am especially indebted to John Cort, who was eventually to read and comment on the entire manuscript for this book. In a similar fashion, the idea of viewing Swami Vivekananda against the backdrop of the 1893 Parliament of Religions, which forms the core of chapter 2, was originally presented as a paper at the Midwest American Academy of Religion in 1993. I recall that Richard Seager was present at the time and that he raised tough questions for me regarding Vivekananda's role at the parliament; I was later to find his own work on the World's Parliament extremely helpful. Later on, Steve Prothero read a draft of this chapter and I remain grateful to him for his excellent suggestions.

In the spring of 1995, a semester's leave funded by the Joyce Foundation and Illinois Wesleyan University gave me my first real opportunity to take up an in-depth study of eclecticism and modern Hindu discourse. I want to thank Alan Hodder and Tim Bryson for sharing their work with me at this crucial juncture. That spring Martin Srajek and I often took the time to lunch together. More often than not we talked about eclecticism, examining it in light of his interest in critical theory and my interest in South Asia. I have to think that this book looks the way it does in large part because of those conversations. One other conversation partner at a somewhat later stage in the writing was Matt Dusek, who took time out of his senior-year class schedule to meet regularly with me. I can't thank him enough for his careful reading, tough questions, and fertile bibliographic suggestions.

In 1995 I was fortunate to receive a Joyce Foundation Summer Travel Grant that allowed me to return briefly to Calcutta to expand upon research for chapter 5. That trip was made all the more memorable by the fact that I was able to make my way to India after first visiting Japan on a faculty enrichment trip sponsored by the Mitsubishi Motors Corporation. I remain profoundly indebted to my hosts, Wako Takayasu and Junzo Ishino, for that leg of the trip. As always, in Calcutta I received the hospitality and assistance of Uma Das Gupta of the United States Educational Foundation in India, as well as Aditi Sen of the American Institute of Indian Studies. Additionally, I benefited from the many kindnesses of Anurag Sanyal and his family. I remain especially grateful to Vijay Misra for a memorable tour around Mallick Bari.

In the spring of 1997 a University Fellows Summer Research Grant from Illinois Wesleyan supported work toward the eventual completion of the manuscript. After that, the time came for the book to find its way in the world. If it had not been for the enthusiastic support and encouragement (not to mention critical feedback) I received from Wendy Doniger, this book might never have come to be. If no other book has had a fairy godmother, this one has.

I would especially like to thank, at Oxford University Press, Cynthia Read for so eagerly endorsing the book and Cynthia Garver for seeing to its careful production. Several anonymous readers also commented on the manuscript and to all of them I am grateful; I wish I could have fully addressed all their concerns. My thanks to Jennifer Cross for preparing the index.

Many of my colleagues at Illinois Wesleyan took an interest in this project from an early date. Among them, I want to thank two especially. First, Carole Myscofski has supported my work as both department supervisor and friend. I want to thank her not just for helping me obtain financial support for my project but for modeling a commitment to excellence in teaching and scholarship. Second, Janet McNew, Provost and Dean of the Faculty, deserves my gratitude for providing funds to defray the costs associated with the final production of the book.

Finally, I come to my family—though they've been here all along. Alison and Gerrit are my mainstay; because the history of this book overlaps our history together, it is theirs as much as it is mine. Selden Richardson did the drawings for the book and I can't thank him enough. The rest of my family is in here as well, in one way or another, but I dedicate this book especially to my mother and my father. It wouldn't be fair to hold them responsible for it, but it surely wouldn't be what it is if it weren't for their love and support.

A Note on the Treatment of Names and Terms

In the treatment of Indian names I have opted for commonly accepted forms rather than orthographic accuracy—for example, Rammohun Roy, Keshub Chunder Sen, and Rajnarain Bose. However, I have endeavored to render Sanskrit and Bengali terms, as well as the titles of any works in these languages, in orthographic transliteration.

CONTENTS

Eclecticism and Modern Hindu Discourse

1

Introduction

Meaning is a shaky edifice we build out of scraps, dogmas, childhood injuries, newspaper articles, chance remarks, old films, small victories, people hated, people loved.

—Salman Rushdie

The mere fact that historians of religion have dedicated little intensive study to the phenomenon of eclecticism would seem in itself a sufficiently good reason to devote some attention to it. However, I would be less than honest if I were to say that's why I began this project. As it turns out, I started looking at the problem of eclecticism for somewhat different reasons; only subsequently did I come to the realization that this was territory that had not been heavily reconnoitered by my scholarly forebears and contemporary colleagues in the study of religion. Let me begin, then, by simply outlining the genesis of my interest in the phenomenon of eclecticism, especially in its modern Hindu manifestations. Two sets of remarks should serve to suggest how this book came to be written as it did.

First, my principal research interest for the last decade or more has been the dynamics of cultural encounter and religious change in modern India, especially colonial Bengal. In a previous book (1996) I attempted to chart the vectors of cultural change in mid-nineteenth-century Calcutta, with an eye toward accounting for some of the conditions and concerns that have shaped the development of modern Indian social and religious reform movements. In that book, the great Hindu apologists—like Rammohun Roy, Keshub Chunder Sen, and Swami Vivekananda—are present, but are kept waiting in the wings. This is because my goal in that book was primarily to fill in the setting within which the lives and work of such individuals must be situated. Nevertheless, my concern has always been to allow these figures to move to center stage. The present book affords them this opportunity. In it I invite them onstage to share with us their penchant for an eclectic mode of discourse.

Anyone even remotely familiar with the writings of Rammohun, Keshub, or Vivekananda—not to mention the religio-political rhetoric of leaders and statesmen like Mahatma Gandhi and Sarvepalli Radhakrishnan—will undoubtedly have been struck by how freely and confidently they construct their religious philosophies from the full range of the world's religious wisdom. In the most fundamental sense, this is what I call their eclecticism. In what follows I will explore ways to be more precise about this term, but here I simply want to indicate how the problem initially appeared to me. Having thus been struck, as it is hard not to be, by the eclecticism of the modern Hindu apologists, I was struck further by the realization that very few people have attempted to provide an explanation for, or interpretation of, this remarkable characteristic of modern Hindu discourse. Though the phenomenon has been right under our noses, scholars of South Asia, and historians of religion more generally, have scarcely paused to give it much scrutiny. To be sure, many have observed the eclecticism of a Rammohun or a Gandhi, but few seem to have paused long enough to ask why it is that both Rammohun and Gandhi (alongside a score of other modern Hindu apologists) share this discursive strategy.[1]

One of those who did ask this sort of question was Agehananda Bharati, who wrote an essay nearly thirty years ago on the question of eclecticism in modern Hindu apologetics (Bharati 1970). It is doubtful whether the essay fundamentally changed how anyone viewed the dynamics of modern Hindu discourse, although Bharati's use of the "pizza effect" (1970: 273)—a clever shorthand invoked to account for the popularity of reformist ideas in India only after they have been endorsed by admirers abroad—has been fairly widely cited (most recently by Flood, 1996: 267–68). Given the relative unimportance of Bharati's essay, it will no doubt strike some as odd that I shall focus here on his analysis as a foil for my own reflections. Nevertheless, I do so both because it was Bharati's essay that first sparked my interest in this phenomenon and because it seems to me that what we have in his essay is a shot across our bow. Up until now we've been steaming ahead as if it were never fired; the time has come to slow down and see what the fuss is about.

What Bharati attempted to do was to call our attention to the importance of eclecticism within modern Hindu discourse. Beyond this, he proposed a set of criteria for interpreting it. Since that time no one has bothered to ask if his is the best way or the only way to view the matter. In particular, it seems important to me to situate the genealogy of modern Hindu eclecticism within a larger framework—one that would help us understand not only its origins and significance within South Asian culture but also the history and problematics of the very categories and tools we use to discuss such eclecticism.

This brings me to my second set of remarks on the origin of this book. As a scholar of religion writing at the tail end of the twentieth century, I have seen my academy transformed by the theories and methods of poststructuralism, postmodernism, postorientalism, and postcolonialism. It would take a singular act of will to ignore what all this means for my work as a scholar and a teacher. While I can sympathize to a degree with the aversion felt by many of my peers toward the jargon of contemporary theory, I am just as impatient with such an attitude when it forecloses on the possibility for profitable reflection. In the study of South Asia, there is much that can be gained by a judicious application of recent critical theory. The present book represents my attempt to illustrate this point. In it I hope to demonstrate how the interpretation of modern Hindu discourse can profit from linking the concerns of postmodern critical theory to those of the history of religion and the study of modern South Asia.

As surely as my reading of Bharati's essay alerted me to the centrality of eclecticism in modern Hindu discourse, my reading of postmodern theory called to my attention the prominence of eclecticism (or pastiche, as it is sometimes called) within contemporary literature, theory, and the visual arts. It was precisely this discovery that sent me back to the particulars of my own research into modern Hindu discourse and to the issues that had prompted Bharati to write his essay. One author in particular who contributed greatly to my rereading of Bharati was Salman Rushdie, in whose work the concerns of postmodern theory and postcolonial identity are so tellingly dramatized. Like Bharati, Rushdie plays an important role in this book—both as unwitting instigator and as foil. The reader will presently see how I have attempted to carry out the argument of this book in the realm between these two interpretive positions. Working in this somewhat hybrid and somewhat conflicted realm, I have brought forth a book that is part intellectual history of modern India, part reflexive meditation on the practice of Indology, and part foray into contemporary critical theory. The single thread that ties these various parts together is my investigation into the meaning and interpretation of eclecticism, a concept whose history and usage is, as we shall see, itself fraught with ambiguity.

How, then, should I go about getting some purchase on this concept, for which I have thus far given only the most minimal definition?

I might begin by simply stating something that most of us will agree on at the outset, which is that the concept of eclecticism comes heavily freighted with normative baggage. Unpacking this baggage will be part of my task in what follows. Before that, however, I would like to engage an issue on which most of us will find less initial agreement: the question of how the phenomenon of eclecticism relates to the equally problematic phenomenon of syncretism. This is a difficult question. Many of us simply use the two terms as if they were synonymous, or we view eclecticism as a subset of syncretism; in either case we tend to assume that the former may be understood in light of the latter. Still others—Denis Diderot, for example—have occasionally turned things around and proposed that syncretism is in fact an apprentice to eclecticism, which suggests a rather different view of the matter (see Donini 1988: 2). Just how important is it for me to weigh in on this question? Since this is a book about eclecticism, could I not simply decree that I will not concern myself with the phenomenon of syncretism and be done with it?

I am afraid the matter cannot be put off that easily. At the very least I need to offer a brief definition of syncretism, which might serve as a rationale for my decision to treat eclecticism independently.

With respect to the meaning of syncretism, certain pieces of evidence have been much discussed: the fact that our sole reference from antiquity comes from Plutarch's reference to the Cretan's decision to unite in the face of a common enemy (e.g., *sun-kretismos*); the subsequent creation of a false etymology in Greek from *sun-kerannumi* to account for the sense of "mixing together"; the accretion to the term—notably in the Christian context—of the pejorative sense of *illegitimate* mixing, as in the corrupting of something originally pure, like the Gospel; the attempt by nineteenth-century historians of religion and twentieth-century phenomenologists of religion to use the term as a category for describing contexts of religious encounter and fusion; and the debate among more contemporary scholars as to the continued utility of a concept whose career has been so checkered.[2]

Clearly we can have little use in the history of religions for a concept of syncretism that is freighted with theological judgment; we may therefore agree fairly quickly to dispense with any usage that views the phenomenon as an attempt to water down or corrupt an authentic faith. However, even when disabused of its normative character, it proves far more difficult to reach a consensus on whether syncretism may be adopted as a meaningful descriptive category. As John Carman suggested more than thirty years ago, there is significant variation in usage even among historians of religion. Does the concept best refer solely to a context like the Hellenism of late antiquity, or can it be extended to characterize religious systems in India, China, or Japan? Is syncretism a "conscious joining together of different religions" or is it the "organic growing together of religions"?[3] Does syncretism name "an interaction of different religious forms" or a "basic religious attitude toward such interaction" (Carman 1964: 38)? Should we follow the likes of Gerardus Van der Leeuw and Joachim Wach in viewing every religion as a syncretism?

While there is something attractive about granting to syncretism the widest possible descriptive applicability, it might almost be argued that in doing so we rob the concept of its meaning. After all, if it is used to describe the process of encounter and synthesis through which all religions grow and change, then to speak of religious syncretism is something of a tautology.[4] One is pleased to find that the author of the entry on "Syncretism" in *The HarperCollins Dictionary of Religion* arrives at a similar verdict, concluding, "In view of the fact that no historically known religion has begun in a vacuum but has instead readily drawn on valuable aspects of existent traditions in which its members found meaning, one must conclude that the term at this time has little taxonomic value" (Smith 1995: 1043). Unfortunately, after reporting this conclusion, the dictionary proceeds in the very next entry to resurrect the recently deceased term in order to apply it to the case of religion in Japan. The entry, "Syncretism (Japan)," begins by announcing, "The combining of various religious forms has been a major feature of Japanese religion throughout history" (Smith 1995: 1043). But in light of the immediately preceding entry one is tempted to ask: Are Japanese religions unique in this regard? Why not the religions of China or Middle

America? The ancient world? Christianity? Buddhism? Don't we find "the combining of various religious forms" throughout all religious history? If so, wouldn't we be justified in saying that there really is no pure religion? As the general entry on syncretism only too clearly suggests, the fall into history—and thereby into syncretism—precedes creation, if you will.

For my purposes there is no need to argue this point further, but simply to use its basic logic to suggest some guidelines: (1) the historian of religion has no business using the category of syncretism as a normative category; (2) if it is to be used, then it will serve as a kind of shorthand for the idea that religions are culturally constructed and are continually transformed through "the combining of various religious forms"; and (3) if so used, then the concept should be carefully distinguished from other concepts, most notably eclecticism. That is, if syncretism is used to refer to broad processes of historical change and systemic interaction among religions, then eclecticism should be used to refer to something else. What I propose is that we use eclecticism to denote not patterns and processes of historical change, but a particular method of change—a method based on conscious selection—and the systems of criteria and classification that may (or may not) guide this method. To follow this distinction, syncretism names a historical process, while eclecticism names a method of interpretation and appropriation.

One further distinction that will be increasingly relevant as I proceed: whereas eclecticism and syncretism both operate through processes of selection, what distinguishes syncretism is the additional feature of reconciliation. That is, it is not sufficient, when speaking of syncretism, to refer only to the process of encounter and appropriation; one must also speak of merging, accommodation, or amalgamation.[5] Syncretism involves blending, synthesizing, or harmonizing; this is what lies behind the spurious etymology I mentioned above: *sun-kerannumi*. The author of the dictionary entry on syncretism in Japan apparently has this phenomenon in mind when speaking of "a more deliberate mode of syncretism" that works by claiming there is "an underlying similarity or cosmological connection between two or more traditions" (Smith 1995: 1044). The awareness of such a similarity is what justifies the attempt to merge or reconcile the traditions in question. In the case of Japanese religious history, the author cites the theory that the Shinto *kami* are the manifestion of the original nature (*honji suijaku*) of the Buddhas and Bodhisattvas.[6]

This usage is widespread, and there seems little point in trying to argue for its complete rejection. However, I would like to suggest that even in this sense the term should be used with care—not only to avoid making everything a syncretism, but more important, to avoid missing what may be the most interesting thing about how such syncretisms come about, namely, by a method of selection and classification. As the dictionary entry puts it, what drives such a process is someone's awareness of similarities or connections. I would like to suggest in what follows that it is the positing of such connections that drives the method of eclecticism. And it is this method that should be of interest to the historian of religion. Why this connection and not another? How do we, in the words of Richard Mulcaster, come to posit "the likeness of unlike things" (see Lewis 1964:1)? My contention is that by moving too quickly to the language of syncretism in such cases, we may miss out on what is most fascinating and/or problematic about this phenomenon. We may also, in some cases, perpetrate an outright error of description. In chapter 5 I shall argue that this is precisely what has happened in the case of the Bengali reformer Keshub Chunder Sen. Keshub is routinely viewed as a syncretist. However, I shall attempt to demonstrate that this not only violates his own self-understanding; it also obscures what is most interesting about his work.

By setting down these guidelines, we can begin to appreciate the need to view eclecticism in its own right. In the field of religion, at least, eclecticism more often than not appears as a rather idiosyncratic method of interpretation practiced by specific individuals and adopted by specific groups under an individual's guidance. This is simply to reiterate the view that eclecticism names a method of *conscious* selection, a method imbued with intention and purpose. Syncretism, as in Japan, cannot be so described—at least not across the board. And yet, we all too often find such a sense being given to syncretism, as in the aforementioned dictionary entry, where we read that "Shinto borrowed magic from Taoism" (Smith 1995: 1043). On the surface, this sounds as if it describes a method of conscious selection that accords with my definition of eclecticism. However, at work in such a formulation is a pernicious form of reification—nay, personification—of religion. Since when do *religions* act with a sense of intention and purpose? There will not be many in the academy who will go along with such a view of religion, except in the most casual kinds of conversation. But, then, we need to be more than casual in the way we use our categories.

Now it may well be, as the entry continues, that "religious institutions in Japan have been used ad hoc by individuals and groups for the various needs of individual and collective life" (Smith 1995: 1043). If we examine such cases we may find that these various and idiosyncratic acts deserve to be called eclectic. Few will deny that the Japanese take a pragmatic view of religion, in which what one does religiously depends on what one finds effective or personally meaningful. Thus it is routinely said that in Japan one is born Shinto and dies Buddhist. In between, one may well opt for a Christian marriage ceremony, spend some time in Zen training, or participate in one of the so-called new religions (see Reader 1991). Over time, the net result of such eclectic borrowing and ad hoc religious practice has led to the kind of merger the author of the dictionary entry wished to note between Shinto and Taoism. We may wish—if we are so wedded to the concept—to apply to this overall historical tendency the label of syncretism; but then we would no longer be speaking of eclecticism as a method of conscious selection.

One problem is that, in the broadest sense, we are all eclectics; we all make choices. This is not really the point, though. The point with eclecticism is that sometimes we make choices in remarkable ways and for apparently unlikely reasons. I am not being particularly eclectic if I choose to walk down the street on Sunday morning to worship in the Lutheran Church on the corner. I am being decidedly more eclectic if I go to church after chanting the thousand names of Viṣṇu and I return to sit *zazen* before lunch. What mark this behavior as eclectic are precisely the disjunctions and surprising juxtapositions it manifests.

To say that my behavior makes perfect sense as a lived set of choices, we do not need to invoke the concept of syncretism, with its connotations of centrifugal cohesion. My life is not a mixing bowl or a food processor. It might be better compared to a kitchen cabinet: it has a few shelves that provide hierarchy and order (though even these can be rearranged or removed). On the shelves there may be a variety of tubs, boxes, and bottles; some of these may even be nested inside others. But all these compartments and containers can be arranged countless ways, to include or be included in other containers; furthermore, containers can crack open and break, so that flour ends up in the rice and olive oil on the spice jars. The point is, I put things in these various spaces and I move them around according to my acquisitive compulsion, my discriminatory choices, and my daily needs. This is an eclectic system that incorporates disparate elements as they are, not a syncretic one that attempts to reshape those elements or reconcile them within some *tertium quid*.

And it is precisely in this apparent failure of eclectic practice to arrive at some higher synthesis that many locate its deficiency. According to this view, synthesis represents advancement, and the eclectic, by failing thus to advance, merits our condemnation or scorn. Thus we can find critics who will tell us that eclecticism "is almost the opposite of creation. Information and scholarship, on which it is based, are essentially different from deep synthesis. . . . Eclecticism does not suggest a new order of things" (Bhattacherje 1944: 3). It was precisely their attempt to create a new vision of the world that led C. S. Lewis to wax eloquent about the zeal of medieval scholars to organize, codify, synthesize, and harmonize—that is, to build "a syncretistic Model" (see Lewis 1964: 10–12).[7]

This is precisely the logic that has led some (most notably his admirers) to make a syncretist out of a reformer like Keshub. That is, if we want to say that what Keshub did by way of manipulating the teachings of Muhammad, Jesus, Buddha, and Caitanya was *creative*, then we feel compelled to label his work syncretistic. Only the critic would dare impugn Keshub's name by calling him an eclectic.[8]

It turns out, however, that Keshub viewed his work as a species of eclecticism. If one takes the time to read his speeches and writings, the operative word in them is eclecticism, not syncretism. Here is one of those troubling discoveries that suggest to us just how much baggage gets carried along in the categories we apply to those we study. If Keshub saw himself as an eclectic, then why has he been styled a syncretist? If we choose to honor his self-understanding as an eclectic, then are we sure what he meant by this term? Does it correspond to what we mean by it? Are we, for instance, going to concur in the verdict that eclecticism is uncreative? If not, then how are we going to account for its creativity? Keshub provides an excellent occasion for raising these questions, and I shall return to him when I examine the eclectic reformers of nineteenth-century Bengal. Here it is perhaps enough to be alert to the fact that eclecticism is not about abstract systems of merger and homogenization, nor is the latter alone the only way to understand creativity. What we must attend to when looking at eclecticism are methods of choice, patterns of desired connections and accepted disjunctions. We are interested not in synthesis but in selectivity—for the selectivity of the modern Hindu eclectic is a form of self-construction. And it need hardly be pointed out that self-construction is by definition a creative process.

In order to suggest how we got ourselves in such a bind with eclecticism and how we might begin to rethink the problem, I turn now to the two foils for this study, Bharati and Rushdie. As I have already indicated, my interest in the phenomenon of Hindu eclecticism developed in response to Bharati's 1970 article, "The Hindu Renaissance and its Apologetic Patterns." I therefore would like now to examine that essay. However, let me first make clear my purpose in doing so.

In many respects, Bharati's name operates in this book as a metonym for a particular mode of Indological interpretation. However, I do not credit him, nor do I blame him, for creating that paradigm. It could well be argued that his work has not been nearly as influential in shaping scholarly attitudes to modern Hindu thought as that of the German Indologist, Paul Hacker.[9] While I shall indeed have occasion to consider Hacker, the point I wish to make is that it was Bharati who happened to write an essay that problematized the phenomenon of eclecticism within modern Hindu discourse. This alone would have more than justified my foregrounding of his essay, were it not that Bharati also stands for an approach to the study of South Asia based squarely in the positivism of post–World War II social science. It is the convergence of these two facts that makes him such an apposite foil for this study. And since one of Bharati's concerns was to evaluate the effect Hindu eclecticism had on the formation of contemporary patterns of resurgent Hindu consciousness, it seems entirely appropriate, in these days of renascent Hindu nationalism, to reconsider his conclusions. I hope that all of these concerns will resonate in the reader's ear when I go on to discuss Bharati.

There is another characteristic of Bharati's work that recommends it for my purposes: the almost palpable tone of self-assurance with which he writes. Adopting the role of qualified interpreter, he was nothing if not forthright. When coupled with his wide learning and broad personal experience of India, such self-assurance meant Bharati could be both on target and offhand. The essay in question illustrates this dual tendency very nicely. In "The Hindu Renaissance and its Apologetic Patterns," Bharati combines a wide-ranging and heuristically valuable characterization of modern Hindu apologetics with a finely grained and at times downright acerbic depiction of its idiosyncrasies.

It will help here if I simply highlight the essentials of Bharati's critique of Renaissance discourse. To begin with, the Hindu Renaissance (also known as the Indian Renaissance) to which Bharati refers may be understood in two basic senses: first, as the name for the period of colonial history—beginning around the turn of the nineteenth century and running up to the attainment of Indian independence in 1947—that is associated with widespread and multiform attempts by Indian thinkers to revive, reform, and redefine the Hindu tradition; and second, as the overarching designation for a range of discursive styles and strategies ('idioms' is the term Bharati prefers) found among the urban, highly educated, typically high-caste, reformers, educators, preachers, and savants who together, if not always in unison, formulated the apologetic presentation of Hinduism during this period. In the simplest of terms, the goal of these Hindu intellectuals and religious leaders was to assert the dignity and meaningfulness of the Hindu worldview during a period marked by colonial subjugation and Christian missionary polemics. The basic presuppositions and goals of this Renaissance mode of discourse were Bharati's principal concern in his 1970 essay—just as they are mine in the present book.

Turning to the essay, I can safely say that Bharati is most on target when he zeros in on the discursive role of "one of the constantly occurring canonical quotes" of Renaissance Hinduism, namely, the Vedic mantra *ekaṃ sad viprā bahudhā vadanti* (*Ṛg Veda* 1.164.46), which he translates as "Truth is one, wise men call it by various names" (Bharati 1970: 282). This text, says Bharati, has been "milked for all its worth" in modern Hindu apologetics, its logic supposedly underwriting other quasi-canonical assertions such as "God is One, worship him universally," or (we might add) Gandhi's "All religions are true."

Bharati explains the prominence of such mantras within Hindu Renaissance discourse in terms of the "modern Indian desire for total solutions." That is, the modern Hindu desires religious answers that are "ultimately convertible into terms for *mukti* (salvation)," and anything else—be it the particularities of Indian scholastic philosophical systems or the dialectics of Western analytic philosophy—is rejected out of hand (Bharati 1970: 284). Among holistic solutions, none seem to be favored more than the revamped metaphysics of Advaita Vedānta. Bharati correctly points out that the makeover of Vedānta in Renaissance apologetics owes much to the preaching of Swami Vivekananda, and I shall certainly explore Vivekananda in some detail in chapter 3. Suffice it to say here that for Bharati, a consideration of the rhetoric of Vivekananda (and of a host of lesser gurus of the colonial and postcolonial era) provides us with enough evidence to hand down an indictment of Renaissance apologetics on the charge of rampant eclecticism. As he puts it,

> Antagonism toward scholastic, traditional, and primary-source-oriented Hinduism goes so far that non-Hindu religious idioms are frequently preferred to orthodox parlance. Simplistic statements about the love of Christ, the renunciation of Jesus, or *sūfī* Islamic mystics occur rather more frequently in Renaissance talk than reference to brahmin masters of the commentary. Not only the Ramakrishna Mission Centers, but most of the less prominent *āśrams* which cater to the modern apologist refer to the Cross with greater ease than to the theological categories of Sanskrit commentary. (Bharati 1970: 285)

In bringing forward his charge that a "hypertrophic eclecticism pervades the apologetic of modern Hinduism," Bharati wished to call attention to the modern Hindu's unrestrained passion for connecting just about anything and everything to the Hindu view of life (1970: 285). Thus Vivekananda's Hinduism appeals to the Buddha and to Thomas à Kempis, and Sarvepalli Radhakrishnan garners support from Plotinus and the theories of Albert Einstein, while Gandhi quotes the Sermon on the Mount. One of the things that disturbs Bharati is that these and other thinkers apparently saw no problem in gathering under the umbrella of Hinduism a wide range of themes drawn from modern science, philosophy, and the world's religions. However, to Bharati such juxtapositions tend to look "quaintly anachronistic and solecistic," especially when one encounters books with titles like "Liberation in Pringle-Pattison and Buddha" (1970: 284).

But as should also be clear by now, another thing that disturbs Bharati is that such eclectic inclusivity did not extend equally to all aspects of either Indian or Western thought. On the contrary, Hindu apologetic discourse appears undeniably selective. This selectivity troubles Bharati on at least two accounts. The first is simply that, as we have seen, the modern Hindu took little to no interest in analytic philosophy. And yet, to Bharati it was "intellectually inhibiting" for Indian university students to be offered only the totalizing systems of Berkeley and Hegel and not the positivism of Ayer or the linguistic philosophy of Wittgenstein (Bharati 1970: 284).

However, the other more troubling aspect of Renaissance selectivity in Bharati's estimate is that its preference for "simplistic statements about the love of Christ" ultimately leads to a repudiation of what he refers to in the passage cited above as the "orthodox parlance" of the "brahmin masters." Here Bharati plays the part of the aggrieved Indologist who is outraged at the way modern Hindus play fast and loose with—when they don't simply ignore—what he takes to be the genuine or authentic traditions of learning enshrined in the primary texts he and his scholarly cohorts have worked so hard to edit, translate, and situate historically. Bharati raises his objections not only in the name of Indology but also in the best interests of the orthodox *paṇḍits* themselves, since as far he can tell, the "agents of the Renaissance mistrust and dislike both" (1970: 285).

It is precisely Bharati's self-portrait as the scholarly expert and voice of authentic Hinduism that recommends his essay as a foil to consider the status of eclecticism in the eyes of Indology. What Bharati claims to discover is that for all its inclusivity, there is in fact much that is left out of modern Hindu apologetic discourse. Most important, Bharati feels compelled to point out that what Vivekananda and other Renaissance apologists call Hindu religion is in fact largely discontinuous with traditional or authentic Hinduism. As an expert Indologist, Bharati claims to speak for those who really know India. In the words of John McGowan, Bharati exercises the "interpreter's privilege," which stakes its claim on the assumption that since "agents are not conscious of their own motivations," the interpreter must not shy away from advancing "claims that would not meet with the agents' consent" (McGowan 1991: 48). And Bharati is certainly not one to shy away; he is brutally frank about what strikes him as the amusing dynamics of Renaissance apologetics. And his advice to his readers is much the same: Don't you be fooled by this stuff, either!

As I have noted, Bharati is by no means the only scholar to hold such views regarding Hindu apologetic discourse. I daresay that if I had not had a similar response to this discourse from time to time, this book would never have been written. Those of us schooled in the Euro-American mode of Indology, with our philological training and our presumptions of the primary canons of South Asian religion, stand shoulder to shoulder with Bharati. We are troubled by the same questions of authenticity. It is this very anxiety that fuels the present investigation.

However, at the same time, we are removed from Bharati by nearly three decades, during which our disciplines have undertaken much reflexive introspection. Bharati's mode of Indology is by no means a thing of the past, but his positivistic, social-scientific reading of Hindu apologetics clearly reflects trends in scholarship on India typical of the 1960s and 1970s, when the question of India's potential for modernization exercised the imagination of many a scholar. Could India modernize? And if so, would Hinduism prove to be an impetus for or a brake on such change? What would become of the caste system in a modern, democratic India? These and related questions were the bread and butter, so to speak, of scholars trained in Bharati's generation and disciplinary matrix.

What makes Bharati's essay rather unique, of course, is the way it pays special attention to the significance of eclecticism within modern Hindu discourse.[10] Bharati directly relates the specific problem of eclecticism to the more general concern with modernization. The question thus becomes: How has Hindu eclecticism impinged on the goals of modernization? It is precisely this combination in Bharati of a general scholarly suspicion and a particular concern with eclecticism that makes his essay so valuable in the present context. What we discover is that we have to wrestle not only with the problem of eclecticism as identified by Bharati but also with the presuppositions of the scholarly paradigm out of which Bharati launches his assault on Hindu apologetics.[11]

Looking back at Bharati's critique, one is reminded of those readers of *Midnight's Children* who eagerly pointed out to Salman Rushdie all the factual errors he had committed in the book—such as having Ganesha record the *Rāmāyaṇa* at the feet of Valmiki or having Lata Mangeshkar sing on All-India Radio in 1946. Rushdie has noted that there always seemed to be "an undertone of pleasure" on the part of the one pointing out such errors, a pleasure in having gotten the better of the writer (Rushdie 1991: 23). Bharati seems to take the same sort of pleasure in sending up modern Hindu eclecticism.

This is one of those points at which a reading of Rushdie proved so helpful to me as I struggled with Bharati's verdict. In pausing to consider Rushdie's response to his wiser-than-thou critics, I began to see a way I might formulate a reply to Bharati. What Rushdie did, in effect, was to throw cold water on his critics. He simply asked them what they would say if he told them he actually intended to commit the errors they had detected. What's more, Rushdie asked the same critics if perhaps they were the ones who had erred, by failing to get the point of *Midnight's Children*. This is not a historical novel; it is not about facts and dates, but about memory and self-construction. *Midnight's Children* forces us, in fact, to reconsider just how reliable our memories are. The point is, it all depends on what you mean by 'reliable.' If you mean, "How accurately does my memory represent historical events?," then I might have to admit that mine is occasionally none too accurate. (For his part, Rushdie claims to remember how when he was a boy everyone worried about the Chinese marching into Delhi, even though he knows he could not have been around for such a memory!) On the other hand, if you mean, "How well does my memory serve to provide my life with meaning?," then I might say it is quite reliable indeed. In *Midnight's Children*, Rushdie asks us to appreciate the fact that—as troubling as it may be to some—we are all engaged in everyday acts of "unreliable narration" (Rushdie 1991: 25). This is precisely how we give meaning to our lives.[12]

Obviously it will not do to respond to Bharati on behalf of modern Hindu apologists by saying that what they are up to is a business of writing unreliable history, philosophy, or theology. However, the example of *Midnight's Children* is illustrative: The point that Rushdie made, in offering to us the world of Saleem Sinai, is that the truth of this world is far too important to be undone by a mere weather report. It is Saleem's truth, "and only a madman would prefer someone else's version to his own" (Rushdie 1991: 25).[13] When it comes to meaning, it seems we face a choice: Do we make our lives fit the facts, or do we make the facts fit our lives?[14] Do we wish to side with Bharati or with Rushdie? Does it have to be one or the other? These are crucial questions to bear in mind as we explore the dynamics of modern Hindu eclecticism.

Rushdie writes from the postcolonial perspective of a South Asian living in the United Kingdom. In some respects his situation is analogous to the Indian living under colonial rule. Certainly the colonized Hindu could agree with Rushdie when he says that "to be an Indian writer in this society is to face, every day, problems of definition" (Rushdie 1991: 17). And the questions Rushdie poses to the South Asian living in Europe are the mirror image of those asked by modern Hindu apologists like Vivekananda or Radhakrishnan:

> How should we discuss the need for change within ourselves and our community without seeming to play into the hands of our racial enemies? What are the consequences, both spiritual and practical, of refusing to make any concessions to Western ideas and practices? What are the consequences of embracing those ideas and practices and turning away from the ones that came here with us?

All such questions, Rushdie concludes, amount to asking: "How are we to live in the world?" (1991: 17–18).

Just as Rushdie would have us understand more clearly the world out of which and against which he writes, we would do well to attend more carefully to the colonial world in which Hindu apologetics must be situated. Considered against the background of its colonial origins, the putative errors of modern Hindu eclecticism may turn out to be truths to live by. As odd as many of these truths may seem to the social scientist or the historian, they are truths far too powerful to be outdone by the weather reports of text-critical scholarship, cranial measurements, or census results. Whether we take the case of postcolonial multiculturalism or colonial domination, Rushdie helps us appreciate how easy it is to go mad, if by 'mad' we mean 'accepting the truth someone else has given us.' When we view madness in these terms we are hard-pressed to find anyone more mad than the colonized Indian—educated in the colonizer's tongue, clothed in pantaloons and leather shoes, served with tea and biscuits, and edified by the works of Macaulay. No wonder the cosmopolitan Babu of Calcutta was such a butt for jokes within popular culture.

This much Bharati should have recognized. After all, he was able to see a connection between the dynamics of Renaissance apologetics and what he called the "delicate novelty of the Renaissance ego" (Bharati 1970: 287). Unfortunately, Bharati viewed the emergence of the modern Indian ego largely in terms of modernization theory—the transition from a precolonial ideology, in which the individual qua individual is not granted infinite value, to a modern ideology of the "dignity of an empirical, social, and autonomous individual." For Bharati and others who share his confidence in social-scientific method (see Madan 1987), the eclecticism of the Renaissance is one factor impeding the emergence of just such a modern Indian individual. The individual cannot emerge because, as Bharati argues, Hindu eclecticism is predetermined in its selectivity. It has a normative canon that includes idealism and Vedānta but excludes analytic philosophy. As a result, it hinders the "choice of personal, experiential variegation" (Bharati 1971: 285). In other words, by being too choosy Hindu eclecticism banishes choice—or so it seems to Bharati. If it sounds paradoxical to find fault with "rampant eclecticism" for being too selective, Bharati apparently saw no such paradox. The paradox *is* striking, however, and deserves closer scrutiny—for here is one of the problems that animates this study: the problem of freedom and the individual subject or self.

To raise the problem of the individual is to raise a contested issue indeed. Bharati's model, which presupposes both the nonexistence of the precolonial Indian self and the colonial emergence of the modern self, is currently vulnerable to assault on either flank. The once-authoritative claims of Orientalist scholarship regarding the absence of the precolonial Indian subject have now been rendered suspect, thanks to the work of Edward Said and others. In response, new attempts to define what Ronald Inden calls the "subject-citizenry" of ancient India have been undertaken. And while we need to beware of simply projecting the bourgeois individual back into Indian history, it is beyond dispute that today we can talk about subject-agency in a case where Euro-American scholars and philosophers have hitherto only acknowledged "patiency" (see Inden 1990: chap. 6).

However, at the very moment agency/subjecthood is recovered in one domain, it threatens to vanish in another. Thus alongside attempts to reevaluate the precolonial self, we find the status of the newly emergent Indian self being called into question by postmodernist scholars who have declared the death of the bourgeois subject. When reading the works of the postmodernists, it is sometimes difficult—as Frederic Jameson has noted—to decide whether they mean to suggest that the once-existing bourgeois subject has finally passed away, or that such a subject never really existed in the first place (1984: 63). It hardly matters in the present context, since in either case the verdict is dim for the Indian self; at the hour of its birth it is handed a death certificate. As Simon During has noted, this is one of those points where postcolonialism, which is all about selfhood and identity in the wake of colonization, does not sit well with postmodernism (cited in Docherty 1993).

During's observation is an important one. On the one hand, it suggests that what is at stake in the tension between Bharati and Rushdie is not merely a matter of epistemology, but the very meaning of and possibility for selfhood. Both Bharati and Rushdie are deeply concerned with the possibilities for Indian self-definition in the (post)colonial context. On the other hand, During helps us see how dangerous it can be to map intellectual fault lines in terms of simplistic dichotomies.

If I have begun by contrasting Rushdie with Bharati, then now is the time to acknowledge how the contrast can be blurred. Thus, in During's terms, as a postcolonial writer, Rushdie must perforce find aspects of his work at odds with the postmodern assertion that the subject is dead; at the same time, for all that Bharati's scientific rationalism can be sneered at from a postmodern perspective, his concern for the Indian subject makes his analysis of Hindu apologetics highly relevant to the discussion of postcolonial selfhood. Taken together, the work of these two thinkers suggests that as we wrestle with the meaning of the Indian self, we must be prepared to shuttle between the postmodernist awareness of the constructed character of all knowledge and the postcolonialist struggle to construct a sense of identity. Clearly no blithely unilinear model of psychosocial development can do justice to the complexities of life under the contested conditions of colonialism. The work of Rushdie allows us both to call into question Bharati's know-it-all modernism and to amplify his analysis by taking more seriously the stresses, strains, and lingering psychological tensions produced by colonial rule in India. Thus, if the Renaissance ego is delicate, as Bharati suggests, is this due to its infancy or to the fatigue and disorientation induced by the stresses of colonial life?[15]

In the problem of eclecticism we have one feature of modern Hindu thought that allows us the opportunity to wrestle with such a question. Bharati chose to read eclecticism as a univalent term, finding in it a significance that could be fairly easily tagged—and subsequently written off. However, to begin to situate the dynamics of modern Hindu eclecticism within an appropriate semantic, philosophical, and historical matrix is to find ourselves immediately at a loss for the kind of easy answer offered by Bharati. In this book I shall attempt to enter into this matrix by covering ground as far afield as later Greek philosophy; ancient Indian ritual and epistemology; the philosophies of Diderot, Kant, and Hegel; the crisis of modern historicism; the logic of modernism and postmodernism; the various eclecticisms of Bengal's so-called Renaissance; and the place of the bungalow in the colonial and postcolonial world. What we shall learn about eclecticism along the way should be enough both to reveal the inadequacy of Bharati's judgments and to promote a more searching inquiry into the colonial origins of modern Hindu eclecticism.

If I have looked to Rushdie for guidance along the way, it is because he is self-consciously eclectic. His most interesting characters—like Saleem Sinai and Zeeny Vakil—often live eclectically (see Rushdie 1991: 16). From characters like these we learn just how one person's madness can become another person's truth. To put it bluntly, I contend (contra Bharati) that what is called for when considering modern Hindu discourse is a healthy respect for the very excesses of its eclecticism.

At the same time, I also recommend an equally healthy suspicion for what Bharati rightly took to be the constraining principles of selectivity at work in such eclecticism.

In other words, I see this book as an exercise in dialectics. My approach to eclecticism will oscillate between appreciation and skepticism, between a yes and a no. Along with Bharati (if in somewhat different terms) I must be prepared to consider some of the unfortunate consequences that follow from the totalizing agenda of Hindu eclecticism—above all, the potentially violent dynamics of exclusion or destruction that accompany certain recent Hindu attempts at self-definition. However, at the same time, it may be necessary to move quickly to jettison other aspects of Bharati's critique of Renaissance apologetics. For instance, his fixation with authenticity is increasingly hard to defend today and it prevents us from seeing how modern Hindu discourse fulfills the postcolonial quest for identity through its very selectivity.

Having said all this, however, the goal of my dialectic approach is not to produce a higher truth. Rather, my understanding of dialectics owes something to the concept of negative dialectics developed by Theodor Adorno. Inspired by Adorno's critique of philosophical systems, I submit that we must resist the temptation to bring the questions raised herein to a definitive solution; final, definitive closure may well be both impossible and undesirable. When it comes to eclecticism in modern Hindu discourse, the truth will always be found in agreement with, and in opposition to, the conclusions of Bharati. As I shall attempt to argue in the Conclusion, we will do best if we can make ourselves comfortable while shuttling between the poles—not in any point of balance or stasis, but in the continual transit between suspicion and respect, affirmation and denial. As is the goal with Adorno's negative dialectics, we must forestall "closure and reconciliation" (Jay 1984: 53).[16] Happily, Rushdie can contribute to this aspect of my endeavor as well. In his call for a paradigm of knowledge that avoids foundationalist language, he urges us to avoid the temptation to speak of what Hindu discourse should or should not include. Likewise he has suggested that we not rush to decide once and for all what the legitimate principles of eclectic selection should be. We make up our rules, says Rushdie, as we go along.

2

"Difference Relates"

Eclecticism Past and Present

An Eclectic is a philosopher who tramples underfoot prejudice, tradition, seniority, universal consent, authority, and everything which subjugates mass opinion; who dares to think for himself, go back to the clearest general principles, examine them, discuss them, and accept nothing except on the evidence of his own experience and reason; and who, from all the philosophies which he has analysed without respect to persons, and without partiality, makes a philosophy of his own, peculiar to himself.

—Denis Diderot

There are many ways to answer the question, Who or what is an eclectic? The French *philosophe* Denis Diderot described the eclectic as someone who makes up his own philosophy by drawing freely upon his own experience and using his own reason as a guide. In the epigram here, Diderot announces that the eclectic is someone who is not afraid of trampling over dogma and authority if that's what it will take to make "a philosophy of his own." By endorsing eclecticism as an enlightened philosophy, Diderot wanted to emphasize that it promised a way to break free from dogmatism, that it guaranteed one the liberty to construct a philosophy based purely on one's experience and the rational study of human history (Braun 1973: 153).

When Diderot says an eclectic is a philosopher who dares to think for himself, these words obviously resonate with the famous reply given by Immanuel Kant to the question, "What is enlightenment?" Enlightenment, wrote Kant, is our liberation from self-incurred tutelage, from bondage to all the externals that would determine us instead of allowing us to be self-determining, or autonomous. The motto for true autonomy is *sapere aude*—'dare to know'—and it suggests just how closely reason and freedom are joined in Kant's system (Taylor 1986: 5).[1] We see the same interplay between freedom and reason in Diderot's definition of the eclectic cited above, which only serves to further remind us how much Kant and Diderot shared as guiding voices of the Enlightenment. It is worth asking, then, whether these two thinkers are in agreement in their views of eclecticism.

It turns out that Diderot's understanding of eclecticism was shaped by the earlier work of a now little-known eighteenth-century historian of philosophy, Jakob Brucker, whose *Historia critica philosophiae* appeared in 1742.[2] In this immensely influential text, Brucker advanced the claim that the finest fruits of eclecticism had been produced in the seventeenth and eighteenth centuries in the work of such philosophers as Bacon, Descartes, Hobbes, and Leibniz (Donini 1988: 19–20). What Brucker pointed out about these thinkers, and what appealed so strongly to Diderot, was that their eclecticism amounted to a repudiation of sectarianism and a rejection of external authority. As Diderot understood it, these were thinkers who dared to think for themselves. Thus far it would seem that Diderot's understanding of eclecticism harmonizes well with Kant's injunction, *sapere aude*.

However, when we scratch a little harder, we uncover an important difference between Diderot and Kant. As it turns out, these two great thinkers could not have been further apart in their evaluations of eclecticism. Unlike Diderot, Kant did not think one could construct a viable system of philosophy by simply relying on what Diderot called the evidence of one's own experience. To the contrary, in the penultimate chapter of *The Critique of Pure Reason*, Kant contrasts what he calls *cognitio ex datis*, or historical knowledge, with *cognitio ex principiis*, or rational knowledge. In Kant's terms, the former effectively describes Diderot's conception of eclectic knowledge, which is gleaned from a variety of external sources. However, according to Kant, no matter how impressive one's mastery of the world's doctrines and philosophies, the knowledge produced by such mastery is doomed to remain imitative and therefore essentially unproductive. Since the eclectic's knowledge does not arise directly out of the subjectivity of the thinker, but depends upon the heteronomous force of external influence, it cannot promise life and freedom. Rather, in basing his philosophy upon such knowledge, the eclectic becomes little more than a plaster replica of a living person (Braun 1973: 222).

Kant therefore urged that we review our very conception of reason by giving up our view of the mind as a passive receptacle for knowledge in favor of a view of the mind as both active and synthetic. True freedom could come only when knowledge was grounded not in external sense-data but in the "synthetic activity of the knowing subject" (Taylor 1988: 5). In other words, by recognizing the a priori character of reason, one achieved complete autonomy—freedom from bondage to the external direction of the Other. Thus in Kant's view, the key to enlightenment lay in removing from one's discipline anything borrowed or heteronomous. To achieve autonomy was thus to achieve a kind of purity (Taylor 1992: 3).

It may fairly be said that between Diderot and Kant lies the destiny of eclecticism in the modern world, a destiny fraught with ambiguity.[3] From Diderot and the *philosophes* comes our esteem for the free-thinking, iconoclastic eclectic. From Kant and the subsequent trajectory of German idealism comes an opposite response: the complete repudiation of eclecticism (Braun 1973: 222).

We are thus faced with a dilemma: Can religion be both eclectic and rational? If it were simply a matter of choosing whether one wanted to join the Diderot camp or the Kant camp, our response to this question might be a little more straightforward. Unfortunately, the problem is messier than this, since it can be shown that Diderot himself contributed in a roundabout fashion to the negative estimation of eclecticism among modern thinkers.

To illustrate this we need to consider very briefly the history of modern interpretations of later Greek, or Alexandrian, philosophy during the period from the first century BCE to the third century CE. The philosophers of late antiquity—Plutarch, Galen, Ptolemy, Cicero, Seneca, and the rest—can be ranked among the greatest eclectics the West has known. They borrowed freely from Platonists, Aristotelians, and Pythagoreans alike to advance their own positions. The question is, How are we to assess the value of their eclecticism?

The one scholar who did the most to shape twentieth-century attitudes toward the Alexandrians was Eduard Zeller.[4] Zeller viewed the developments of later Greek philosophy as framed chronologically by the earlier achievements of the Stoics, Epicureans, and Skeptics and by the subsequent flowering of Neoplatonism. By comparison, the thinking that occurred between these grand high points could only be called pedestrian or uncreative. For Zeller, Alexandrian philosophy represented the very exhaustion of thought itself. Considering such a verdict, it comes as no surprise that, thanks to Zeller, the philosophers of the later Greek period have tended to be something of an "embarrassment to intellectual historians" (Dillon and Long 1988: 1). They seem "too muddle-headed or light-minded to stick to the principles of any one of the four main Hellenistic schools" (Dillon 1988: 104).

If there is a single word in Zeller's vocabulary that sums up his negative assessment of later Greek philosophy, it is *eclecticism*. What is most ironic about Zeller's condemnation of later Greek eclecticism is that in a very real sense he owed it to none other than Diderot, the Enlightenment's great advocate of eclecticism. As strange as it may seem, Diderot—for all that he trumpeted the virtues of eclecticism—found fault with the eclecticism of the later Greek philosophers. Of course what bothered him was not their eclecticism as such, but the fact that they had betrayed the promise of eclecticism by leading it into what he took to be the dark alley of syncretism. That is, Diderot accused these ancient philosophers of being too quick to reconcile or harmonize the opposing schools of their day. In short, they were guilty of creating systems. And as Hegel was to note rather wryly, in Diderot's France anything that smacked of *systeme* was "synonymous with narrowness of views" (Hegel 1955: 401). What troubled freethinkers like Diderot was that the systems created by the eclectics of late Hellenism wound up becoming platforms upon which to establish new sects (Donini 1988: 21). Thus despite his affinity for eclecticism, Diderot ended up by giving eclecticism a bad name in what might otherwise have been one of its crowning historical manifestations. We can therefore hold him partially responsible for Zeller's views.

But to fully appreciate the force of Zeller's repudiation of eclecticism, one must turn to Kant and, after him, Hegel. We have already had a chance to observe the important difference between Kant and Diderot regarding the possibility of working eclectically with the data of experience and history. It turns out that Hegel, no less than Kant, had his own principled objections to eclecticism. For Hegel, eclecticism could offer no tenable philosophical position. It was superficial and, as such, it was "utterly to be condemned." No matter how intelligently one selected bits of philosophy in one's search for the best, one always ran the risk of losing "consecutiveness of thought." And once such continuity was lost, thought itself perished (Hegel 1955: 400–401).[5] In other words, for Hegel, eclecticism amounted to a denial of the integrative force of philosophy and the truths of historical development.

Ironically, while he condemned eclecticism, Hegel did not join in Diderot's criticisms of the Alexandrian eclectics. For whereas Diderot saw in the Alexandrian philosophers a betrayal of eclecticism in the name of systematicity, Hegel saw in them the triumph of unifying, integrative philosophic vision. Just how much Hegel differed from Diderot in his estimation of the Alexandrian philosophers is apparent when he praises their work as "a deeper knowledge of the philosophical Idea" (Hegel 1955: 402). Hegel thus sought to restore the good name of the Alexandrians, which had been tarnished by *philosophes* like Diderot. As for the use of the term *eclectic* in this case, Hegel was prepared to accept that it was here to stay; the French had already seen to this. Nevertheless, Hegel would not accept the negative estimation of this eclecticism. For according to Hegel, it was the Alexandrian's ability to integrate a wide range of philosophies that had prepared the way for the grand vision of the Neoplatonists.

By this point, one gets the sense that the later Greek philosophers are becoming almost incidental. Instead, we have begun a game of pitting system and reason against the selectivity of eclecticism. By the time of Zeller, eclecticism is the loser. In the final coup, Zeller adopted from Diderot a cynicism toward later Greek philosophy and combined it with Hegel's disdain for eclecticism as superficial non-thought. Thus the "critical and open approach to inquiry" that Brucker had originally admired in Descartes and Leibniz became in Zeller's work something "opprobrious" (Dillon and Long 1988: 5; Donini 1988: 23). To this day, eclecticism must struggle against this opprobrium. Suspicion of eclecticism remains for many the definitive word. When you get down to it, eclecticism is frequently seen to be a bad habit (Kidney 1974: vii). It is accused of being lazy, sloppy, uncreative, and rationally unsatisfying. Its appetite is apparently unrestrained, while its synthetic vision seems hopelessly feeble.

However, having traced the genealogy of such prejudice back to Brucker and Diderot by way of Hegel and Kant, we begin to appreciate something Hegel himself took great pains to make clear: every philosophical position has a history. There is no natural position on truth or beauty, nor is there a natural position on eclecticism. Philosophies may be understood as arising from and situated in their particular historical contexts. A quick look at the Alexandrian quest for reconciliation or at the Enlightenment ideal of "daring to know" suggests how historically complex has been the application and evaluation of eclecticism. Insofar as we live in a world bequeathed to us by both Diderot and Kant, we are faced with the challenge of searching out the possible relationships that might exist between the methods of eclecticism and the principles of reason.

As I suggested in the introduction, only a dialectical approach to the problem—one that emphasizes difference, as in Derrida's conception of *différance*, as opposed to the Hegelian goal of *Aufhebung*, or synthesis—is going to help. In any case, as heirs to the legacy of both Diderot and Kant, we appear to have little choice but to shuttle between them. Of course, even this will scarcely be an adequate solution, since by now the larger implications of the Enlightenment goal of daring to know have themselves been called into question by a variety of postmodern critics.

But in this latter recognition may lie some hope. If what Jean-Francoise Lyotard has called "the postmodern condition" represents a new historical context, perhaps within this context eclecticism must find a new valuation.[6] In fact, there are clear signs that it already has. We might well take Salman Rushdie as our example. We have already seen that his fiction and critical essays—widely hailed as major contributions to postmodern literature—evince a genuine pleasure in eclecticism (nicely dispelling the illusion that the eclectic somehow suffers from a lack of creativity).[7] At the same time, Rushdie recognizes the challenges posed by coming around to the eclectic's way of life. Rushdie makes this challenge palpable when he asserts that to understand his work one must open wide and swallow the whole world. Not only must our appetite be grand, but also our nerves must be sound, since we are asked to tolerate the disjunctures, the ruptures of context, the apparent betrayals of meaning and errors of memory occasioned by the eclectic's selective habits of borrowing. In other words, whether one can stomach such fare is in large part a matter of one's tolerance for difference, selectivity, and at times, even violence. In the latter regard, at least, eclecticism is a bit like war—it tends to take the best and leave the rest (see Rushdie 1981: 335).

This appears to be one instance in which Rushdie has the scholars on his side, since philologists note that in the ancient world the verb *eklegein*—from which we get the words *eclectic* and *eclecticism*—was in fact used to communicate the act of selecting the best from among any group of things. That a philosophical position could be constructed by combining ideas from a variety of sources was "by no means unusual in the classical world" (Dillon and Long 1988: 4). Aristotle refers to Plato's system as a blend of Parmenides, Heraclitus, Socrates, and the Pythagoreans; Xenophon refers to Socrates' speaking of selecting (*eklegometha*) ideas from ancient wise men (Donini 1988: 15 and 17). But, as Pierluigi Donini has recently pointed out, the ancients never referred to such cases as eclecticism; the latter was a term they reserved for the act of "deliberately planning to select some doctrines out of many philosophies and fit them together" (1988: 16). It is in this latter sense that Diogenes Laertius refers to the work of Potamo of Alexandria—the classic exemplar of ancient eclecticism.[8] And Clement of Alexandria seems to have meant something similar when he explicitly identified his method as being *eklektikon*, or eclectic.

Obviously the eclectic is perfectly happy picking up a little of *this* and has no qualms if this also means casting off the rest of *that*. As an eclectic, I select, I choose (*ek-lego*). If I choose one thing, then I do *not* choose something else. And if that something else happens to stand in close proximity to—or worse, is actually connected to—that which I mean to choose, then it is easy to see how the process of selection can quickly turn violent. It is a bit like Odette's problem when she began to lie to her lover, Swann; confronted by him, she had to find something to say, but unfortunately all she had at hand was the truth. Nevertheless:

> She broke off from it a tiny fragment, of no importance in itself, assuring herself that, after all, it was the best thing to do, since it was a verifiable detail and less dangerous, therefore, than a fictitious one. "At any rate, that's true," she said to herself, "which is something to the good. He may make inquiries, and he'll see that it's true, so at least it won't be that that gives me away." But she was wrong; it *was* what gave her away; she had failed to realize that this fragmentary detail of the truth had sharp edges which could not be made to fit in, except with those contiguous fragments of the truth from which she had arbitrarily detached it, edges which, whatever the fictitious details in which she might embed it, would continue to show, by their overlapping angles and by the gaps she had forgotten to fill in, that its proper place was elsewhere. (Proust 1982: 303)

What Odette apparently ignored was the violence involved in disarticulating truths one from the other; she failed to see how the torn edges and empty gaps in her story betrayed the sham of it all. We can relate this to the complaint we frequently voice ourselves when we object that a particular phrase, image, or piece of music has been *wrenched* or *torn* from its context. Rather ironically, then, it turns out that the shadow side of the eclectic's laziness and lack of creativity is in fact her aggressive and unrestrained manipulation of the truth. The eclectic's appetite knows no bounds—and this can be shocking.

While eclecticism as a method or a school of thought has never been recognized as such in India, there is an interesting (if somewhat arcane) lexical example from Sanskrit that may help us think about the nexus between selection and violence. In Sanskrit, when one selects something—a passage of verse, for instance—that action is designated by the verbal root *hṛ* (take) coupled with the prefix *ud* (up). The process of selection is thus known as *uddhāra*, or 'lifting up.' The word *uddhāra* suggests both extraction and recombination, both of which actions are central to the creation of literature. The paradigmatic example of *uddhāra* would have to be the composition of the sacred Vedas by the sage Vyāsa, who selected and arranged the myriad Vedic mantras.[9] In speaking of such an endeavor, what is selected out of one context and reintegrated into a new context may be said to be *uddhṛta*, or 'lifted up.' Thus we find that the aphorisms on worldly morality attributed to the sage Cāṇakya are said to have been selected (*uddhṛta*) from a variety of authoritative sources (*Cāṇakya-rāja-nīti*, v. 1).[10]

When we consult the ancient lexicons, we find that the past participle *uddhṛta* can be used when speaking of water that has been drawn from a well (*Amarakośa*, v. 90). This is important, since it suggests that the process of selection carries all the gentle and restorative connotations of pulling up a cool bucket of well water on a hot Indian afternoon. Equally delightful is the idea of skimming off the cream from a fresh pot of milk, which is yet another way of metaphorically suggesting what is at work in the semantics of *uddhāra*. What you get when you read a compendium, or *saṃkalana*, like that of Cāṇakya's moral maxims, is the very best there is to offer, the crème de la crème. In Sanskrit we would call such cream the *sāra*, or 'essence.'

The quest for essences has a long history in India. One notable early example can be found in the opening lines of the Chāndogya Upaniṣad, where the sacred syllable *oṃ* is praised as the very essence of essences:

> The essence of things here is the earth.
> The essence of the earth is water.
> The essence of water is plants.
> The essence of plants is a person (*puruṣa*).
> The essence of a person is speech.
> The essence of speech is the Rig ('hymn').
> The essence of the Rig is the Sāman ('chant').
> The essence of the Sāman is the Udgītha ('loud singing').
> This is the quintessence of the essences, the highest, the supreme, the eighth—namely the Udgītha . . .
> The Udgītha is this syllable "Om." (Hume 1931: 177)

The hierarchical paradigm established here, whereby one engages in a progressive reduction (or ascent) to a fundamental (or supreme) essence will be taken in subsequent centuries and applied to all forms of knowledge and behavior, from lovemaking to morality.[11] Thus when Cāṇakya's words were collected to produce an epitome of ethics and worldly conduct, the text was considered to be a *nīti-sāra*, or 'essence of morality' (*Cāṇakya-rāja-nīti*, v. 3). The process that brought this cream to your table could, by extension, be called *sāroddhāra*, or 'extracting the essence.' This would make the person doing the extracting the *sāragrahī*, the 'one who grasps the essence.' Thus the Indian eclectic becomes, as it were, a *sāragrahī*—one who dives into the ocean of riches and resurfaces with a handful of jewels.

It is intriguing, though, that behind or alongside this set of meanings stands a second, less benign set of meanings. To return to the ancient lexicons, we find that *uddhṛta* can also be used in the sense of tearing something out by the roots (*Abhidhanaratnamālā*, v. 4.27). Thus, in the last act of the classical Sanskrit drama *Śakuntalā*, the king is praised for destroying a host of demons who had threatened the serenity of Lord Indra's heaven. To describe the rout of the demons, the poet Kālidāsa employs the compound *uddhṛta-dānava-kaṇṭaka*, which means something like 'those thorns (*kaṇṭaka*) that were the demons (*dānava*) have been uprooted (*uddhṛta*).' One commentator, Rāghava Bhaṭṭa, notes that "by using the word *uddhṛta* in this context [the poet] suggests the utter extermination of [the demons] by a destruction aimed at their very roots" (*Abhijñāna-śākuntala*, v. 7.3). Clearly this word *uddhṛta* can also carry some fairly violent connotations.

Surely there are times when it is good to perform violent extractions, as the passage from *Śakuntalā* itself suggests. Removing a troublesome thorn; pulling out a tooth that has gone bad; extracting an arrow; or plucking serpents from the sea, as does the heavenly Garuḍa—these are all cases of *uddhāra* that bring comfort, health, and safety. But what about the attempt to extract the heart of something—be it of a philosophy or a living creature? Is it not necessarily going to do fatal damage? If the eclectic promotes a process of interpretation based on *uddhāra*, then at what point does the violence of such selection become problematic? Can we so blithely pluck things from their contexts? A fish pulled (*uddhṛta*) from the sea will die—as Lakṣmaṇa reminded his brother, Rāma, when the latter suggested leaving him and Sītā behind (*Rāmāyaṇa*, 2.53.31 [Vrajajīvan Prācyabhāratī ed.]). If, like war, the eclectic takes the best and leaves the rest, what are we to make of all the casualties?

Interestingly, it is difficult to locate a single instance in which an Indian author or commentator has objected to the violence inherent in the process of *uddhāra*. Rather, the process of selection, distillation, and compilation seems to have gone its merry way in India. Alongside the phenomenon of compendia like those of Cāṇakya, we might consider the literature of the Purāṇas, whose eclecticism is unarguably "conspicuous" (Bailey 1987: 106). Or we might examine a text like the *Yogaśāstra*, written by the cosmopolitan Jain scholar Hemacandra (ca. 1088–1173). In this text the author quotes freely from a variety of non-Jain sources such as the *Manusmṛti*, the *Devī Purāṇa*, and a work on love by Vātsyāyana; what's more, while Hemacandra may quote Manu disapprovingly in one instance, elsewhere he refers to him with apparent approval.[12] Hemacandra appears to practice selective appropriation with no second thoughts.

The picture changes somewhat with the advent of the colonial era. To be sure, Indian authors and commentators continued to select and extract in familiar ways, but with the arrival of the Europeans new standards for judging such selectivity also came into play. One begins to note, in particular, genuine disparities between what others have called the "polytheistic" vision of South Asian culture and the "mono-mania" of Western civilization—these are nowhere more clear than in the tensions between Hindu eclecticism and biblical religion.[13]

One early and notable case occurred in Calcutta in 1820, when the polymath Bengali reformer Rammohun Roy locked horns with some of the first Protestant missionaries to preach the Gospel in Bengal. With his pride in Sanskrit and the Vedas, his training in Arabic and Persian, his fluency in English, and his knowledge of biblical Greek and Hebrew,

Roy represented something of a living testament to eclecticism. As a religious reformer, his goal was to promulgate a more rational and humane religion. As an eclectic, or *sāragrahī*, his method was to draw freely upon his great wealth of knowledge and experience. Accordingly, one of his earliest projects was to work a bit of selective reconstruction on the New Testament by drawing forth from the Gospels only those sayings of Jesus that he felt accorded with reason and offered guidance in morality. What emerged was a selective portrait indeed.

In writing *The Precepts of Jesus: The Guide to Peace and Happiness*, Rammohun consistently excluded anything that smacked of mystery, miracles, Trinitarianism, or church dogma. From Rammohun's perspective this may have been nothing more than the age-old method of *sāroddhāra*, the distillation of the essence of the Gospel. Tellingly, one Bengali scholar calls the fruit of Rammohun's efforts a *saṃkalan*, or 'compendium,' reminding us of the *nīti-sāra* of Cāṇakya (see Bandyopādhyāy 1972: 54). However, from the perspective of an evangelical missionary the matter was far more problematic. Joshua Marshman, for one, was infuriated by the violence of Rammohun's selective method. He took great pains to respond to Rammohun's project and to demonstrate how it threatened to "greatly injure the cause of truth" (see Thomas 1969: 1). The note of injury here is not coincidental, I think. For what Marshman accused Rammohun of doing was *tearing* the teachings of Jesus from their appropriate context (see Hodder 1988: 137). What to Rammohun looked like the benign act of drawing water from a well could only strike an evangelical Christian as the violent act of ripping out the living truth of the Bible by the roots.

Needless to say, Rammohun's goal was not a violent one. He merely hoped to arrive at a "simple code of religion and morality" that would be free of superstition and sectarian bias (Roy 1906: 485). How his selective treatment of the Gospels contributed toward this end is made clear in his introduction to *The Precepts of Jesus*. There he notes that "in matters of religion" it is typical for "learned men of particular sects" to "pay little or no attention to opposite sentiments" on account of their "prejudice and partiality." To counter this tendency, Rammohun advocated an openness to the "simple enumeration and statement of the respective tenets of different sects" (1906: 484). Common sense and human reason, freed from the shackles of tradition and prejudice, should guide us toward the appropriation of religious truth.

We begin to sense how profoundly Rammohun had imbibed the values of the Enlightenment. When viewed from this angle, the work of our Indian *sāragrahī* turns out to be not all that different from that of Rationalists, Deists, Unitarians, and Transcendentalists in Europe and America, who frequently resorted to methods of selective appropriation in advancing their own philosophies. Alongside Diderot, one thinks of Voltaire, who always claimed to have been an eclectic, freely appropriating, from any sect of religion or any system of philosophy, whatever appeared to him to be true (Michel 1984: 44). Somewhat later, on the other side of the Atlantic, Emerson proffered to Americans a similar principle, proclaiming in the pages of *The Dial*:

> Each nation has its bible more or less pure; none has yet been willing or able in a wise and devout spirit to collate its own [bible] with those of other nations, and [thereby] sinking the civil-historical and the ritual portions to bring together the grand expressions of the moral sentiment in different ages and races, the rules for the guidance of life, the bursts of piety and of abandonment to the Invisible and Eternal. (Emerson n.d.: 324; see Richardson 1995: 379)

Emerson's confidence that the world's many bibles could be carefully emended so as to bring forth the universal truths of religion and morality reminds us distinctly of Rammohun. And, in fact, Emerson had been aware of Rammohun's work since the early 1820s (see Richardson 1995: 43). However, in order to explain the logic of Emerson's approach to scripture, we need not necessarily posit a direct influence of Rammohun upon Emerson (as is done by Hodder 1988). Instead, we need only appreciate the common wellspring of Enlightenment rationalism and anticlericalism that fuels their work.

It is precisely the global diffusion of this intellectual impulse that explains the remarkable fact that at almost precisely the time Rammohun brought out his *Precepts* in Calcutta, Thomas Jefferson, a world away in America, was engaged in a similar endeavor. Inspired by Unitarian preachers like Benjamin Rush and Joseph Priestly, Jefferson set out in the first decade of the nineteenth century to extract from the Christian New Testament what he called "the most sublime and benevolent code of morals which has ever been offered to man" (Jefferson 1989: 17). As Jaroslav Pelikan has remarked, it gives one pause to imagine Jefferson confidently at work in the White House, razor in hand, with Greek, Latin,

French, and English testaments laid out before him (Jefferson 1989: 149). The so-called Jefferson Bible that eventually emerged from his endeavors with a razor and a pot of glue is a selective emendation of the Bible grounded in the Enlightenment quest for a rational and universally valid religious worldview. It is a work entirely in harmony with the spirit of Rammohun's work, and made all the more remarkable because there is no evidence linking the one to the other.

Jefferson, Rammohun, Emerson, Voltaire—all sought to grasp the true essence of religion that had either been perverted or forgotten over the centuries. Like Saleem Sinai, they were dangerous madmen; yet like Saleem, they were after truths they could call their own—the only kind that deserved to be called authentic. While Saleem worked from memory, they worked with the tools of common sense, impartiality, and rational consistency. Such tools were up to any task, whether it was deflating myths, stripping off the husks of dead tradition, or polishing the imperishable kernels of truth. At the same time, these tools promised universal human understanding, since it was expected that, human reason being everywhere the same, all that was needed was a clear, unvarnished perspective on truth. Thus while seeking truths of their own, these eclectics could dream of revealing truths for all. Here was one of the great beauties of eclecticism as practiced by many eminent moderns—it aimed at harmony and reconciliation, whether it was doctrinal, philosophical, or cultural (see Hutchison 1976: 26).

Still, for all its conciliatory promises, eclecticism—like *uddhāra*—has a darker, violent side. How the modernist eclectic will arrive at his universal truths boils down to his perspective on what some have called the problem of the One and the Many, which is the fundamental problem of difference (Hassan 1985: 127). Do we assert universality over the dead body of difference? Does the One envelope or destroy the Many? Can we acknowledge the Many and still strive for the One? Perhaps it could be argued that the reconciliation attempted by the eclectic reveals a creditable openness toward difference. After all, Emerson listened not just to Leibniz but to Confucius and the *Bhagavad-gītā* as well. Borrowing the language of Raimundo Panikkar (which I shall explore in more detail in chapter 4), we might call this the democratic mode of eclecticism, in which the eclectic professes to listen with equal interest to a wide range of voices.

However, as Panikkar has suggested, eclecticism can also wax aristocratic, by imposing a hierarchical principle for evaluating the evidence it selects (see Panikkar 1975). We notice this tendency especially among modern eclectics who work in the name of universalism. The universalism of the aristocratic eclectic works hierarchically; it classifies according to a scale of greater and lesser truths. For this reason it can easily assume the form of inclusivism. According to inclusivist logic, differences of philosophy, custom, and ritual are overlooked in the name of some universal principle. If difference is admitted, it can only be in a subordinate fashion. This is a discursive strategy used by the likes of modern Hindus, American Transcendentalists and Christian universalists alike. For the modern Hindu, the all-embracing principle is *brahman* and insofar as it is the root of reality, then all religious truths find their ultimate home there. (I shall take up Paul Hacker's analysis of such discourse in chapter 3.) For the Transcendentalist, Leibniz and Confucius speak not out of their differences, but in a single voice granted to them by the poetic mind of the interpreter. And for their part, Christian inclusivists have been known to acknowledge the existence of truths within Hinduism—but only when those truths are read through the higher truth of Jesus Christ.

The point is, if the eclectic chooses to pursue such a strategy he must face a double indictment: Not only is he already under suspicion for violently uprooting truths from their contexts; now he is charged with attempting to strong-arm diversity into a totalizing program. In other words, what starts out looking like an open and friendly philosophy ends up having a rather aggressive and aggrandizing shadow side (Hacker 1983: 19). As one nineteenth-century Indian critic of eclecticism remarked, the kind of unification achieved by the inclusivist is a bit like "the union between the tiger and the lamb when the latter was in the former!" (Bose 1884: 409).

The problem of inclusivism therefore illustrates the double bind faced by the aristocratic eclectic: such a method not only does violence to context but also supports a violent attempt to encompass other viewpoints. We see this illustrated time and again in modern Hindu apologetics, when an author begins by plucking a verse from the Vedas to serve as a proof-text for his universalism. I have already had occasion to note how troubled Bharati was by the modern Hindu appropriation of the Vedic mantra, "Truth is one, though the wise call it by many names."[14] Armed with such a motto, the Hindu eclectic feels empowered to use this proof-text as an interpretive umbrella under which to gather any or all of the world's diverse faiths. And so, when Swami

Prabhavananda begins his commentary on the Sermon on the Mount, his ingenuous admission that he has no bona fides as a biblical scholar becomes all the more striking by being coupled with his unapologetic appropriation of the Gospels in the name of his own brand of Vedantic inclusivism:

> I am not a Christian, I am not a theologian, I have not read the Bible interpretations of the great Christian scholars. I have studied the New Testament as I have studied the scriptures of my own religion, Vedanta. Vedanta, which evolved from the Vedas, the most ancient of Hindu scriptures, teaches that all religions are true inasmuch as they lead to one and the same goal—God-realization. My religion therefore accepts and reveres all their great prophets, spiritual teachers, and aspects of the Godhead worshipped in different faiths, considering them to be manifestations of one underlying truth. (Prabhavananda 1964: 13)

Here, in a nutshell, is the phenomenon of inclusivistic eclecticism that Bharati found at once amusing and disturbing.

This is the point at which it becomes important to reflect upon how—from the time of Rammohun—Hindu apologetics has been profoundly tied to the prevailing discourse of Enlightenment reason and modernist humanism, with its fundamental suspicion of difference. If the project of modernity is understood as the rational quest for purity, harmony, and autonomy, then we must recognize to what degree modern Hindu discourse participates in this process. Especially when practiced in conjunction with an aggressively inclusivistic philosophy, the Hindu eclectic's goal can largely be seen as one of overcoming both the complexity of Indian religious phenomena and the diversity of the world's religions so as to arrive at a definition of Hinduism as an autonomous and internally coherent entity. Clearly this goal was not formulated simply in response to a rational or intellectual problematic, but emerged out of the psychological and political vortex of colonialism. But this only heightens the significance of the fact that the quest to define and defend Hinduism in the face of European/Christian power should have followed a modernist approach to the problem of the One and the Many. As we shall see in chapter 6, the modern Hindu quest to construct a religious and political home has necessarily involved it in the same sorts of exclusions and repressions that accompanied Enlightenment attempts to suppress or encompass diversity in the name of unity.

Heterogeneity proves troubling to the modernist, who dreams of the homotopia. As Demetri Porphyrios has pointed out, homotopia can be envisioned as an immutable grid. Its perfectly ordered coordinates promise to provide answers to all our questions—even before they are posed. In this respect, the homotopia lives up to the almost magical promise of Enlightenment rationality as described by Horkheimer and Adorno: "the process is always decided from the start" (1972: 24). Porphyrios resorts to an architectural illustration to help us visualize the power of the homotopia. He refers us to the high modernist architecture of Mies van der Rohe and Le Corbusier, in which the cityscape became a geometric grid studded regularly with functional cubes. In such architecture, we can actually see the "passion to homogenize." The passion generated in the heart of the modernist by such a grid was due precisely to the conviction that its "immaculate homogeneity" was a function of its universality. It was as if, "by gridding space, one safeguarded against all accidents or indiscreet intrusions, and established instead an idealized field of likeness. Were it not for the sudden intervention of a curtain wall, that magic screen of the grid could, in fact, extend forever, enveloping the whole world and cleansing it of all its irregularities" (Porphyrios 1982: 1). In other words, we are invited to read modernism as a vision of pristine unity grounded upon a universal grid. Mies van der Rohe's famous remark that architecture "is the will of the age conceived in spatial terms" (quoted in Harvey 1989: 21) takes on a heightened significance when one realizes how much the modernist project has invested in constructing homotopias.

As Porphyrios suggests, the grid provides an excellent metaphor for modernism because it suggests the convergence of both the structural and the ethical canons of modernity. If homotopias reject difference—if they seek instead familiarity in continuity—then what they seek is the enlightened goal of purity we saw emerging from Kant's critique. Purity is both beautiful and true, because it is autonomous and rational. Cubes, crystals, grids, geometry—their appeal for Le Corbusier is readily apparent in what he wrote of Paris in the 1929 work *The City of Tomorrow*: "Imagine all this junk, which till now has lain spread out over the soil like a dry crust, cleaned off and carted away and replaced by immense clear crystals of glass, rising to a height of over 600 ft. . . , open to light and air, clear, radiant and sparkling" (quoted in Collins 1965: 235). That there is more going on here than mere aesthetics is suggested by Le Corbusier's own fascination with a Pythagorean vision of the universe, with the peculiar evolutionary grid of theosophy, and with the almost Manichaean worldview of his Cathari heritage (see Taylor 1992: chap. 4).[15] Clearly purity for Le Corbusier is also a quasi-religious goal.

The modernist, then, aimed to create utopias, "untroubled regions" where we might comfortably stroll along the grid of uniformity "always discovering little hidden clues that alluded to the unified constitution of the world" (Porphyrios 1982: 2). It is easiest to picture the grid as a building or a plan for a city, but the grid might just as easily be a Unitarian Universalist hymnbook, whose selections from Vietnamese Zen Buddhist prayers, the *Bhagavad-gītā*, and the *Tao te ching* are made to provide—despite their many and manifest differences—those precious clues to the "unified constitution of the world." In calling upon such a diverse set of religious data to provide the sense of a universal human tradition, today's Unitarian effectively practices a modernist mode of eclecticism. The goal is to provide the grid of the homotopia, according to which diversity is crystallized into a pattern that promises unity and closure of meaning.[16]

We find quite a different view of the world when we turn to the "certain Chinese encyclopedia" written by Jorge Luis Borges and cited by Michel Foucault in the now-famous passage from *The Order of Things*. Here is a testament not to unified meaning, but to the impossibility of wrapping up meaning in any neat fashion. Here, in a word, is what Foucault calls the *heterotopia*. Following Foucault, we can say that the heterotopia represents a state in which "things are 'laid,' 'placed,' 'arranged' in sites so very different from one another that it is impossible to find a place of residence for them, to define a *common locus* beneath them all" (Foucault 1973: xvii–xviii). Unlike the homotopia, such a space is disturbing, not the least because, by abandoning the syntax that is supposed to hold everything together, a heterotopia makes it "impossible to name this *and* that" (1973: xviii).

If the comfort of homotopia lies in always knowing where you are—and therefore where others should be—the problem with heterotopia is that it provides no coordinates. In the words of Charles Baudelaire, one has *ni etoile ni boussole*, neither star nor compass. Baudelaire used this expression in the middle of the nineteenth century to voice his discomfort with the eclecticism practiced by the painters of his day (Baudelaire 1968: 251). What he bemoaned was the lack of a universal gird, some set of coordinates by which to navigate and, thus, to find meaning.

We find a similar complaint voiced by Samuel Taylor Coleridge, who condemned the "immethodical" eclectics of his day for their disregard of the grid. For Coleridge, eclectic and system represented mutually exclusive categories; by dismissing the demands of the system, the eclectic made light of the rigors of logical coherence. Eclectics are the sort who

> choose whatever is most plausible and showy; who select whatever words can have some semblance of sense attached to them without the least expenditure of thought; in short whatever may enable men to take of what they do not understand, with a careful avoidance of every thing that might awaken them to a moment's suspicion of their ignorance. (Coleridge 1969: 192)

Concluding with a great flourish Coleridge added:

> This alas! is an irremediable disease, for it brings with it, not so much an indisposition to any particular system, but an utter loss of taste and faculty for all system and for all philosophy. Like echoes that beget each other amongst the mountains, the praise or blame of such men rolls in vollies long after the report from the original blunderbuss. (Coleridge 1969: 192–193)

Such a diatribe epitomizes the complaint of the systematic philosopher of the homotopia against the violent disjunctions of eclecticism.

In some respects it is odd to find poets like Coleridge and Baudelaire repudiating eclectics. Both men contributed in significant ways to the evolution of the modernist temper; in fact it was Baudelaire who early on equated the spirit of modernism with the spirit of relentless change, with the giddy sensation produced by the continual rejection of past ideas, norms, and fashions. At first glance we have to wonder what grid could withstand Baudelaire's vision of frenzied change. It would seem he might have given a warm welcome to the gridless world of heterotopia. And yet, it was Baudelaire, too, who reminded us that change was but "one half of art, the other being the eternal and immutable" (in Harvey 1989: 10). With this qualification, Baudelaire effectively reintroduced the grid, since the only way to approach the eternal and immutable, apart from the unifying theology and metaphysics of the Middle Ages, was through what Jürgen Habermas has called the objective science, universal morality, and autonomous art that derived from the Enlightenment (Harvey 1989: 12; see Habermas 1983: 9).

It is important to register this point about Baudelaire's modernism, since it assists us in our quest to view modernity dialectically—in this case, as a ceaseless exchange between stasis and change, being and becoming, the One and the Many. In making this point I have been guided by the work of David Harvey, who suggests that out of Baudelaire's formulation flowed, as it were, "two currents of sensibility" that have shaped the meaning and expression of modernity (Harvey 1989: 275). The one stream aims to achieve human liberation by overcoming history and change through the rational organization of reality; this is the stream of heroic modernism à la Le Corbusier—of universalism and the grid. The other stream seeks not to overcome history, but to recover our orientation to it through museums, libraries, crafts movements, and collecting; this is the stream of William Morris and Louis Sullivan—of the particular and the place.

Harvey points out that the combination of these two streams thus provides both an escape from historicism and its fullest expression (1989: 24). In other words, modernism has all along been divided against itself. If the meaning of modernity itself has been contested by moderns, if Le Corbusier could object to William Morris, then we begin to see how other modernisms may clash—notably, Bharati's and that of the modernist Hindu. In the latter case, the debate has largely been about history. Indeed, historicism has played an important role in guiding the judgments of Indologists—Bharati included—on the meaning of Hindu culture, as we shall see in chapter 4. It has provided them with a tool for judging the flaws of eclecticism, for condemning its universals from the standpoint of history's particulars. However, it turns out that eclecticism can be practiced from within either modernist stream—universalist or particularist. In chapter 5 I will draw upon such an awareness in arguing for a nonmonolithic view of eclecticism.

Harvey's analysis is also helpful for reflecting on how all forms of modernist eclecticism have been transmitted, revised, or questioned from the perspective of postmodernism. After all, eclecticism remains very much in the air, whether it be in medicine and psychotherapy, or in art, architecture, and religion. And our responses to it continue to reflect a range of tensions. Robert Venturi's eclectic design for the new Sainsbury Wing of the National Gallery in London is a case in point. Praised by some for its ability to reconcile the classicism of monumental Trafalgar Square with the vernacular of the side streets, the annex has been roundly criticized by others as a joke made in poor taste. Has the new wing undermined the classical integrity of the original building, or has it instead achieved some continuity between the museum's earlier form and its present-day context? As one critic noted, it often appears to be a case of "damned-if-you-do-and-damned-if-you-don't" (MacAdam 1991).

The popular writings of Deepak Chopra offer another telling instance of our present-day dilemma regarding eclecticism.[17] Chopra's best-selling books on healing the body and mind reflect his own cross-cultural background and training as a physician. A credited practitioner of Western allopathic medicine, Chopra has also been trained in Indian Ayurvedic traditions. Not surprisingly, then, his answers to questions about health and well-being are couched in the analyses and remedies provided by both traditions. What is more, he communicates his therapy by means of a discourse that freely and unapologetically juxtaposes Hindu metaphysics and American self-help jargon, much the way Prabhavananda juxtaposes the Gospels and Vedānta. In the case of both authors, it was the cultural encounters of the modern period, coupled with the ideology of modernism, that made their work possible. And yet, the same ideology of modernism might lead others to question the validity of their work. Modernist historicism stands up to modernist universalism.

To offer but one final example of the continuing dilemma of eclecticism, we might turn to the 100th anniversary of the Parliament of the World's Religions celebrated in Chicago in 1993 (I shall consider the original parliament in chapter 3). At this event the problem of eclecticism became especially visible for historians of religion. The 1993 Parliament of the World's Religions brought together spiritual leaders and scholars from around the globe in what might be called a New Age extravaganza (Toolan 1993). Naturally the 1993 parliament attracted Buddhists, Christians, Hindus, Jews, and Muslims; after all, representatives of these traditions had been publicly sharing grievances and testing truths for at least the last 100 years. What was new, however, was that the parliament also welcomed Sikh, Baha'i, and Native American Indian spokespersons, not to mention futurologists, witches, devotees of Isis, and various practitioners of neopaganism. Registration forms elicited such self-descriptions as "Jewish Hindu witch" or "Catholic Hindu" (Steinfels 1993). With such a list of participants it is easy to imagine that the 600 or more papers, seminars, and performances presented ranged over philosophical and soteriological ground that would have been unthinkable in 1893. A perusal of presentations finds North American Indian spirituality making common cause with Taoist wisdom and Judaism in a quest for a "greener" religion. Likewise, explorations of the spiritual assets of astrology, near-death experiences, and cinema were offset by presentations in which UFOs, the big bang, and the double helix were written into the New Age mythology. I have admittedly chosen the most outlandish examples, but it nevertheless remains the case that today—as Americans increasingly take to yoga, sweat lodges, and Tai chi, alongside more mainstream religious commitments—such combinations appear less and less unusual. This is what religion has come to mean in America: the spiritual smorgasbord. As a recent piece of journalism put it, many of us are out for "religion a la carte" (Lattin 1993).

It is hard not to slip into parody when cataloging such manifestations of eclecticism. The question is, Should we be turning up our noses at the participants at the 1993 parliament or dancing with them under the full moon in Chicago's Grant Park? Should we be laughing at the creator of the Sainsbury Wing or with him? As we have seen, the modernist as practitioner of the pure grid feels justified in looking askance at the likes of Venturi, Chopra, and the spiritual seekers of the 1993 parliament. As one scholar has put it, the modernist "disdains the artifacts and conditions of the New Age" (Wyschogrod 1990: xiv).

However, the question remains, What will the postmodernist say? If nothing else, over the last twenty years or so scholars, artists, and critics have begun to consider that perhaps the joke has in fact been on the modernist. For the sake of convenience we might call such voices "postmodern," acknowledging up front that, as with "modernism," there is plenty of room for interpretation and disagreement on the meaning of the term.

Deciding precisely what the postmodern position is with respect to modernism is a difficult matter. In the most general terms we might take the "post" in postmodernism to simply reflect an attempt to gain some critical distance on modernism. But this leaves obvious questions: Is postmodernism a late phase of modernism—that is, post*modernism*? Is it a crisis taking place within modernist ideology? Could it simply represent the foregrounding of themes already present in the background of high modernism, as it were (see Jameson 1983, 1984)? Or are we better off viewing postmodernism as a turning away from modernism entirely—that is, *post* modernism (see Harvey 1989: 113)? And if it is the latter, then in which direction are we turning? Is it a form of neoconservatism (Habermas 1983)? Are we returning to premodern values or is an entirely new worldview and socioeconomic reality coming into being? As the literature on postmodernism proliferates, so, too, do the various answers to these questions. For the interests of this book, I prefer to emphasize what Mark Taylor has rightly called the "inextricable interrelation of modernism and postmodernism" (1992: 194–196).

Nuances of meaning notwithstanding, in an important sense postmodernists stand for the creation of alternatives to modernist perspectives on such problems as authenticity and change, synthesis and juxtaposition, the One and the Many (see Connor 1990: 80). We might simply say that postmodernists are, after Foucault, advocates of heterotopia.

Understanding this, it hardly comes as a surprise to find that eclecticism (or pastiche, as it is frequently called) is routinely identified as a hallmark of postmodern theory and praxis (see Collins 1995; Ahmed 1992; Jameson 1983; Rose 1991; Wyschogrod 1990; McGowan 1991).[18] If we adopt the interpretive perspective of poststructuralism—as indicative of, but not coextensive with, postmodernism—we can see why this is so. Poststructuralists insist that all we find around us is the endless play of signifiers—what we might call "wall to wall" textuality (see Fish 1989: 303). If this is the case, if we are unconstrained by any ultimate signifieds, the door is clearly thrown open to juxtaposition. As Mark Taylor has pointed out, unlike in the modernist homotopia of reason, there is no Archimedean point in a poststructuralist world, no privileged code, no center to grasp; "perspectives are radically relational," opposites are nonexclusive, and "meaning is irreducibly relative" (Taylor 1984: 173). Not altogether sympathetically,[19] Frederic Jameson has written,

> What would happen if one no longer believed in the existence of normal language, of ordinary speech, of the linguistic norm (the kind of clarity and communicative power celebrated by Orwell in his famous essay, say)? . . . In that case, the very possibility of any linguistic norm in terms of which one could ridicule private languages and idiosyncratic styles would vanish, and we would have nothing but stylistic diversity and heterogeneity. (1983: 114).

Might as well come right out and say it: nothing but eclecticism. In such a world, modernist concerns about purity, autonomy, historicity, and accuracy are ruled out, because meaning is no longer understood as the best possible representation of some world that really exists "out there." Modernist concerns with authenticity or authorial intention are likewise dismissed. The "subject," or the humanist "self"—that autonomous personality with a unique vision, voice, and style—has been declared dead. The work of art or of literature is out of the creator's hands;

it is but one more text whose meaning will shift as it encounters ever new texts and contexts.

Faced with such a fluid, unstable, shifty conception of our world, we are told that the proper response is not to hang on (since there is nothing to hang onto); rather, one should simply let go and enjoy the playful freedom of heterotopia. And predictably the eclecticism of the postmodern is nothing if not playful: one need only look at Frank Gehry's design for the Frederick Weisman Museum at the University of Minnesota in Minneapolis or at James Stirling's Neue Staatsgalerie in Stuttgart (see Fig. 1). The postmodernist fondness for play is also apparent in the way analogies with music and dance punctuate postmodern works. Scholarly introductions become 'preludes,' which is to say a kind of 'foreplay' (from *ludere*, 'to play'), while definitive conclusions are abandoned in favor of open-ended 'interludes' (see Wyschogrod 1990 and Taylor 1984). There is no quest for the closure of the grid, but simply an appeal to join the dance of meaning.[20]

Considering this penchant, we might well want to rush out and join the New-Agers for a quick dance. It is not quite that simple, however, since the postmodernist also has significant grounds for being uneasy about eclecticism. If eclecticism and the Enlightenment go hand in hand, as Diderot seemed to suggest, then the postmodernist will be looking at eclecticism with the same suspicion reserved for the Enlightenment project. To be specific, the eclecticism of modernists like Rammohun, Emerson, and Jefferson is not only individualistic in its method, but universalist in its dreams of global reconciliation. If the bourgeois individual has been reduced to the status of an ideological construct and universalism has been condemned as a dangerous form of totalizing exclusion, then these aspects of modernist eclecticism begin to look dubious indeed. Finally, the eclectic may well be accused of the same "commodious" appetite that characterizes the acquisitive zeal of modern capitalism. Albert Borgmann suggests that over against such a destructive appetite, postmodernist culture chooses to advocate another set of values, which favors less "hyper" styles of consumption (1992).[21]

It is important to bear these suspicions in mind, especially since they allow us to situate the problem of modern Hindu eclecticism within a rich and potentially rewarding critical matrix. The advantage of reading Bharati's critique of modern Hindu apologetics from the vantage point of postmodern theory is that we are able to imagine a new context in which we might appropriate some of his concerns about the relation-

Figure 1 Neue Stattsgalerie, Stuttgart. Drawing by Selden Richardson. Used by permission of the artist.

ship between the Hindu tradition and the modern Indian self. In envisioning a move outside modernist discourse we can discern more clearly not only the internal dialectic that characterizes the logic of modernism but also the complex relationship that must exist between modernism and its postmodern critique. In the end, we may find ourselves compelled to adopt a more nuanced approach to Bharati's reading of eclecticism, granting the force of his objections to the totalizing approach of neo-Hindu idealism, while dwelling critically on the inordinate trust he seems to place in historicism and the discourse of authenticity.

But if we are to arrive at either of these conclusions, we must first devote ourselves to a variety of tasks. To begin with, we would do well to investigate in more detail the discourse of Swami Vivekananda, since his work epitomizes the kind of Renaissance apologetic Bharati found so vexing. It is to Vivekananda that I shall therefore turn in the next chapter. After familiarizing ourselves with Vivekananda it will be well worth asking after both the roots of his eclecticism in the Indian context and the response to such eclecticism on the part of modern Indologists. Chapters 4 and 5 will take up these tasks, by examining isolated instances of eclectic thinking from the ritual world of ancient India to the cosmopolitan milieu of colonial Bengal. Following this, in chapter 6, I will offer a rather lengthy meditation on the dynamics of self-construction in the colonial and postcolonial Indian context. It is my hope that together these four chapters will provide the information and interpretive perspective we require to arrive at a more nuanced reading of modern Hindu eclecticism.

3

Swami in Wonderland

Vivekananda's Eclectic Hermeneutics

The invention of legitimacy makes choice *the key determinant of value in a world of semiotic excess.*

—Jim Collins

Try to imagine a lone Indian holy man disembarking in Vancouver in July 1893 after a long voyage from India by way of Ceylon, Malaya, Singapore, Hong Kong, and Japan. He is dressed in the robes of a monk, but he is dragging with him the steamer trunks and wardrobe of a modern tourist. Hardly has he come ashore than he boards a train for Chicago. The journey will take five days. He has already been traveling for a solid month and has been overwhelmed by the sight of modern battleships in Penang, pigtailed children and fabulous Buddha-images in China, picturesque gardens and bustling factories in Japan. Now he gazes out at the towering mountains of western North America and watches as they gradually give way to cool green forests, expansive prairies, and sprawling farms. What could possibly be going through his mind when his train finally rolls into the sprawling city of Chicago?

Though he undoubtedly feels lonely, our holy man feels anything but invisible. It must seem as if all of Chicago is eyeing him "on account of his unique attire in Mandarin colors." Throughout his visit to the United States his visage ("bronze" and "fine"), not to mention his getup ("a robe of pink silk, fastened at the waist with a black sash, black trousers and . . . a turban of yellow silk"), would attract endless comment:

> He is a large, well-built man, with the superb carriage of the Hindustanis, his face clean shaven, squarely moulded regular features, white teeth, and with well-chiselled lips that are usually parted in a benevolent smile while he is conversing. His finely poised head is crowned with either a lemon-colored or a red turban, and his cassock (not the technical term for this garment), belted in at the waist and falling below the knees, alternates in a bright orange and rich crimson. (CW 3: 471)[1]

What an opportunity he must have presented to the porters and touts swarming through the station!

Such is the picture one draws of Swami Vivekananda's arrival in the United States in 1893. He had come in all his "Oriental" splendor to Chicago, because he had heard there was to be convened in that city a World's Parliament of Religions in conjunction with the World Columbian Exposition (the Chicago World's Fair). It was his plan to attend the parliament on behalf of the people of India and to give voice to the religious vision of the Hindus. His arrival and his apparel bear noting not simply because of the striking incongruity of the former, but also for the eclectic flair of the latter. However cosmopolitan they may have been, Calcuttans of his day rarely wore turbans, and wandering holy men were seldom found wrapped in colorful silks and dapper slacks. Here, in other words, was a man with a flair for presentation as well as a keen desire to fit the part of the "eminent Oriental" expected by his American hosts (CW 3: 486). He had to be an authentic Hindu, even if it meant making it up as he went along. How he made himself up, and under what circumstances, are precisely the questions I want to raise. In pursuit of such questions, we are led into the heart of Hindu apologetics and are brought face-to-face with our own presuppositions about authentic Hinduism and the eclecticism of Renaissance discourse.

The significance of Vivekananda's presence at the parliament can scarcely be exaggerated. For better or worse, the image of our turbaned visitor holding forth to awestruck crowds has become the canonical representation of America's encounter with Asian religion and of India's proclamation of spiritual pride. However, as much as this epoch-making moment has been reviewed and replayed, very little attention has been devoted to the broader context within which Vivekananda's visit took place. And here I mean not simply the parliament, which was only recently revisited in depth during the celebration of its centenary in 1993, but the Chicago World's Fair as a whole. One welcome exception is Richard Hughes Seager's book *The World's Parliament of Religions*, which goes a long way toward situating the parliament within the larger Columbian exposition. What Seager does, apart from orienting us to the broader institutional contexts within which the parliament was situated, is to explore what might be called the entire Columbian myth that lay behind the fair.[2] Acknowledging the important contribution Seager has made in this connection, I would like to pursue some further reflections on the curious fit between the World's Parliament and the Chicago World's Fair.

What we find when we examine the planning and layout of the fair is a modernist microcosm, a theme park for the age of industry, the progress of nations, and the harmony of mankind. As a subset of this celebratory cosmos, the World's Parliament offered yet another microcosm, something like a symphony of world religions, or a "Museum of Faiths," to borrow the title of a recent review of the parliament by Eric Ziolkowski (1993). Ziolkowski's phrase is particularly apt for, as he demonstrates, there was a tension in the parliament between offering an occasion for interfaith colloquy and providing a site for the display of religious specimens. Whatever goals of modernist universalism may have inspired the parliament, these were offset by an equally modern urge to catalog and exhibit the treasures of human culture.

It is into this mix that I must introduce our traveling swami—not simply as yet another wide-eyed visitor, not simply as a crowd-pleasing orator, but also as a self-appointed representative of Hindu culture. Situating Vivekananda in this fashion prompts me to ask, What might we discover if we were to examine the fit between his own purpose in coming to the parliament and the logic of this modernist museum? That is, what correlations exist between the philosophical worldview of our visitor, the religious vision of the parliament, and the larger dynamics of the World's Fair?

Considering what must have been the extreme disorientation felt by Vivekananda upon arriving in Chicago, I find it extraordinary that the very next day he set out to visit the fair, which had only recently opened. With all else that might have distracted or fascinated the curious visitor about the impressive metropolis of Chicago, it was the fair that galvanized Vivekananda. It's as if he had to go.

It is hard at this remove to recapture what must have been the enthusiasm and awe he felt as he first approached the sprawling grounds.

Among his few recorded comments on the fair is the observation that it was a "tremendous affair," a spectacle that required ten days to be seen in full (CW 5: 11).

"Tremendous" seems like an understatement, when one considers what had been planned and brought to realization on Chicago's Midway. No sooner had Chicago been selected for the honor of holding the World Columbian Exposition than planning began in earnest toward the creation of an exposition that would be the mother of all expositions. A fever of invention began to take hold of would-be architects and planners, a fever that yielded some truly bizarre proposals and a no-less-bizarre finished product. Before the fair had even opened, its supporters were so awed by the spectacle they had planned that they made bold to announce, "In its scope and magnificence the Exposition stands alone. There is nothing like it in all history" (see Burg 1976: 75).

Consider for a moment some of the flights of fancy inspired by the prospect of a Chicago exposition:

- There was one designer who envisioned erecting an enormous tentlike structure that would house the entire exposition—it would be 3,000 feet in diameter (an area equivalent to seven city blocks); its roof would be suspended from a central pole, 1,000 feet high.
- Another visionary proposal was for a tower that would put the Eiffel Tower to shame. The proposed spire would be 1,500 feet tall (as opposed to the Eiffel's 984), and inside it would be housed the world's largest music hall; and, lest that not seem grand enough, a 5,000-room hotel.
- Someone else suggested creating a 450-foot giant, kneeling like Atlas and holding a gigantic globe on his back. Inside the globe, the plan called for building an assembly hall with a capacity of 10,000 to 15,000 people.
- Yet another proposal called for something to be known as the Water Palace. David Burg describes it in the following manner:

> The Water Palace would have been a large circular structure, topped off with a steel and glass dome, on which would be mounted replicas of Columbus's three caravels and over which would tumble an enormous volume of water which would plummet into a moat around the base of the dome that would harbor a historical exhibit of naval architecture—all to be illuminated by electric lights. (Burg 1976: 80)

- Finally, as if this were not enough, one proposal called for buying the Coliseum in Rome and shipping it to Chicago, where it could be reassembled, stone by stone!

These are just some of the ideas that flitted through the feverish dreams of planners and engineers. Clearly the emphasis was on *big*, but not just for bigness' sake. Size spoke of triumphal encompassment. Indeed, many of these proposals reflect a desire to encompass huge public spaces—assembly rooms, hotels, and music halls—within an enormous structure. Here was the desire to be inclusive made manifest, an exercise in the global, an effort at totality. Admittedly, this was not a uniquely American exercise. Rather, it suggests something about the phenomenon of the modern world's fair. As one Frenchman remarked of the Paris Exhibition of 1889, "une Exposition universelle est une totalisation" (quoted in Levin 1986: 31). What we have to reckon with is that any world's fair is a quintessential expression of triumphal modernism; in it the grand narrative is spread out across the landscape.

Still, the 1893 Chicago World's Fair was the Columbian exposition, and in its goal of presenting America to the world we do witness the unique expression of American modernism. This is especially evident from what actually materialized out of the many visionary proposals submitted in advance of the fair. While it is easy to see why the proposals mentioned above never progressed beyond the drawing board, what was eventually created was hardly less fantastic. Here, again, are some facts to ponder:

- The size of the fairground alone was staggering: 200 buildings arranged over carefully planned and landscaped grounds of over 600 acres—nearly six times as much land as at the great Paris Exhibition of 1889. Indeed, someone calculated that to see everything in the fair even once quickly, a visitor would need to spend three weeks and walk about 150 miles (Applebaum 1980: 5).
- Nearly every account of the fair dwells upon the grandeur and enormity of the Manufactures and Liberal Arts Building. Never mind bringing the Coliseum from Rome, for the Manufactures Building ended up being four times as large as the Coliseum, with seating for 300,000 people. Contemporary observers remarked that the entire army of Russia could be mobilized across its floor, or that one could have fit inside this hall the U.S.

Capitol, the Great Pyramid, Winchester Cathedral, Madison Square Garden, and St. Paul's Cathedral (Burg 1976: 97).

- Finally, to power the fair's astounding range of technological invention—which included enormous fountains, searchlights, and exotic kinetoscopes—Westinghouse was called on to build a power-generating facility larger than the one then supplying the business district of Chicago. It was the largest employment of electrical power in the nineteenth century (Burg 1976: 98).

Even this quick sampling of the fair's attractions serves to illustrate that the real marvel of the fair was its architecture and planning (Applebaum 1980: 7). At the official dedication in October 1892, the president of the corporation responsible for bringing the fair into being remarked that the overall spectacle of the fair afforded a scene of "beauty and grandeur unrivaled by any other spot on Earth" (see Burg 1976: 106). Certainly, when contrasted with the dark and gritty reality of the railyards and factories of Chicago, the gleaming, unpainted facades and well-manicured vistas of the fair presented to the sore eyes of fairgoers a sight of pristine glory. It is precisely because of this sparkling freshness that the architecture of the fair came to be known as the White City style.

Stylistically, White City architecture represented an extension of the Beaux Arts tradition, amplified, however, by a noted propensity for mixing a range of styles drawn from Greek and Roman antiquity, Byzantium, and the Italian Renaissance. Perhaps the single best example of such eclecticism was Louis Sullivan's Transportation Building, which incorporated into its Beaux Arts framework elaborate ornamentation drawn from both Islamic and Byzantine architecture. The result of such eclectic selection and juxtaposition is strikingly evident in Sullivan's Golden Doorway, known to fairgoers as the Gate of the Sun (Applebaum 1980: 58; see Fig. 2).

Indeed, the World's Columbian Exposition is said to have amounted to "a show of power" for eclecticism in architecture (Kidney 1974: 18). It must be noted that this was due not solely to the prominence of the White City style, but also to the fact that the fair was awash in styles, periods, and traditions. Beside the monumental classicism of the Beaux Arts buildings one could find Spanish towers in honor of Columbus, the French Gothic of the Marine Café, a replica of a Japanese monastic building, and an electrical display mounted by Western Electric in what purported to be an Egyptian temple. Likewise one could puzzle over the combination of a Dutch pavilion perched on the shores of a canal on

Figure 2 The “Golden Doorway” of Louis Sullivan’s Tranportation Building at the World’s Columbian Exposition, Chicago. Drawing by Selden Richardson. Used by permission of the artist.

whose waters floated Venetian gondolas and a Norwegian Viking boat. This latter set of juxtapositions was by no means unique. The entire fair was an orderly jumble, in which Old Vienna, the streets of Cairo, and a Laplander village were "packed together cheek by jowl in an exceedingly confined—not to say confused—space."[3]

To some, the White City style itself appears "disconcertingly eclectic" (Applebaum 1980: 11). But why is such eclecticism disconcerting? In the previous chapter I commented on modernity's ambivalence regarding eclecticism. In this connection I would suggest that the critic's discomfort with the White City style reflects one pole of the modernist response to selectivity. In other words, it is the same discomfort Baudelaire experienced when viewing painting in midcentury Paris. As he surveyed the work of contemporary painters, Baudelaire claimed to detect a regrettable lapse into eclecticism—regrettable because he viewed it as normless, feeble, and superficial (Baudelaire 1968: 251). And yet, while both Baudelaire and the critic disconcerted with the White City share one typically modern response to eclecticism, we must acknowledge that the eclecticism of the White City is itself a hallmark of modernism. Its selectivity is the flip side of the fair's attempt at universality through inclusion. We find ourselves caught between the chaotic juxtapositions of the museum and the static universalism of the grid.

At this point it may do well to return to our visitor from India, who has just arrived at the White City. It would hardly be an exaggeration to say that the swami had landed in wonderland—a kind of crazy-quilt universe of styles and traditions stitched together from scraps gathered from around the world and across time. In thinking about the significance of the visit of Swami Vivekananda to the World's Parliament of Religions, one can scarcely help considering the rather striking relationship that pertains between the fantastic eclecticism represented in the architecture and exhibits of the fair and his own eclectic mode of religious world-construction. What does he make of what he sees and hears, tastes and feels, as he moves around the grounds, into and out of the many buildings and exhibitions?

Something of what he must have experienced has been suggested in his official biography:

> He was struck with amazement at the wonders he saw. Here all the latest products of the inventive and artistic mind of the entire world had been brought to a focus, as it were, for examination and admiration. He visited the various exposition palaces, marvelling at the array

> of machinery, at the arts and products of many lands, and, above all, at the energy and practical acumen of the human mind as manifested by the exhibits. (*Life of Vivekananda* 1: 400)

In subsequent days, we are told, Vivekananda "continued to frequent the Fair, eager to absorb all that was of value. He was fascinated by the splendour and perfect organization of it all" (*Life of Vivekananda* 1: 400).

And yet the Swami's response cannot be taken as the normative one. To many other contemporary observers the organization of the fair was far from perfect. Unlike Vivekananda, they found the rampant excesses of eclecticism difficult to stomach. One such visitor was Henry Adams, the grandson of John Quincy Adams. Henry visited the exposition twice during the summer of 1893, and he later recorded his opinions of it in his autobiography, *The Education of Henry Adams*: "The Exposition itself denied philosophy. One might find fault till the last gate closed, one could still explain nothing that needed explanation. . . . Since Noah's Ark, no such Babel of loose and ill-joined, such vague and ill-defined and unrelated thoughts and half thoughts and experimental outcries as the Exposition, had ever ruffled the surface of the [Great] Lakes" (quoted in Badger 1979: 120). Adams seeks in the exposition the assurances of the grid; he looks for system. However, he finds only looseness and disorder. That Adams could voice such deep reservations, while others praised the fair for its grand evocation of unity amid diversity, merely reminds us how modernism is divided against itself. It finds itself torn between the particulars of history and the universals of reason.

Seager's study does a good job of highlighting the ways this fundamental tension was given concrete manifestation at the fair. Most telling, perhaps, is the contrast between the particularism of the chaotic Midway Plaisance and the universalism of the classical facades of the so-called White City. Seager sees in this the manifest tension between a fascination with what is "merely particular" and the grand vision of enlightened universalism (Seager 1995: 25, drawing upon Rydell 1984).

It is this tension between the particular and the universal that gives greater force to the problem and the practice of eclecticism. As one contemporary observer noted, what you had at the fair was "the civilized and the savage world to choose from—or rather to take one after the other" (quoted in Seager 1995: 28). In other words, even though the grand Columbian myth was framed against a backdrop of universal reason and enlightenment, its evocation at the fair was brought about through a climate of random juxtaposition. Not surprisingly, as Seager points out, this tension between rational universals and historical particularity could work to undercut the avowed goals of the fair. For when one channels the ideals of freedom, enlightenment, and inclusivism into the particular rubrics of Christian millennialism and evolutionary progressivism, the end product turns out to be a mixture of racism, xenophobia, and exclusivism.

We confront this tension directly when we examine the program created for the World's Parliament of Religions, whose putative goal was to inaugurate a new era of "tolerance, cooperation, and peace" (Badger 1979: 125–126). To bring these universalist dreams to life, the parliament was in fact encouraged to adopt an eclectic approach. The World's Fair Congress Auxiliary (which oversaw the procedural planning of the twenty departments within the World's Fair, including the Department of Religion) had decreed that no one species of truth would be privileged at the fair. Rather, the goal would be to give equal opportunity to "all varieties of thought" while studiously avoiding all debate, controversy, difference of opinion, or conflict of ideas (Badger 1979: 98). In terms of the parliament, this guaranteed not only that there would be no judgment or condemnation of religious worldviews, but also that there would be no grand effort toward synthesizing all the religious positions presented. What one found within the parliament, then, was what one found presented magnificently across the rest of the fairgrounds—wild and wonderful juxtaposition.[4]

It was to this eclectic paradise that Vivekananda had come to represent India. Even though he arrived in America with no official invitation to the parliament, his own determination, a bit of luck, and some kind friends won him a place on the program (see *Life of Vivekananda* 1: chap. 21). The odds of his being recognized as a delegate were certainly improved by the fact that it was India he claimed to represent rather than Borneo or Paraguay. Among his broad-minded American friends in the salons of Cambridge and Chicago's Lake Shore Drive, India was perceived to be absolutely unique in being "the hugest standing Parliament of Religions in the world" (Barrows 1893: 78).

Furthermore, from the perspective of Vivekananda's followers it must have seemed entirely appropriate that Vivekananda should represent India at the parliament. After all, this grand parliament was nothing but the physical enactment of the spiritual truths of religious unity that had been embodied and taught by Vivekananda's teacher, Sri

Ramakrishna. According to his disciples, Ramakrishna had realized the highest states of mystical union with God, known in Sanskrit as *samādhi*. Not only this, but he also had supposedly found, in his quirky, unlettered, and unorthodox fashion, that these states of perfect, egoless bliss could be attained by any number of religious paths. He himself was thus viewed as a kind of spiritual eclectic, who was driven by a relentless inner compulsion to test the viability of various Hindu—not to mention Muslim and Christian—methods of religious practice. As one contemporary admirer of Vivekananda exclaimed:

> What better equipment could one have who was to represent before the Parliament of Religions, India in its entirety—Vedic and Vedantic, Buddhistic and Jain, Shaivic and Vaishnavic and even Mohammedan? Who else could be better fitted for this task than this disciple of one who was in himself a Parliament of Religions in a true sense? (*Life of Vivekananda* 1: 392)

This admirer claimed to see a unique fit between the wisdom Vivekananda had learned from Ramakrishna and the religious vision the Chicago parliament claimed to promote. That Vivekananda and the fair seemed to mirror one another was indeed noted by some at the time. In one of the White City novellas spawned by the fair, there is a Hindu character whose pink turban and transcendental philosophy made him "a sort of embodied apotheosis of the Midway" (quoted from Clara Burnham's *Sweet Clover*, cited in Seager 1995: 28). Can we help seeing Vivekananda behind this sketch?

Both Vivekananda and the midway, then, became famous for their jumbled display of diversity; both represented a kind of wonderland. Scholars like Robert Rydell and Richard Seager have helped us get inside the Columbian myth-making and modernist euphoria that account for the curious chaos of the Midway, but there is more still to be said about the logic that defines Vivekananda's world. Curiously enough, Vivekananda helps out in this regard by explicitly conjuring up Alice's looking-glass world, in which he finds a suitable metaphor for his own religious vision. Though the reference is admittedly a passing one, it bears exploring as an avenue into the swami's eclectic universe.

At one point during one of his American lecture tours, Vivekananda found himself in the position of having to introduce to a New York audience one Hindu perspective on the nondual nature of ultimate reality. From this perspective, what the Jew or the Christian takes to be a real and divinely ordained creation is in fact nothing but the illusory superimposition of diversity onto the ultimate, nondual reality known as *brahman*. According to a well-known phrase, *brahman* is real, the world is false (*brahman satyaṃ, jagan mithyā*). If this is the case, Vivekananda argues, then all the apparent laws and connections that we claim to discern within creation are in truth nothing but a dream of order, a mirage of seeming connectedness. In reality, there are no connections in this world; connections require multiple entities to connect, but multiplicity is mere illusion.

We can imagine that this was a difficult first lesson in Vedānta philosophy for Vivekananda's New York audience. Well might the swami have searched for a metaphor or an image through which to make the lesson more concrete. The illustration he settled on, with a typical eclectic flourish, was Lewis Carroll's *Alice in Wonderland*. Why? It is difficult to say at this remove; perhaps Vivekananda felt this was a piece of contemporary literature with which his audience would be familiar. Then again, it might be that Vivekananda had a better reason than this. We must remember he was in need of some way to illustrate to his audience a radically different perspective on reality. He needed to take them through to the other side of the looking glass of *māyā*, or illusion. He needed to unsettle their assumptions about the world and their experience of it enough so that they might be able to grasp the truth of a nondual metaphysics. Until he could accomplish this, his audience would remain confused and unconvinced regarding Vedānta—just as they remained unsettled by the topsy-turvy world Alice discovered through the looking glass. Toward this end, Vivekananda told his listeners that what they took to be the most troubling feature of *Alice in Wonderland* was what pleased him the most—namely, that "there is no connection there" (CW 3: 23). The point he wanted his listeners to take home was that they were in fact that very moment living in a kind of looking-glass world; their confident structures of religious truth and dogma were in fact built upon shifting sands. There are no more stable realities or constant connections here than in wonderland. In other words, he was asking them to let go of their dogmas to envision other patterns of truth and meaning.[5]

This unanticipated reference to Alice, as well as Vivekananda's startling commentary cited here, are both highly suggestive. Here is the eclectic spirit at its best. To begin with, we have all the striking juxtapositions of the scene—an Indian holy man introducing a group of New Yorkers to the philosophy of Vedānta by means of *Alice in Wonderland*.

But equally important are the implications he draws from his illustration regarding the benefits of an eclectic worldview. Since there are ultimately no connections in this world, we may feel free practically to find connections when and where we will. Here is one way to avoid the charge of violence that might be leveled at the eclectic: Since none of the apparent relationships that structure our world—be they of history, physical contiguity, or cause and effect—have any reality, there can be nothing violent about severing them one from another; nor can it be any less real to reconfigure the elements of our world in radically new and unprecedented ways. Obviously for someone like Vivekananda, who was engaged in defining a new religious path, the implications were clear: Evidence to support the validity of one's path may be adduced as and where one will.

As Gandhi was later to conclude, if all phenomena are ultimately false, then all religions may just as well be said to be true. None can claim to speak of or represent reality; at the same time, all spring from humanity's legitimate attempt to wrestle with transcendence (see Gandhi 1962). Precisely because of the relative truth of the world's religions, human beings are free to pick and choose among them as necessary. Hinting at the age-old metaphor of extracting essences, or *sāroddhāra*, Vivekananda said we should be like bees who gather nectar from hundreds of flowers but are never confined to a single blossom (CW 1: 474). Anyone who has delved into the *Complete Works of Swami Vivekananda* will know how this basic rule manifests itself in his essays, lectures, and correspondence. Again and again we watch Vivekananda move smoothly from the teachings of the Buddha to those of Jesus and back again to a commentary on the *Bhagavad-gītā*. And every time we notice him setting up such juxtapositions, we wrestle with the temptation to dismiss them as the unsystematic and antihistorical musings of an overactive imagination.

Vivekananda was fond of saying that we always move from truth to truth and never from error to truth. Some have called this the "stepladder" view of truth, according to which we ascend to ultimate truth by mounting the rungs of relative truths.[6] Such a view echoes the thinking of John Stuart Mill, from whose work Vivekananda learned a great deal. Mill records in his autobiography how he came to develop "a most decided bent" toward eclecticism. He notes with disapproval the type of temperament that made one quick to take up the fight whenever confronted with an opposing viewpoint. In such circumstances, one "rushed eagerly" to demonstrate the errors of the opponent. For his part, Mill preferred to take a more conciliatory approach; rather than turning every philosophical disagreement into a battle between truth and falsity, it was more rewarding to search for "the truth which is generally to be found in errors when they are anything more than paralogisms, or logical blunders" (Mill 1981: 156). Elsewhere Mill refers to his method as one of "practical eclecticism," by which he means a procedure of gradually bringing people to higher or better philosophical positions by first finding what is good in their original opinions (Mill 1963: 42). As it turns out, there is more than a hint of Mill in Vivekananda's practical Vedanta, to which I shall turn shortly.

To better understand this interpretive philosophy as it applies to Vivekananda, we might return to the metaphor of the stepladder and try to improve on it. For while the image of the ladder adequately captures the idea that all truths on the way to ultimate truth are only provisional, it also introduces an unfortunate sense of sequence; that is, to reach the higher rungs, one must follow the preordained order of the rungs beneath it. Admittedly, one could skip over a rung or two, but even so the metaphor leads us to infer that the rungs thus skipped have somehow been encompassed in the act of reaching to the rung above them.

To avoid this implication—and thus to give greater credit to the idea of religious choice that we find in Vivekananda—we might think instead of a shallow ford in a stream. In keeping with the age-old Indian metaphor of salvation, our goal is to cross to the other shore. However, the current is swift and the waters cold. Our best bet is to make use of the many stones that jut up from the roiling waters. By negotiating our way carefully from one to the other we may eventually make the other side. But we must bear in mind, too, that the stones are scattered throughout the riverbed; and they come in all shapes, sizes, and conditions. Some are large, some are small; some are wobbly, some are firm; some are smooth and dry, others are awash with water and very slippery. Furthermore, there is no absolutely correct sequence that must be taken to reach the other shore; one may even need to double back or zigzag in order to finally reach safety. Who you are, what you are wearing, when and where you cross, how brave you're feeling—in the end, all these factors will determine the stones you choose. The point is, for all of us to cross successfully, there need not be a single, overarching bridge—only careful individual choices guided by experience and forethought.

This multiplicity of paths was not something Vivekananda bemoaned. What would be the point? The fact of diversity within creation was fundamental and undeniable. As the Vedic creation myths tell us, in the beginning ultimate being was all there was. But it became lonely; it longed for a second. Therefore, from the depths of solitude, the ultimate expressed the desire to be many. Creation—our world—stems from this wish for plurality. As Vivekananda put it, "Unity is before creation, diversity is creation" (CW 4: 372). This being the case, we should not try to force the issue of unity, to try to paper over the cracks and broken fragments of reality. Diversity is not ugly. "Difference is the sauce of life; it is the beauty, it is the art of everything" (CW 4: 127).

Taking the diversity of our cosmos as a blessing, we realize what great wealth we possess, what wonderful opportunities there are to pick and choose: "I do not deprecate the existence of sects in the world. Would to God there were twenty million more, for the more there are, there will be a greater field for selection" (CW 1: 325). Enrolled as we are in the grand pageant of diversity, we are free to choose. In terms of religion, as Gandhi was to say, "while we adhere to our own faith, we have every right to adopt acceptable features from any other faith." No doubt Vivekananda would also have agreed with Gandhi's immediate amplification of this assertion: "It is not only a right; it is a duty we must discharge" (Gandhi 1962: 3). To be human, for Vivekananda and Gandhi—as for so many other modern Hindu thinkers—is to feel the right and even the duty to define one's world eclectically. "We leave everybody free to know, select, and follow whatever suits and helps him" (CW 4: 357).

Vivekananda was astute enough to know that he would need to provide an adequate justification for his philosophy of eclectic borrowing. This is surely one reason why he invoked *Alice in Wonderland*. Nevertheless, Alice alone could not rise to the defense of Vivekananda. To find support among his listeners, Vivekananda would have to face more directly the question of what criteria one uses in selecting from among the world's religious data. This we find him doing in a remarkable passage written as a preface to his Bengali translation of *The Imitation of Christ*, by Thomas à Kempis. Here he offers not only a further justification for his eclectic method, but also a more formal statement of the criteria that should guide the eclectic in making selections. Once again we must marvel at the range of the man's resources and the confidence with which he recruits to his cause everyone from Lewis Carroll to Thomas à Kempis.

Clearly Vivekananda recognized how skeptically his readers might respond to his eclecticism. Some might, for instance, ask what business a Hindu swami had translating a piece of medieval Christian devotional literature. Such a choice might have seemed especially problematic to his fellow Indians at a time when the nationalist impulse was to look for inspiration not from Europe but from India's own cultural record. It is in anticipation of such objections that Vivekananda explains to his Bengali readers the choice of this work for translation. And on one level his explanation is quite simple: He admits quite frankly that his interest in *The Imitation of Christ* reflected his own personal attachment to the figure of Jesus Christ—an affinity fostered not only by his father's eclectic religiosity but also by his own education at one of Calcutta's most respected Christian colleges (see Raychaudhuri 1988: 223 and 244).[7]

This leaves unanswered, however, the charge that such Christian literature can have no significance for a Hindu. More to the point, does one cease to be a Hindu if one begins to look to Christ—as so many Indians feared when first confronted by Christian preaching? Vivekananda's response to these concerns is to cite (albeit somewhat inaccurately) a Sanskrit aphorism that he attributed to the Vaiśeṣika school of philosophy, namely, *āptopadeśavākyaṃ śabdaḥ*. He interpreted this aphorism to mean that any teachings promulgated by so-called *siddha puruṣa*s, or "perfected souls," have a "probative force" equivalent to the highest form of verbal testimony, known in some Indian schools of philosophy as *śabda pramāṇa*. In other words, the teachings of perfected souls constitute a form of revelation. But what is more, Vivekananda pointed out to his readers that the ancient ritualist Jaimini had observed that such perfected souls might be born "both among the Aryans and the Mlechchas" (CW 8: 160–161). To Vivekananda, all of this amounted to saying that saving wisdom is not the sole property of specific holy texts or specific religious traditions; rather, religious truth is a function of any individual's spiritual perfection. The perfected soul is one who has realized the truth. And evidence of such a realization can be found among Hindus and non-Hindus alike. Therefore, when one finds such perfected souls, one legitimately looks to them for authoritative truths.

The passage in which Vivekananda sets forth this view is as revealing as it is brief. It tells us something not only about Vivekananda's rather selective and haphazard way of dealing with his sources, but also about the very methodology of selection he wishes to authorize. The Sanskrit aphorism he most likely had in mind was *Nyāya Sūtra* 1.1.7, which reads, *āptopadeśaḥ śabdaḥ*. We might translate this aphorism as, 'Verbal testimony is the instruction of a reliable person.' On the one hand, Vivekananda's attribution of this aphorism to the Vaiśeṣika school is understandable, since Nyāya and Vaiśeṣika are customarily viewed as coordinated philosophies, the former offering an epistemology, the latter an atomistic ontology. On the other hand, we must pause to give further thought to what is at stake in Vivekananda's intrepretation of this aphorism. It turns out there are important differences among Indian philosophical schools regarding what is known as *pramāṇa*, the valid means for acquiring knowledge.[8]

The interesting thing about Vivekananda's attribution of this aphorism to the Vaiśeṣika school is that Vaiśeṣika does not accept any form of verbal testimony (*śabda*) as a valid means of knowledge (or *pramāṇa*). According to Vaiśeṣika philosophers, only perception and inference are recognized as valid means of knowing. The philosophy of Nyāya, by contrast, does accept verbal testimony as an independently valid means of knowing. According to Nyāya, such testimony may come to us either from the Veda—whose trustworthiness is unimpeachable since it was created by God—or from an *āpta*, or 'reliable person.'[9]

This slight confusion on Vivekananda's part is interesting principally in light of the considerable emphasis he places on the concept of the *āpta*. As his comments from the preface to his translation of *The Imitation of Christ* suggest, it is the possibility of the *āpta* appearing anywhere and at any time that allows us to conclude that the words of Jesus (and, by a similar logic, of Thomas à Kempis) can carry religious meaning for Hindus. The wisdom of the *āpta* is universally accessible and meaningful because it does not depend for its authority on the supposed sacrality of any given scripture. The truth of such testimony is linked only to truths of human experience. For Vivekananda, the paradigmatic example of such spiritual realization is the Yogi, the one who has seen the truth through meditation:

> We are all of us struggling towards knowledge. But you and I have to struggle hard, and come to knowledge through a long tedious process of reasoning, but the Yogi, the pure one, has gone beyond all this. Before his mind, the past, the present, and the future are alike. . . . He does not require [himself] to go through the tedious processes for knowledge we have to; his words are proof, because he sees knowl-

> edge in himself. These [Yogis], for instance, are the authors of the sacred scriptures; therefore the scriptures are proof. If any such persons are living now their words will be proof. (CW 1: 204)

Vivekananda was careful to add that for someone's words to attain this status as proof, we must be able to verify that (1) their conduct is unselfish and holy, (2) they have experience of matters beyond the senses, and (3) what they say does not contradict reason and experience (CW 1: 204).

Vivekananda admitted that Indian philosophers "go into long discussions about Apta-vakya and they say, 'What is the proof of their words?'" He recognized that for centuries philosophers had asked, On what grounds should we trust the testimony of the *āpta* and just how far should our trust extend? Notwithstanding this awareness, Vivekananda seemed content to sidestep such debates. It was enough for him to affiliate his thought loosely with the aphorism about verbal testimony.

Interestingly enough, his description of the *āpta* turns out to accord rather well with the Nyāya position on such questions. The Nyāya school asserts that all forms of valid knowledge are valid only by reason of extrinsic causes, a position which is known as *parataḥ-prāmāṇya-vāda*. In effect such a view holds that when, for example, Margaret tells us it is snowing outside we should trust this statement only if such trust is justified by what we can infer from her character and past behavior. Knowing that Margaret has never lied before leads us to trust her testimony. By similar reasoning, we say that the Vedas offer reliable testimony about the path to salvation beause we know they were created by the Lord, who is incapable of falsehood.

The curious thing is that while he apparently adopts the Nyāya position in his remarks on *The Imitation of Christ*, Vivekananda not only erroneously traces the aphorism to the Vaiśeṣika school but also goes on to complicate the picture by invoking the name of Jaimini, the author of a ritualistic text known as the *Mīmāṃsā-sūtra*. Jaimini's aphorisms on the exegesis (*mīmāṃsā*) of Vedic scripture and on the performance of ritual action form the basis for yet another philosophical school, known as Pūrva Mīmāṃsā. The Pūrva Mīmāṃsā, or the 'earlier' exegesis, is so designated to distinguish it from Uttara Mīmāṃsā, or the 'later' exegesis, otherwise known as Advaita Vedānta.[10] Despite important differences in terms of soteriology, Pūrva and Uttara Mīmāṃsā share much in common—including an unshakable trust in the sacrality and autonomy of the Vedas. For both schools, Vedic truth is valid in and of itself. It is so because it is eternal and authorless (*apauruṣeya*). This trust in the intrinsic validity of Vedic testimony is reflected in the general theory of knowledge endorsed by these two schools of thought, known as *svataḥ-prāmāṇya-vāda*. Unlike the *parataḥ-prāmāṇya-vāda* of the Nyāya school, *svataḥ-prāmāṇya-vāda* holds that valid knowledge is intrinsically valid—it needs no other supporting evidence. In other words, the conditions that produce knowledge also account for its validity.

Like the Pūrva Mīmāṃsā of Jaimini, the Uttara Mīmāṃsā (or Advaita Vedānta), especially as taught by the eighth-century philosopher Śaṅkara, holds Vedic testimony to be absolutely self-evident. There is no room for doubt, and there is no need for extrinsic validation, as there is in Nyāya. What is more, no other *pramāṇa* can call into question the validity of Vedic testimony regarding saving knowledge (Rambachan 1991: 46–47). As for non-Vedic testimony, Śaṅkara admits that while such knowledge is also valid, its validity depends upon some other source of knowledge. This is because, unlike the Vedas, such testimony is of human origin (*pauruṣeya*). Thus, if someone tells you that fire is cold, you would have to reject such testimony on the grounds that your perception of fire indicates just the opposite. However, if the Vedas tell you that your true self is other than your psychophysical identity, such testimony would have to be accepted as valid, even though it contradicts your everyday experience of selfhood. The bottom line is that for Advaita Vedānta no other *pramāṇa* can invalidate Vedic testimony.

The point of this brief excursus on Indian epistemology is to problematize Vivekananda's view of the testimony of inspired individuals, or *āpta*s. The goal is not so much to indict him for failing to achieve consonance with any particular classical system, but simply to highlight the eclectic pragmatics of his discourse: a bit of Nyāya here, a bit of Mīmāṃsā there. And—as we shall see—why not throw in a touch of the Buddha's heterodoxy to boot? It strikes us as odd to find Vivekananda juxtaposing such disparate authorities in his quest to universalize the means of attaining saving knowledge. The violence of his eclecticism can get a bit dizzying at times:

> If, brethren, you begin with the Sutras of Gautama, and read his theories about the Aptas (inspired) in the light of the commentaries of Vātsyāyana, and go up to the Mimāmsakas with Shabara and other commentators, and find out what they say about the *alaukikapratyakṣam* (supersensuous realisation), and who are Aptas, and whether every

> being can become an Apta or not, and that the proof of the Vedas is in their being the words of such Aptas if you have time to look into the introduction of Mahidhara to the Yajur-Veda, you will find a still more lucid discussion as to the Vedas being the laws of the inner life of man, and as such they are eternal. (CW 4: 340)

What are we to make of this jumble of authorities? As we tumble through this passage, struggling to gain a grip on the syntax, we wonder if we are reading systematic philosophy or pseudoshastric obfuscation.

Anantanand Rambachan has looked carefully at Vivekananda's hermeneutics and he finds them troubling—if only because they simply do not square with the acknowledged tenets of Advaita Vedānta, the system proclaimed and propagated even today in the organizations founded by Vivekananda. Alert to the kind of pragmatic calculus apparently at work in the preceding quotation, Rambachan points out that when lecturing in India, Vivekananda tended to follow carefully the doctrine of the impersonal authority of the Vedas. For instance, Rambachan cites a passage from an address given by Vivekananda in Kumbakonam, in which Vedic revelation is distinguished from the scriptures of the world's other great religions on the grounds that the Vedas alone have no personal founder. In the case of scriptures associated with historical figures like Moses and Jesus, one need only begin questioning the historicity of the founder and the whole scriptural edifice eventually crumbles. By contrast, Hinduism for Vivekananda is a religion based on eternal principles preserved in the words and sentences of the Vedas and not on the contingent testimony of historical personages (Rambachan 1994: 59; see CW 3: 183).

Speaking in Lahore, Vivekananda put it most plainly: "[W]e believe the Vedas to be the eternal teachings of the secrets of religion. We all believe that this holy literature is without beginning and without end, coeval with nature, which is without beginning and without end; and that all our religious differences, all our religious struggles must end when we stand in the presence of that holy book" (CW 3: 372–373).

How different this is from the view of the Vedas one finds when one looks at Vivekananda's talks outside India. In such cases, as Rambachan points out, Vivekananda emphasizes not the eternality of the Vedas but the fact that what the Vedas enshrine are spiritual laws analogous to natural laws. We may refer, appropriately enough, to the paper on Hinduism presented by Vivekananda at the parliament in Chicago: "Just as the law of gravitation existed before its discovery, and would exist if all humanity forgot it, so is it with the laws that govern the spiritual world. The moral, ethical, and spiritual relations between soul and soul and between individual spirits and the Father of all spirits, were there before their discovery, and would remain even if we forgot them" (CW 1: 7). The point is, while Vivekananda stayed quite close to what Rambachan calls the "traditional orthodox position" when in India, he was apparently content to leave this perspective behind when addressing non-Indian audiences (Rambachan 1994: 60).

Rambachan does not accuse Vivekananda of inconsistency. Instead, he suggests that Vivekananda knew exactly what he was up to. While it made good strategic sense for him to endorse the impersonal authority of the Vedas among Hindus at home, no such caution was necessary abroad. Thus we may suspect his preferred view of the Vedas emerges in his addresses outside India, which treat them as the record of spiritual discoveries made by remarkable human beings. In this view, the authority and status of the Vedas are viewed as purely secondary to the experience that created them. They are like maps; they spark our curiosity, but they can give no direct knowledge of the countryside. This can only be had by experience (Rambachan 1994: 44; see CW 1: 185).

Elsewhere Vivekananda recounts a conversation he had with a "very holy man," who pointed out to him that an almanac may predict the annual rainfall, but no amount of squeezing can make rain fall from the book. "So until your religion makes you realise God, it is useless. He who only studies books for religion reminds one of the fable of the ass which carried a heavy load of sugar on its back, but did not know the sweetness of it" (CW 1: 326). Once again, we have the appeal to direct experience. This, as Rambachan rightly points out, is the "pivot" of Vivekananda's metaphysics, the point he "unfailingly hammered." Religious truth is obtained "only by an experience of direct perception or apprehension, not by inquiry into words and sentences of any revelatory text" (Rambachan 1994: 61).

Just how much Vivekananda was prepared to distance himself from the scriptural exegesis of Śaṅkara is clear from remarks addressed to a group of listeners in upstate New York. Accusing Śaṅkara of resorting to sophistry in order to make the sacred texts support his philosophy, Vivekananda added: "Shankara says: God is to be reasoned on, because the Vedas say so. Reason helps inspiration; books and realised reason—or individualized perception—both are proofs of God. The Vedas are, according to him, a sort of incarnation of universal knowledge" (CW 7:

41). To this Vivekananda replied: "Vedanta is necessary because neither reasoning nor books can show us God. He is only to be realised by superconscious perception, and Vedanta teaches how to attain that" (CW 7: 41). And from where did Vivekananda derive his warrant for making such an assertion? Not from Śaṅkara, but (in good eclectic fashion) from the Buddha. For according to Vivekananda it was the Buddha who taught us: "Believe no book; the Vedas are all humbug. If they agree with me, so much the better for the books" (CW 7: 41).

Returning now to Vivekananda's appeal to the *āpta*, we see that the experience of the *āpta* serves as a map to guide us onto the path in search of saving knowledge. Whether the testimony of the *āpta* is enshrined in a scripture like the Veda or is found in the spiritual guidance of Thomas à Kempis, it serves the same purpose. In any case it is not the testimony, but the possibility of our verifying it in our own experience, that counts. In this regard Vivekananda is a modern humanist. He trusts that humans are the same everywhere, with the same faculty for experiencing the saving knowledge of ultimate truth.

Rambachan's problem with this is that quite apart from the strategic quality of Vivekananda's pronouncements on the Vedas, he has diverged radically from the position of Advaita Vedānta, which he is himself supposed to have helped to revive in the modern era. The most obvious point of this divergence is in Vivekananda's elevation of experience (*anubhava*) to a status of authority higher than scripture. That such an interpretive move could be attempted in the name of Śaṅkara, who is as ardent a scripturalist as Jaimini, is ironic, surely. But it is more than that, for as Rambachan has pointed out, the impact of Vivekananda's reconstruction of Advaita Vedānta has been felt with an almost global force. One might survey scholars from Sarvepalli Radhakrishnan to R. C. Zaehner, as well as countless popular works on Hindu philosophy, and find Vivekananda's paradigm fully in place. In Hinduism, we are told, experience is the reigning concept, with revelation reduced to the status of a provisional guide (see Rambachan 1991).

For the historian of philosophy as well as for the student of so-called comparative mysticism, Rambachan's observation is extremely noteworthy. It warns them both that they may have been misled into viewing the Hindu tradition through a pair of spectacles tinged by one particular—dare we say idiosyncratic?—interpretation of Hindu monism. No less than Bharati, Rambachan wants to call our attention to the biased lens of modern Hindu discourse in this respect. Both scholars wish to challenge the authenticity of Vivekananda's Vedānta; both wish to expose the errors associated with all forms of Vedantic inclusivism that have stemmed from such an interpretation.

And yet we might well ask, Who ever said Vivekananda's goal was to propagate Śaṅkara's Advaita Vedānta? As Rambachan himself points out, Vivekananda never performed that most fundamental of tasks for the Indian philosopher of any school, which is to write commentaries on the great triad of the Upaniṣads, the *Brahma Sūtra*s, and the *Bhagavadgītā*. Not only did Vivekananda never directly comment on the texts commented on by Śaṅkara, but also, the only commentary he wrote was on the *Yoga Sūtra*s of Patañjali—a text whose experiential import was undoubtedly its greatest asset to him (Rambachan 1994: 7–8). This being the case, can we really accuse Vivekananda of trying to pass himself off as a latter-day Śaṅkara? Without a doubt, this has been the message of his own followers within the Ramakrishna Mission and the Vedanta Society. However, the politics of legitimation in this case seem fairly patent (see Neevel 1976); and in any case need we lay the blame for this at Vivekananda's door? What's more, it is difficult to overestimate the significance of the pride generated among colonial-era Indians by the portrait of Vivekananda as the one who not only revitalized the legacy of Śaṅkara's message but also used that very message to win the hearts of modern European philosophers and spiritual seekers.

What is far harder to imagine is that Vivekananda would be moved by our complaints that his reading of Advaita Vedānta was not entirely accurate. After all, here is a man who appealed to the renunciation of Jesus, who emulated the rationalism and independence of the Buddha, who claimed Kapila (the legendary founder of Sāṃkhya philosophy) was the greatest philosopher India had known, and who studied at the feet of a rustic devotee of the goddess Kālī. On his own admission his work was "constructive" (CW 3: 195, 213–220).[11]

Above all else, Vivekananda viewed his work not as systematic, but as practical: "The dry, abstract Advaita must become living—poetic—in everyday life. . . . That is my life's work" (CW 5: 104–105). Confronted with the task of challenging the norms of religion and society in India and of propagating a universalist Hinduism for the spiritual regeneration of the entire world, his interpretive rules of thumb were not validated by painstaking correspondence with a given system of epistemology or metaphysics. They were generated out of the very pragmatics of his life and preaching. Let us not forget that this was the man who coined the phrase and cobbled together the discourse known as "practical Vedanta." If not practical, religion to his mind was but a matter of empty words and meaningless forms. By contrast, a practical religion was, very simply, one that helped other human beings; it was grounded in this world, the very place where people experienced joy and suffered humiliation. To attempt to determine in some final way whether the inspiration for such an inner-worldly orientation came principally from liberal Protestantism, Rāmānuja's Viśiṣṭādvaita, or Tantric Hinduism is surely to miss the point (see Bryson 1992 and Neevel 1976). All such vocabularies—and many more—come into play in Vivekananda's discourse. As the architect of practical Vedanta, Vivekananda felt absolutely free to "[u]tilize the things of this world" (CW 4: 241).

In any case, we did not enter into this chapter in hopes of identifying the absolute origins of Vivekananda's eclecticism. The robes of the holy man are never made of whole cloth, but are stitched together from discarded rags. So it was with Vivekananda's eclectic philosophical robes; they were a complex pastiche of threads and patches. Born into the grand parliament of Indian culture, tutored in the cosmopolitan classroom of colonial Calcutta, transformed by the magnetism of a modern mystic, and impelled by that experience to become India's missionary to the West, Vivekananda burst into world renown on the stage of the World's Parliament of Religions. The parliament was itself a microcosmic counterpart of the eclectic macrocosm of the 1893 fair, which was itself but a microcosm of the grand modernist narrative. Like the larger fair, the parliament represented an attempt both to evoke and to plot the possibilities for harmony in the modern world. Placing Vivekananda in that context allows us to identify some striking correlations between the cultural logic of the fair and his own eclectic worldview.

It seems that Vivekananda could not have found a better platform from which, and background against which, to broadcast his own religious message. If, in looking at either the wonderland of the fair or the worldview of the swami, we are struck by the seeming chaos of it all, we might well recall the words of the nineteenth-century French eclectic philosopher Victor Cousin: "When all around us is mixed, complex, and mingled together, when *all contrarities exist and exist well together*," can our worldview be any different? Can our thought avoid being eclectic, "when all around it is so . . . ?" (1872: 271).

4

What's the Connection?

India's Eclectic Heritage

For the modernist predicament, often epitomised in Yeats's words—"Things fall apart: the centre cannot hold"—we have the dialectical answer: "Things fall together, and there is no centre, but connections."

—Charles Jencks

Faced with the curious hermeneutics of Vivekananda, we find ourselves tempted to ask both where he got them and how we are to make sense of them. His appeals to the classical philosophical rubrics of India certainly suggest there are deep roots for his eclecticism within Indian soil; and yet, the dynamics of colonialism and the demands of Hindu apologetics suggest the determinative conditions were entirely modern. Surely we must hold these two contexts in tension. But then what? Will we have accounted fully for the origins of Vivekananda's eclectic worldview? Perhaps not, but then again, that probably shouldn't be our goal. Rather, by juggling the relative significance of the ancient and modern roots of Hindu eclecticism we can more importantly equip ourselves to take on our second question: How are we to make sense of such eclecticism? With this goal in mind, I would like to use this chapter as an occasion to venture briefly into ancient India—not in quest of the origins of eclecticism, but as a means for highlighting the problematics of positing connections between apparently disconnected things. At points along the way, I shall also have to pause to consider how Indologists have construed this problematic, especially as it relates to the problem of historical truth.

As it turns out, the theory and practice of eclecticism has an old and venerable pedigree within the South Asian context (see O'Flaherty 1980: 6). In highlighting a few moments from within the Indian tradition, my goal will not be to posit a genetic relationship between the discourse of the modern Hindu apologist and the thought world of the ancient Indians. Instead, it will be to open up a field of inquiry into what is at stake in the game of *sāroddhāra*. What intellectual problems does it pose? And how might ancient and classical Indian reflections on these problems assist us as we attempt to wrestle with modern Hindu eclecticism? What might we gain, for instance, by viewing Gandhi's claim that "all religions are true" as a contemporary refrain of what Max Müller dubbed the "henotheism" of the ancient Vedas? When Gandhi praises one religion without detracting from the truth of all the others, is he akin to the Vedic poet who sings of the supremacy of first one god and then another? Notice, I do not want to ask whether Gandhi is the heir of Vedic religious discourse; clearly he is and he isn't. What I want to ask is, What insights into modern Hindu selectivity do we gain by viewing it in light of ancient Indian religious thought?

And let it be noted that we need not confine the heritage of Indian eclecticism to the Vedas. We find eclecticism among the heterodox—the 'scorners of the Vedas' (*vedanindaka*)—as well. Isn't the fundamental goal of Nāgārjuna's Mahāyāna Buddhist dialectic of form and emptiness to undercut any absolutist point of reference (O'Flaherty 1980: 6)? And what about the distinctly Jain view of truth known as *anekāntavāda*, or 'the doctrine of plural perspectives'? According to the classic illustration of this view, if four blind men are led up to different parts of an elephant and are asked to decide what they are touching, there is no way to say any of them is either right or wrong in identifying the object as a wall, from one perspective; a rope, from another; and a pillar, from yet another. The point is, reality may be described any number of ways, and so the Jain theory of meaning is also known as *syād-vāda*, the doctrine of 'may be' (*syād*).[1] Recalling Hemacandra's eclectic tendency to quote from widely divergent sorts of sources in his *Yogaśāstra*, we realize that what at first glance looked like an idiosyncratic practice in fact represents a core insight of Jain philosophy.

We will return to the ancient world presently, but before doing so it may not be a bad idea to reinforce further the claim that eclecticism is an integral part of the Indian cultural tradition. One way to illustrate this is to consider contemporary Indian approaches to health and well-being, which represent a striking case of what might be called medical eclecticism. As G. Morris Carstairs put it in his book *The Twice-Born*, when it came to medicine "[i]n the village, no statement, and no narrative, was ever felt to be entirely right or wrong, and so none was discarded. Contradictory, incompatible explanations were allowed to co-exist. . . ." This being the case, it is by no means uncommon for the Indian villager to seek the assistance of specialists working in as many as four different medical traditions: a little Ayurveda here, a little Unnani there, some homeopathy today, a little allopathy tomorrow (O'Flaherty 1980: 6). One begins to get a sense for the pragmatics of *syād-vāda*![2]

One is reminded of Mahasweta Devi's short story "The Witch Hunt," in which the tribal priest occasionally and "eclectically" turns to Western science for help in "certain matters." In a wonderful metaphor, tribal and Western medicine run side by side, like the river and the railway tracks—parallel yet distinct, unconnected, and yet clearly related (cited in Bardhan 1990: 266–267). This metaphor illustrates nicely a point that has also become axiomatic within postmodernism, namely, that "difference relates" (Jameson 1984: 75). We might say that in all its various modes, Indian eclecticism is informed by this seemingly paradoxical notion.

To return now to the world of ancient India, the charter myth for Hindu eclecticism would have to be found within the sacrificial cosmology of the Vedas. The focal point of Vedic religious life was the sacrifice (*yajña*). Over the centuries, the sacrifice was subjected not only to detailed ritual exegesis, but also to sophisticated philosophical speculation, especially regarding its creative power. Thus the elaborate panoply of sacrifices known to us from the Brāhmaṇa texts and the Kalpa Sūtras represent both the ground for and expression of Vedic cosmological reflection. At the heart of such reflection was the quest to put the sacrificer, the sacrifice, and the transcendent world into an ordered—and therefore life-giving—relationship. The "prime intellectual tool" used toward this end was the construction of relationships out of difference (Heesterman 1993: 54). The Vedic seers, or *ṛṣi*s, who sought to ritually construct a cosmos, did so by positing the existence of connections among the elements of sacrificer, sacrifice, and transcendent world.

So exuberantly did the ritualists pursue this end that one scholar has claimed, "According to the Brāhmaṇa-texts anything can be connected with anything else; anything can result from anything; everything is all" (Thite 1975: 5).

It is often the case that the connections established in the texts of Vedic ritualism appear to be strung across the most implausible, even impassable, gulfs. Perhaps the most well-known example of this is found in the opening lines of the *Bṛhadāraṇyaka Upaniṣad*:

> *Om!* Verily, the dawn is the head of the sacrificial horse; the sun, his eye; the wind, his breath; universal fire (Agni Vaiśvānara), his open mouth. The year is the body (*ātman*) of the sacrificial horse; the sky, his back; the atmosphere, his belly; the earth, the under part of his belly; the quarters, his flanks; the intermediate quarters, his ribs; the seasons, his limbs; the months and half-months, his joints; days and nights, his feet; the stars, his bones; the clouds, his flesh. Sand is the food in his stomach; rivers are his entrails. His liver and lungs are the mountains; plants and trees, his hair. The orient is his fore part; the occident, his hind part. When he yawns, then it lightens. When he shakes himself, then it thunders. When he urinates, then it rains. Voice, indeed, is his voice. (Hume 1931: 73; cf. *Śatapatha Brāhmaṇa* 10.6.4)

What we have in this passage is an example of the sacrificial homology, the *bandhu*, or 'connection,' discovered by the *ṛṣi* when he went searching in his heart for the inner meaning of the sacrificial ritual (see *Ṛg Veda* 10.129.4; cf. 10.114.2).

As Brian Smith has pointed out, the significance of this connection-making proclivity of the ancient Indian has long been noted by scholars of the Vedas, albeit in a very curious way. From Max Müller in the nineteenth century, through Sylvain Lévi and Louis Renou in the earlier part of this century, down to scholars like Frits Staal and J. C. Heesterman very recently, scholars have found in the Vedic quest for connections the quintessence of Vedic ritualism. Furthermore, these scholars have long recognized that the practice of constructing ritual homologies eventually led to the grand metaphysical breakthrough found in the Upaniṣads: the identity of the eternal self and ultimate reality (*ātman* and *brahman*, respectively). However, such recognition notwithstanding, these same scholars have tended at best to look down on Vedic homologic thinking as a form of 'prescientific science' (Hermann Oldenberg's *vorwissenschaftliche Wissenschaft*) and at worst to dismiss it outright as irrational twaddle and unrestrained fancy (Smith 1989: 30–33).[3]

Two points bear emphasis. First of all, as Smith notes, these very scholars are the ones who have been responsible for "constructing Vedism" in modern Indological discourse. That is, their judgments have been hegemonic within their discipline, shaping attitudes toward the Vedas among generations of scholars. Therefore it is no small matter when they summarily dismiss the defining intellectual characteristic of Vedic ritualism as a failure of formal, logical, scientific thought. In so doing, these scholars—who claimed to know better—virtually foreclosed the consideration of other possibilities. And this is to say nothing about the implications such attitudes have had for the way Hindus and Hinduism have been imagined in Euro-American scholarship (Smith 1989: 34).

The second point is put quite trenchantly by Smith: Could it be that the ones who have been mistaken about the importance of making connections are not the "Vedic Indians but . . . those who have represented them in this way?" (1989: 34). To put it in terms that will help connect it to the concerns of this study, is it perhaps the case that when we scrutinize the verdict of these scholars we find yet another species of Bharati's critique of modern Hindu eclecticism? That is, does the problem really lie in the rational capabilities of the ancient Indians or does it have more to do with the canons of judgment presumed by the Western Indologist: reason, logic, system, history?

We know the earliest scholars of the Vedas, like Max Müller, were obsessed with a quest for the origins of religion in human history, and that they therefore greatly preferred the poetry of the *Ṛg Veda* to the ritualistic elaboration of the Brāhmaṇas, which developed at a later date. The former was taken to be the urtext and therefore necessarily more authentic than the latter. In other words, the early Indologists were historicists through and through.

Their positivistic historicism was applied with surgical precision to the full range of ancient Indian literatures. As we watch these Indologists search for the "original" core presumed to lie buried beneath the unfortunate excrescences of texts such as the *Mahābhārata*, or as they struggle manfully to rescue the "authentic" philosophy of the *Bhagavad-gītā* from its hopelessly confused textual prison, we are reminded of Jefferson carving away at the Gospels with his razor.[4] Perhaps nothing has troubled Indological historicists more than the body of Sanskrit literature known as the Purāṇas, whose eclecticism I have already had occasion to mention. When viewed through the *textgeschichtliche* grid, the Purāṇas have inevitably appeared philosophically confused and textually corrupt.

Confident that the problem lay with the text rather than the grid, historicist scholars have made it their goal to chart a neat course through the tangled knots of the text. One way to impose such order on these texts has been to reduce them to their component parts, which can then be assigned their own relative chronology and thereby judged for their authenticity. Even today this remains the dominant method of inquiry regarding the Purāṇas, as Greg Bailey has shown (see Bailey 1987).

We encounter the same positivistic historicism in Bharati's critique of modern Hindu apologetics. Like the Indologist studying the Purāṇas, Bharati assumed there were basic facts accessible to the scientific researcher. If these facts were apprehended clearly, they would allow for an accurate account of Indian history and culture. For instance, if one had one's facts straight—as Rushdie's exuberant critics sought to remind him—one would never attribute the *Rāmāyaṇa* to Vyāsa. Nor, as Bharati reminded the Hindu apologist, would one make the mistake of lumping together the monistic philosophy of Śaṅkara and the philosophical idealism of Bishop Berkeley.

In this respect, Bharati's species of historicism differs as significantly from its now-distant Enlightenment progenitors as it does from today's so-called new historicism. The Enlightenment historian was typically a cosmopolitan, whose goal was to search through history for evidence of universal human truths. The modern historian, by contrast, has become enamored of the particulars that serve to manifest historical differences (see Baumer 1977: 253–255). Recognizing this difference is important, since it reminds us of the vicissitudes of post-Enlightenment thought regarding the study of history.

The Enlightenment *philosophes* were primarily skeptics, who viewed history ironically. In this they differed significantly from the positivist historians of the nineteenth century, who used the Enlightenment model of scientific investigation as the grounds for construing historical study as an objective science. The latter view of history is still widely held, as the work of Indologists from the time of Müller to the present demonstrates.

There have been moments of doubt, however. Most notable was the crisis of conscience suffered by historicism in the earlier part of this century. It is customary to associate this crisis with the name of Ernst Troeltsch, who was one of those historians who was troubled to discover that the logic of historicism could be applied to the historian, too. Troeltsch's realization that the discipline of history could itself be studied historically threatened to relativize not only the historian, but also the historian's so-called objective conclusions about history (Baumer 1977: 500). In something of a return to the skepticism of the Enlightenment historians, early-twentieth-century historians began to question whether there was any firm ground for collecting and evaluating the facts of history.[5]

In recent years, the insights of poststructuralism, deconstructionism, postmodernism, and feminist studies have only served to heighten this crisis by bringing to our attention the "textuality" of history and the implication of historical knowledge in the politics of domination and control. As Jonathan Culler so nicely summarizes it, the so-called historical approach "appeals to historical narratives—stories of changes in thinking and of the thoughts or beliefs appropriate to distinguishable historical periods—in order to control the meaning of rich and complex works by ruling out possible meanings as historically inappropriate" (1982: 129). However, the very history that is looked upon as "ultimate reality and source of truth" is itself manifested through "narrative constructs, stories designed to yield meaning through narrative ordering" (129). One is led to conclude, therefore, that history "is not a privileged authority but part of what Derrida calls 'le texte general'—the general text which has no boundaries" (Culler 1982: 130).

The work of Michel Foucault has played a particularly important role in advancing this critical perspective. In Foucault's work we are led to recognize how profoundly the hegemonic discourse of modern reason is invested in positivistic historicism—a discourse that confers identity by what it "forcefully excludes" (McGowan 1991: 121). Likewise, Edward Said's critique of Orientalist constructions of knowledge, itself inspired by Foucault's work, deserves mention here, as does the work of scholars represented under the rubric of subaltern studies. The latter approach, in particular, not only calls into question colonial and Indological forms of discourse about India but also attempts to privilege voices hitherto ignored or suppressed by the "scientific" historiography that has gone hand in hand with the project of Western political and cultural domination.

Of course it is crucial to note that the postmodern turn against the discourse of reason and humanism itself arises out of a profoundly historicist judgment. Foucault, for instance, does not address history from some external vantage point. After all, as he puts it, "there is no outside" (quoted in McGowan 1991: 129). Rather, Foucault is compelled to work from within, pointing to the contingency of all knowledge in a profoundly historicist fashion. In this regard his work, like that of Jacques Derrida, takes advantage of philosophy to undercut the positivist claims of historical research while simultaneously calling upon history to undercut philosophy's "essentialist, idealizing theories and claims to ahistorical or transhistorical understanding" (Culler 1982: 129).

It is precisely the complex and sometimes conflicted relationship between postmodernism and the discourse of historicism that helps explain both the emergence of, and debates about, the so-called new historicism (Newton 1989: 152). Advocates of the new historicism claim that this approach

> sets aside the potted history of ideas, the Marxist *grand récit*, the theory of economic stages, the lock-picking analysis *à clef*, and the study of authorial influence. By discarding what they view as monologic and myopic historiography, by demonstrating that social and cultural events commingle messily, by rigorously exposing the innumerable trade-offs, the competing bids and exchanges of culture, New Historicists can make a valid claim to have established new ways of studying history and a new awareness of how history and culture define each other. (Veeser 1989: xiii)

Sadly, the very certainty of this pronouncement invites criticism. For, once you acknowledge that all historical knowledge is contingent and provisional, you must also forfeit the goal of providing a true account of the world. You can have your textuality or your positivist confidence in empirical data, but one has to wonder whether you can have both. Stanley Fish has in fact asked whether by denying history any "foundation in a substratum of unmediated fact" we lose the opportunity to ever say something "specific and normative"; his own answer is that even while admitting the constructed character of all facts, we may still experience these facts as firm so long as the framework in which they are constructed is not under direct challenge (Fish 1989: 308). In the conclusion I would like to consider whether a perspective like that advanced by Fish might not provide an approach for evaluating the legitimacy of various Hindu eclecticisms.

For the moment, however, it is clear that over the long haul of modernity we notice a dynamic pendulum swing in perspectives on historical knowledge, from the Pyrrhonism of the *philosophes*, through the positivist confidence of nineteenth-century historians, to the crisis of historicism announced by Troeltsch, and back to the re-(de)constructed historicism of the new historicism. The point in noting this dynamic is not to counsel despair, but to bring forward options that will help us decide where we intend to stand vis-à-vis the kind of historical critique advanced against Hindu modernism by the likes of Bharati. A positivist spirit will always tempt us to look for unshakable facts within their own context. However, such contextualism necessarily applies to our own historical science, which may eventually lead us to doubt the firmness of the facts we claim to have discerned. We realize we have seen things this way because it has been in the interests of our scholarly paradigms, our imperial designs, or our masculine identity to so see things. Suddenly, admitting new paradigms or envisioning new political arrangements allows us to imagine other histories—much the way feminist critiques of male-centered notions of "objectivity" have opened the way to confronting the cultural construction of the feminine (Newton 1989: 153).

Considered in this light, especially in terms of the dynamics of power and knowledge, one of the things we come to realize is the way in which positivism and historicism have worked to support the construction of the modern, Western self and its social institutions. Both have provided systems of classification that, by the very act of classifying, have also been systems of hierarchy. Ever since the work of Edward Said, it has become easy enough to comment on the implication of positivist science in the Orientalist project of dominating the non-Western world. Surveys of climate, population, cranial size, and linguistic communities have all contributed their share toward the "scientific" classification of non-European peoples and cultures. Despite—or because of—its attention to the differences among nations, cultures, and peoples, historicism has itself served to support systems of classification that are at the same time systems of hierarchical exclusion. For, once the 'essence' of a people—its *Volksgeist*, to use Hegel's term—has been identified, it may become a powerful tool for asserting the supremacy of one people or the primacy of one culture over another. In one sense, the dark side of the Enlightenment has been precisely its quest for such comprehensive, classificatory knowledge, which time and again has been made to serve the ends of nationalistic identity and power.

To take an example from the South Asian context, one might consider recent debates regarding the historic provenance of Indo-Aryan culture. Did the ancient Aryans migrate into South Asia in the second millenium BCE (as the standard Indological/Orientalist model goes), or were they in fact an indigenous people who exported their culture westward over the Hindu Kush (as postulated in a model that has garnered obvious support from certain Hindutva ideologues)? Though the grounds of the debate have literally been buried in the soils of northwest India for three or four millenia, this is not just arcane archaeology. Rather, there are interested parties who are all too willing to take history hostage until their demands are met. And these parties are not just fanatical cultural nationalists. For even though recent advocates of Hindutva have obvious reasons to hope for the discovery of horse bones in the remains of Harappan Civilization (thereby suggesting that the Vedic Aryan chariot drivers were in fact indigenous to South Asia), Orientalists from Müller to the present have predicated much of their own self-understanding upon a theory of Aryan migration that linked India to their West, India's ancient heritage to their colonial mission.[6]

Colonial empire-building or Neo-Hindu attempts to exclude the non-Hindu from the nation—either way one cuts the cake, one is compelled to admit that the project of historical classification breeds a form of violence. New historicists might take the high road and advise us to avoid perpetrating such violence in our scholarship, but it might well be argued that there is no way for humans to perceive, to think, or to act without such classification. You cannot—it has been said—live an "indeterminate" life (Fish 1989: 311). At first glance, it would appear that Horkheimer and Adorno would endorse this assertion: "Classification," they say, "is a condition for cognition," suggesting the impossibility of thought without exclusionary classification (1972: 220). And yet we must bear in mind that they immediately go on to say that classification is not "cognition itself." Rather, "cognition in turn dispels classification" (1972: 220). We must classify to think, and yet we must not mistake our systems of classification for thought itself. Rather, we must use the very thought so engendered to attempt an assault on its classificatory underpinnings. Does such a dialectical model promise us a way to generate knowledge without getting trapped by the logic of exclusion? If so, how?

One is reminded of Adorno's suspicion of all thought that tended toward reification and his famous pronouncement that "all reification is a forgetting." For Adorno, reification meant the suppression of difference. Consequently, if suppression of difference amounts to a forgetting, then to remember something is *not* to reintegrate it back into a larger whole from which it had been dismembered, but rather, to restore our very awareness of difference and nonidentity (Jay 1984: 68).[7]

This desire to keep in mind the ways one's classificatory schemes tend to foster the forgetting of difference is what gives to Adorno's work its nontotalizing character (Jay 1984: 58). By contrast, what makes the Enlightenment project so troubling is precisely its totalizing character: "For enlightenment is as totalitarian as any system. Its untruth does not consist in what its romantic enemies have always reproached it for: analytical method, return to elements, dissolution through reflective thought; but instead in the fact that for enlightenment the process is always decided from the start" (Horkheimer and Adorno 1972: 24). In this telling passage we are asked to look beyond the aspects of Enlightenment rationality we typically glorify—notably its adherence to analysis and the dissolution of received truths, both of which support the logic of science and the relentless drive toward the new—in order to see that behind this apparent drive toward disintegration there is a profound and troubling inclination toward identity and integration. Ironically, to forget difference in Adorno's terms is to reinstate it in the rigid totalitarianism of our enlightened discourse.

We need to recognize that the great Indologists who established the paradigm for the Western academic study of Indian culture were children of the Enlightenment in a far less rebellious and self-critical way than we are today. For them the Enlightenment was just what it claimed to be: the liberation of humanity from the tyranny of kings, the tutelage of tradition, and the villainy of priestcraft. Indeed, the latter theme provides a dominant trope in much early Indological writing, allowing a scholar like Müller to write off the ritualism of the Brāhmaṇas as a product of "priestly conceit" (see Smith 1989: 32). Working within the myth of Enlightenment progress, the Indologist presumes that between the primitive poetry of the *Ṛg Veda* and the enlightened monism of the Upaniṣads there must stand the priestly mumbo jumbo of the Brāhmaṇas. "We must not forget," says Maurice Winternitz, that "we have here [i.e., in the Brāhmaṇas] only very clumsy works of priests, who had to provide the innumerable sacrificial rites ingeniously thought out by them with similarly innumerable texts and formulas" (1987: 169). Recognizing such presuppositions, we can make better sense of Paul Deussen's claim that one could find in the Brāhmaṇas evidence of the deliberate priestly suppression of the wisdom that would eventually prevail in the Upaniṣads—wisdom he claimed resonated with the philosophy of Immanuel Kant.[8]

Talk about making connections! The Indologist generates his own series of homologies to explain (away) the ritual science of the ancient

Indians, while faulting that science for its excessive appeal to homology. As Brian Smith has noted, the point at which the Indologist writes off the Vedic homology—for its failure to appreciate the logic of difference—is precisely the point where the Indologist reveals his own failure to understand Vedic homology. The goal of the latter, says Smith, is by no means "to *collapse distinctions* but rather to *strengthen connections*" (Smith 1989: 220).

Homologization is a way of explaining that which is unknown (1989: 211). As Freud suggested, the point of making an analogy—however weak it may be—is to help us feel at home. The desire to feel at home is a desire for order and placement—for a cosmos. This is what the Vedic ritualist sought. The Indologist might have recognized that this was his goal as well, as he blithely proceeded to establish parallels between priestcraft in ancient India and medieval Europe or went about identifying Yājñavalkya and Kant.

Of course, to set up an analogy one needs to posit a relationship, and this poses a dilemma: To be put into a relationship, the *relata* must obviously share enough to suggest a relationship, while nevertheless not sharing so much as to collapse the relationship into identity. As Andrew Tuck has recently pointed out, the history of Western attitudes to Indian philosophy exemplifies this dilemma by revealing the epistemological bind involved in all attempts at what he calls "isogetic interpretation" (1990: 30). In order to understand, we have to relate the Other to something familiar, but in the process we also overcome, suppress, or forget the very Otherness of the Other. When Yājñavalkya becomes Kant or when Nāgārjuna becomes Wittgenstein, you end up with an "incongruous pairing of comparativist and objectivist imperatives" (Tuck 1990: 30). You gain something, but you also invariably lose. This was a conundrum the Vedic priests understood all too well.

For the ancient Indian, creation did not yield an orderly cosmos but a chaotic "anti-cosmos" (Smith 1989: 61–62). Order had to be constructed, and this could be accomplished through ritual, whose very purpose was to connect that which is "inherently disconnected" (1989: 51). However, in establishing the necessary connections, the ritualist had to navigate between the Scylla and Charybdis of what Jean-Marie Verpoorten has called "two symmetrical extremes"—namely, homogeneity and isolation.[9] For the connection between two *relata* to be a fertile one—one that bestows meaning and affirms life—the *relata* had to be neither identical nor radically distinct. In the ritualist's terms, one sought to avoid both an 'excess of resemblance' (*jāmi*) and an 'excess of differentiation' (*pṛthak*). If such a condition could not be met, one ended up with either barrenness or fragmentation. For the disorder of the anticosmos to be rectified, one needed to construct "an integrated unity out of distinct but interrelated parts" (Smith 1989: 52–53).

The possibility of accomplishing this feat depended on knowledge of the *bandhu* or *nidāna*—the enigmatic "identification" that has so amused Indologists. In an effort to help us get past the bemusement of the Indologists, Smith proposes we forgo using the word *identification*. He argues that this is not how the Vedic ritualists understood the *bandhu*. For them, to speak of identification was to speak of a *jāmi* relationship, which, as we have seen, could promise nothing but sterility. Smith proposes we speak instead of "resemblance."[10] In choosing this term he means to emphasize that what the ritualist sought to know and enunciate were not identities but "resembling forms of unity" (1989: 74).

That the Vedic ritualist was not interested in relationships of pure identity is conveyed by the language of 'prototype' (*pramā*) and 'counterpart' (*pratimā*) that is used extensively in the Vedic corpus. When the ritualist makes the homologizing remark, "Verily, Prajāpati [the 'Cosmic One'] is the sacrifice," what he means is that the sacrifice amounts to a counterpart constructed to resemble the prototype that is Prajāpati. It is this resemblance that explains its power. "The implications of regarding the sacrifice as the counterpart of the cosmic whole," says Smith, "are obvious":

> The construction of a sacrifice, an ideally continuous and complete entity made out of the joining of discrete parts (rites, performers, implements, offerings, etc.), is a reconstruction of the universe itself in the sense that the one supposedly reproduces—in a different form—the other. They are not identical but resembling forms of unity, sharing the same essence but manifesting themselves differently. The sacrifice is composed of the counterparts to the cosmic prototypes (each element of the ritual being vertically connected to transcendent correlatives), and the sacrifice as a whole is the counterpart to the prototype that is Prajāpati, the universe. (1989: 74)

Constructing such relationships of resemblance was the key to constructing and reconstructing the cosmos. Thus, in a sense, the paradigmatic question for the Vedic ritualist became: "What was the prototype (*pramā*), what was the copy (*pratimā*), what was the connection (*nidāna*) . . . to which the rishis conformed when the sacrifice was born?" (*Ṛg Veda* 10.130.3, cited in Smith 1989: 73)

It is to this question that we might ultimately trace the pedigree of Indian eclecticism to which I referred in the beginning of this chapter. Thanks to what Heesterman has called the "inner conflict of tradition," this question did not remain a purely ritualistic concern. Rather, the scope of its application broadened over the centuries until it eventually came to frame the very "universalistic inclusivism" that has become the hallmark of Indian culture (see Heesterman 1991: 297 and Hacker 1983: 14). How it came to do so is a fascinating problem, and one that bears more than passing consideration, since inclusivism seems to be the evil twin of eclecticism in modern Hindu discourse (see Hacker 1978 and 1983). We will return to this presently.

Clearly, then, the search for *bandhus* in the world of Vedic ritual yielded an intellectual tool of astounding power, since by means of such connections one could ostensibly construct anything out of anything else. For the sacrificer, the network of *bandhus* that mattered most was that which brought into relationship the heavenly (*adhidaiva*), the sacrificial (*adhiyajña*), and the human (*adhyātmā*). In the magical world of ritual speculation, mastery of the coordinates of the sacrifice meant control over the macrocosm of creation and the microcosm of the person. Cosmic order, long life, wealth, and offspring could all be ensured by a proper manipulation of ritual knowledge and action. At the heart of such knowledge was the homology.

As such operations of homologizing knowledge began to take precedence over the action of sacrifice itself, it was only a matter of time until the sacrifice disappeared within the homologizing mind of the sacrificer, and the logic of ritual equivalence produced the all-encompassing homology found in the Upaniṣads—the equivalence of the sacrificer's self, or *ātman*, and the Cosmic One, *brahman*.[11] Such knowledge was all-powerful, and because of this it was liberating; it allowed the sacrificer to finally leave the sacrifice behind, knowing that ultimate well-being lay not in continued ritual performance but in the renunciatory quest for knowledge (see Heesterman 1985: chap. 2). What one sought to know was *brahman*, described by Renou as "a connective energy condensed into enigmas" (as cited in Smith 1989: 72).

While it is precisely such "explicative identification" (Renou's phrase) that is meant by the term *upaniṣad*, Smith is uncomfortable reducing such identifications to enigmas in the way Renou does. After all, Smith's attempt to defend the logic of resemblance against charges of twaddle and mumbo jumbo is largely an attempt to vindicate the rationality and meaningfulness of Vedic thought. In other words, Smith is conscious of the fact that to start talking about enigmas is to fall into the same trap as his Indological forebears did. Here Smith's instincts are good. We need to be careful lest by calling what other people do "enigmatic" or "magical," we cast them in inferior roles with respect to our own supposedly rational practices. Nevertheless, to reclaim the meaningfulness of Vedic ritualism need not necessitate denying its fondness for enigmas; as the Vedas repeatedly attest, the gods love what is enigmatic and obscure (*parokṣa*). Thus if religion is a way of bestowing meaning on life, we must acknowledge that this typically takes place in the face of paradox rather than over its dead body.

J. C. Heesterman has given this fact explicit attention in his work on the transformation of agonistic sacrifice into insulated ritual. Whereas the original sacrifice offered an arena in which to act out the enigma of life and death through a dangerous contest, Heesterman argues that by removing the element of the contest the ritualized fire sacrifice offered no way to resolve the enigma. Instead, the sacrificer has merely replaced "the natural alternation of life and death with an artificial one of his own making" (Heesterman 1993: 31; cf. 74–75). It is in the making of this artificial, ritual world that the sacrificer resorts to the *bandhu*. While there is no need to dismiss this search for connections as mere twaddle, Smith would nevertheless do well to recognize with Heesterman that in the *bandhu* we are faced with a "conundrum"—"that of discrete unconnected entities that yet must be shown to be one single whole" (Heesterman 1991: 298).

What is this, if not the conundrum posed by eclecticism? Positing the likeness of unlike things, eclecticism works by selecting ideas, doctrines, or evidence from a variety of systems, and puts these supposedly unconnected entities to use in creating meaning—regardless of the internal contradictions thus produced.[12] And is it merely coincidental that we have encountered the conundrum of eclecticism in the context of Upaniṣadic monism? As Bharati pointed out, the metaphysics of nondual Vedānta has been the most-favored philosophical position among modern Hindus, who have appealed to the mantra "Truth is one, wise men call it by various names" (*Ṛg Veda* 1.164.46) as the prime scriptural justification for their eclecticism (Bharati 1970: 282; see chapter 1). In other words, what we discover is that there appears to be a very suggestive link between the ritual thought of the ancient Indians and the eclectic strategies of modern Hindus. And by investigating the logic of this linkage we seem, in turn, poised to learn something important about another problematic aspect of the eclecticism of modern Hindu apologetics—the phenomenon of inclusivism.

We owe much of our understanding of modern Hindu inclusivism to the work of Paul Hacker, who, more than Bharati, worked to delineate the discursive strategies of modern Hindu apologetics. Hacker long ago pointed out the important connections that exist between the monism of the Upaniṣads and the central philosophy of what he preferred to call Neo-Hinduism (see Hacker 1983). In an essay published after his death, he cited the example of the well-known dialogue in the sixth chapter of the Chāndogya Upaniṣad between Uddālaka and Śvetaketu concerning the identity of the self (*ātman*) and the absolute (*sat* or *brahman*). This dialogue culminates in the refrain *tat tvam asi*—'That thou art'—one of the so-called *mahāvākya*, or 'great sayings,' cited by Advaita Vedāntins to support their nondual vision of reality. What Hacker saw in *tat tvam asi* was not simply the desire to reduce all phenomena to the single cosmic principle of *sat*, but more important, the desire to claim that "all other speculations concerning the self (*ātman*), truth (*satya*), etc., are ultimately included in the doctrine of *sat*" (Halbfass 1988: 413). In other words, here was the hermeneutical heart of Indian inclusivism: all other doctrines, philosophies, and religions can be subsumed within the monistic view of reality.

In a nutshell, Hacker pointed out that the Chāndogya Upaniṣad offered an authoritative precedent that could be called upon by weaker religious groups whenever they needed to plead the validity of their doctrines. Thus, for example, in a city like Banaras that was virtually dedicated to the god Śiva, a medieval devotee of Lord Rāma like Tulsī Dās could gain a hearing for his poetry by claiming that Śiva himself worshiped Rāma. Or, more to the present point, the colonized Hindu, frustrated by a profound sense of inferiority (*Unterlegenheitsgefühl*) with respect to the colonizer, could compensate for this frustration by invoking monistic inclusivism as the key to religious truth (Hacker 1983: 20). In Hacker's eyes, this strategy of apologetic compensation was one of the defining features of Neo-Hinduism.

It is to Hacker's credit that he was able to suggest a linkage between this "modernistic concern" and the "ancient heritage" of inclusivism (1973: 21). This he was able to do very succinctly, by looking at a common Neo-Hindu interpretation of the *Bhagavad-gītā*. He singled out two passages in particular: verses 20–23 in the seventh chapter and verse 23 in the ninth chapter. The latter reads:

> When devoted men sacrifice
> to other deities with faith,
> they sacrifice to me, Arjuna,
> however aberrant the rites. (Miller 1986: 86)

What caught Hacker's eye was not simply the familiar inclusivism of the Upaniṣads. He was equally fascinated by the fact that a modern Hindu commentator like Sarvepalli Radhakrishnan praised such passages for inculcating the virtue of religious tolerance (Hacker 1983: 16). Here, then, was the link between modern apologetics and ancient cosmology. Like Vivekananda, but with far greater erudition and systematic scope, Radhakrishnan was able to argue how verses like this provided a vindication of the philosophy of Advaita Vedānta, which he took to be the *fons et origo* of all religions. As Hacker put it,

> Thus the Vedānta is the unifying element in the multiplicity of the religious views and practices of Hinduism and of all religions. . . . Now we must remember that Rādhākrishṇan, like more or less all Hindus today, affirms that all religions are equal in their worth or essence or aim. If, however, the hidden goal or centre or essence of all religions is the Vedānta which primarily constitutes the spiritual unity of Hinduism, then all religions are in a way included in Hinduism. This is the most comprehensive application which the principle of inclusivism has ever found. Incidentally, it would perhaps be more accurate to speak of inclusivism in many cases where we are inclined to see Hindu tolerance. (1973: 21–22)

The real thrust of Hacker's position lies in the last sentence of this passage. In a word, he was troubled by the all-too-convenient confusion (*Verwechslung*) of inclusivism with tolerance, which provided the modern Hindu with a means not simply for defending his religion, but also for actively promoting it as the ultimate form of religious experience (1983: 16).

Interestingly, Hacker claimed to see through this strategy in the same way Bharati claimed to know the tradition better than his modernist Hindus did. Thus when Hacker notes that most of Radhakrishnan's books were written for Western readers, it is as if to say: "I see what you are up to, sir." And, like Bharati, he was not going to fall for it. Hacker felt it important to debunk Neo-Hindu inclusivism in the name of his own European, Christian tradition. In particular he wanted to caution against granting to Indians the distinction of having perfected tolerance, since as he saw it Hinduism in particular lacked basic conceptions of freedom and equality that he thought stood behind the true meaning of tolerance (Halbfass 1988: 410). For this reason Wilhelm Halbfass has rightly noted that Hacker's scholarship was by no means impartial (418).

Halbfass has furthermore suggested that what appeared to have troubled Hacker was hierarchy, both within Indian society and within the logic of inclusivism itself. While Hacker acknowledged that it was natural for humans to interpret the unfamiliar in terms of the familiar, he objected to the temptation to subsume the meaning of the unfamiliar under the umbrella of one's own categories (Hacker 1983: 12). Since this is what Hindu inclusivism did, Hacker accordingly denied that it constituted a form of tolerance. Hierarchical tolerance had to be a contradiction in terms. In response, Halbfass has called upon the work of Louis Dumont to suggest that Hacker might have paused to give greater thought to the "pervasive hierarchization" of Hindu culture (Halbfass 1988: 411). Admittedly, such hierarchization can be seen as a powerful means of integration, but following Dumont's analysis it can also be said to offer a guarantee of "qualified recognition and toleration" to that which is integrated (411).

This raises an important issue upon which I have already had occasion to touch: If selection, comparison, and categorization necessarily involve the act of hierarchization, then can inclusivism or eclecticism ever truly work for the modernist goals of universalism, tolerance and reconciliation? Can we respect difference without succumbing to hierarchy? Or, to put it the other way around, is there an acceptable way to conceive difference hierarchically? When we first encountered this problem it was with respect to the implicit prioritizing of Western knowledge in its historicist and positivist modes. We were prepared to question the Indologist's claim to know better. Now, however, Hacker forces us to decide how we will respond to modern Hindu attempts to turn the old Orientalist hierarchies on their head. We find ourselves caught: As postmoderns we are suspicious of Hacker's Enlightenment discourse of reason and tolerance, and yet we remain moderns in our aversion to attempts by Hindu apologists like Radhakrishnan to defend caste as a rational and tolerant division of labor.

It's an awkward tug-of-war—Hacker and Bharati versus Radhakrishnan and Vivekananda. To the former pair we are grateful for identifying the hermeneutical principles at work within Hindu discourse and for spotting their strategic significance within the discourse of modern Hindu apologetics. However, we need to recognize the presuppositions that predetermine both Hacker's and Bharati's conclusions. From our dialectical perspective, we must say that we need Hacker just as we need Bharati, but that we must also find ways to undercut or defuse the agendas that inform their work. We thank them for revealing to us the strategies of eclecticism and inclusivism, as we do for reminding us how deeply the roots of such strategies are planted within Indian culture. It is up to us now to decide to what extent it is true that such strategies deserve our suspicion.[13]

The point that we would do well to bear in mind is that the modern Hindu apologist resorts to eclectic borrowing and inclusivist subordination in precisely the same spirit as did the ancient ritualist—as a means for flexible transformation and reformation. When considering the Vedic world, Smith correctly noted that homologization allows one to "explain the unknown" and to "traditionalize the innovative" (1989: 211). A millennium later the same goal appears to have driven the compilers of the famously eclectic Purāṇas. As a recent commentator has pointed out, "Not only do the Purāṇas avoid innovation and the proclamation of new truths, but, in a positive sense, they also make the original Vedic truth available in a contemporarily relevant way" (Coburn 1984: 37).

Hindu intellectuals and reformers during the colonial period faced a similar challenge; they sought a means not only of assessing and appropriating alien forms of knowledge, but also of arguing for socio-religious innovations while at the same time preserving a sense of cultural authenticity. One way to go about such a task was by homologizing. Those who succeeded most admirably were the ones like Rammohun Roy, who could affiliate the principles of Enlightenment reason and Semitic monotheism to indigenous sources like the venerable canon of Vedic religion; or Vivekananda, who could make humanitarian social service appear to be the traditional prerogative of the Hindu renouncer. This is not to say their claims were objectively or historically valid. As Rushdie might say, the truth of their arguments was far too important to be undone by a weather report. And while Hacker rooted the pyschological origins of apologetic inclusivism in the experience of frustration, we need not begrudge the apologist his strategy for this reason. If anything, we need to be more attentive to the manifold causes and manifestations of such frustration.

Having said this, it can hardly be denied that by enhancing connections among things hitherto never connected, Hindu apologists have at times produced what appear to be disorienting wonderlands of religious imagination. We have already considered Vivekananda's version of *Alice in Wonderland*. Is there really much difference between the predicament faced by the swami's American audiences and that faced by the startled shopper who finds in the local bookstore a slim volume entitled *The Sermon on the Mount According to Advaita Vedanta* (Prabhavananda 1964)? As Vivekananda intuited, both will be led to ask, What's the connection? We might put the same question to Radhakrishnan when he intimates parallels between the ancient Indian quest for liberation, or *mokṣa*, and the theories of Albert Einstein:

> *Mokṣa* is the realization of the purpose of each individual. On the attainment of perfection the historical existence terminates. . . . When the whole universe reaches its consummation, the liberated individuals lapse into the stillness of the Absolute. . . . The world fulfills itself by self-destruction. Einstein's theory of relativity with its assumption that the spatio-temporal system is limited and measurable is not unfavourable to such a dissolution of the world. (Radhakrishnan 1988: 46)

The point is this: we are dealing with something more than simply the quirky rhetoric of a few particular Hindus. It is clear that the fondness for construing enigmatic connections is both deeply rooted in Indian culture and at the same time absolutely characteristic of modern Hindu discourse. Realizing this, we are compelled to wrestle with the enigma rather than deny it or explain it away. When you look at things this way, Brian Smith's objection to interpretations of Indian thought that stress its enigmatic character—while well intentioned—was not entirely well taken. Is there not some grounds for saying—admittedly with a healthy dose of irony—that much of modern Hindu discourse is an enigma?

An enigma may be either meaningless or meaningful; it may provide answers or it may mock them. The difference depends on whether one has built one's world in terms of the enigma, and therefore finds shelter in the comforts of its paradoxes, or whether one stands outside the enigma looking in, puzzled by its oddity and angered by its apparent reluctance to offer admission. Like Mr. Wemmick's home in *Great Expectations*, the enigma looks odd "with its miniature drawbridge, its cannon firing at nine o'clock, its bed of salad and cucumbers. . . ." And yet for all that, its occupants rest assured that this home "could withstand a siege if necessary" (Lévi-Strauss 1966: 17).

The enigma, like the facade of Mr. Wemmick's castle, engenders in those of us who stand outside the same sort of response we have to "other peoples' myths," to borrow a phrase from Wendy Doniger (see O'Flaherty 1988). The challenge in both cases is to make some connection between a strange manifestation and something more familiar. As Doniger suggests, such an endeavor is often facilitated by temporarily leaving the world of visible manifestations and entering the dark cave of archetypes, be they Platonic, Jungian, Marxist, or structuralist (O'Flaherty 1988: 161–166).

This might indeed be a good way to begin making sense of Mr. Wemmick's castle. If we leave aside the "drawbridge," the "cannon," and the "bed of salad," we penetrate to the deeper reality of the ideal form. Entering the cave of archetypes, we realize what we have here is really not so strange or threatening at all; it is simply a house—four walls and a roof over the head. Comforted by the familiarity and ideality of this archetype, we are able to return to the harsher daylight world, where we can begin to ponder the unprecedented, concrete manifestation Mr. Wemmick has given to our ideal form. Because the archetype allows us to see things this way, we can begin to venture comparisons and contrasts. What is the relationship between our split-level ranch and Wemmick's quirky little castle? How does Radhakrishnan's inclusivism compare with my tolerance? Now, as we have already seen, new dangers appear; we inevitably begin to categorize and hierarchize, often making appeals to our chosen archetypes for justification.

As I read Doniger's approach to the study of myth, this is the point when we do best to let go of the archetype—perhaps in part because we know other such archetypes may be advanced. Instead, we choose to plunge into the manifestations. Not without reason, Doniger has for many years styled herself an eclectic in this regard; Freud, Marx, Lévi-Strauss, and others—all offer archetypal tools that can be applied to her object of study, but the very diversity of the tools precludes the chance of one claiming her ultimate or unquestioning allegiance; and for all the panoply of theoretical models, she never loses sight of the particulars, the concrete details of myths in their manifestations. Interestingly, here is the point where we can also link her eclectic approach to the insights of poststructuralism. For the poststructuralist there is no Archimedean point outside things that would allow one to gain final leverage on an issue. One chooses to be eclectic, not by fiat, whim, or stubborn irrationality, but by necessity.

We thus turn to delight in the differences revealed through a variety of manifestations, working as best we can with the tools at hand, and avoiding the temptation to reach for safety to any single tool. We are thrown back into the world of history, economics, politics, culture. We find that the peculiarities of the homes around us are far more interesting than the ideal form of the house. What is more, we begin to discover that we all tend to construct our homes out of "the cultural scraps that are at hand" (O'Flaherty 1980: 7). In a word, we are all *bricoleur*s, a species of builder made familiar to us by Claude Lévi-Strauss.

One of the most significant points about Lévi-Strauss's reflections on the *bricoleur* was that they served to emphasize the degree to which the creativity of mythic thought is always preconstrained. In other words, myth-making involves the continual recombination of the diverse repertoire of *mythemes* that circulates within a culture. The possibilities for such recombination are always limited precisely by the fact that these *mythemes* have been selected or extracted—we might say, *uddhṛta*—from some other language in which they already possessed a specific meaning (Lévi-Strauss 1966: 19). In one sense this can be taken as the pronouncement of a prison sentence upon mythic thought, since it appears that it can never move beyond a single universe of *mythemes* that it continually reorders. However, in another sense once we recognize the preconstrained character of mythic thought we also recognize its liberating potential: as Lévi-Strauss says, mythopoesis protests against the possibility of meaninglessness as pronounced by the strictly linear and progressive thought represented by rational science (1966: 22). By encouraging us to view myth as the transformation of other myths, Lévi-Strauss opened our eyes to the possibilities that exist for making and construing connections. For one thing, he allowed us to see that myths are best studied not in isolation but in juxtaposition with other myths (Sturrock 1979: 35–37).

There is a sense in which these insights dovetail with the understanding of mythic discourse in ancient India. Consider once again the Purāṇas. As we have seen, these texts were not understood to have meaning in and of themselves, but only in relation to the prior wisdom of the Vedas. This has two important implications: First, this suggests that knowing a Purāṇa will necessarily mean knowing its connection with Vedic mythology, and vice versa. This is why one finds it commonly asserted among traditional interpreters that "one should magnify the Vedas with Itihāsa [e.g., the epics] and Purāṇa" (*itihāsapurāṇābhyāṃ vedaṃ samupabṛṃhayet*). We may say, secondly, that the creation of the Purāṇas was understood to be—in Lévi-Strauss's terms—predetermined by the elements of Vedic mythology. The mythic universe is closed, but at the same time it allows for the freedom of new correspondences. Thus, tradition tells us there is no new revelation made in the Purāṇas; rather, Vyāsa (whose very name means,'the Arranger') is said to have compiled the Purāṇas out of a wide range of preexisting myths, tales, and legends (Coburn 1984: 26).[14]

I would like to suggest that our approach to the enigma of modern Hindu eclecticism may benefit greatly from the attempt to view it as akin to the mythopoesis of the *bricoleur*. In fact, when one considers the complex cross-cultural vortex of a city like Calcutta in the nineteenth century, it is hard to picture the indigenous intellectual as anything other than a *bricoleur*. Dhoti-pajama with socks and shoes? Waistcoat, necktie, and turban? How does one sort it out? What to wear and still be oneself? The nineteenth-century Bengali poet Michael Madhusudan Dutt wrestles with this very dilemma: "In matters literary, old boy, I am too proud to stand before the world in borrowed clothes. I may borrow a neck-tie, or even a waist coat, but not the whole suit."[15] What a bind: In matters literary, sartorial, and cultural, the urge toward authenticity competes with the fact of borrowing. It is as if the modern Hindu must say, "I'll never base my authenticity upon something borrowed, and yet I'll never be able to express that authenticity unless I borrow something!" Given this fact, can we avoid thinking of eclecticism as *bricolage*? Can we avoid giving our attention to the myriad preconstraints placed upon creativity? It hardly seems so. And if this is the case, then one of the most pressing questions we can pursue is: What are the principles of selection at work here? In other words, what are the "mechanisms of cohesion" that prevent us from seeing all this as merely "disjointed" (Bailey 1987: 113)? To be blunt, what's the connection?

If there are explicit or implicit rules that govern the eclectic's choices, then it would seem that we should be able to identify these rules and, once they are identified, test their validity. We have seen already that the likes of Rammohun Roy, Thomas Jefferson, and Swami Vivekananda all claimed to base their eclectic methods upon a set of legitimate criteria. For the modernist eclectic, the criterion might be human reason or common sense. It might also be the goal of universal toleration. These criteria were adopted by modern Hindu eclectics as well, but in some cases they also received a further elaboration in terms of the philosophy of Vedantic monism or the epistemological status of the *āpta*. In Lévi-Strauss's terms the criteria that emerged as normative were a function of what was already in the mix. As a form of mythopoesis, the *bricolage* of modern Hindu eclecticism has shown evidence of great creativity and variety. It is to the varieties of modern Hindu eclecticism that I would like to turn in the next chapter.

5

Varieties of Eclectic Experience

The Case of Colonial Bengal

How did the reformers select what they wanted? What, in other words, was the ideological sieve through which they put the newly imported ideas from Europe?

—Partha Chatterjee

While eclecticism, like Hinduism, makes for a handy working category, we must avoid treating it as if it were a monolithic phenomenon. Pierluigi Donini contends that one of the problems with Eduard Zeller's view of later Greek eclecticism was its "excessively generic character," which prevented it from accounting for obvious differences, such as that between the Stoicism of Panaetius and the Neoplatonism of Plotinus (Donini 1988: 27). Donini rightly attempts to correct some of the damage done by Zeller and to offer guidance in the best use of the term *eclecticism* in the future. However, I would question his categorical rejection of Zeller. Granted, we must seek more sophisticated models for capturing the complexity of the phenomenon of eclecticism, but perhaps we can enlist Zeller's help in this cause. We might, for instance, use Zeller as but one tool alongside several others that we have at hand (to borrow Wendy Doniger's useful metaphor). Thus we might juxtapose Zeller with Diderot, who distinguished between what he called experimental and systematic eclecticism—the former consisting of the ceaseless collection of known truths, the latter being the comparison and combination of these truths.[1] Likewise, we might include in our toolbox other typologies that have been suggested—such as comparisons between a rational and an emotional eclecticism, between a frivolous and a scientific eclecticism, or between an eclecticism of convenience and one of conviction.[2] Debates within postmodernism over the playful character of pastiche could prove equally useful.[3]

One recent attempt to distinguish among the varieties of eclecticism has been made by Raimundo Panikkar, in a suggestive if cursory essay that also explores the important differences between eclecticism and syncretism. Interestingly, Panikkar begins his essay by noting that eclecticism is always an "essentialistic" attitude. By this he means that the eclectic tends to use some higher standard of truth—some transcendent reference point—to put different phenomena into relation within a more all-encompassing worldview (Panikkar 1975: 53–55).[4] Perhaps not surprisingly, given his familiarity with the metaphysics of Advaita Vedānta and with the religious history of modern India, Panikkar's view of eclecticism resonates strongly with the decidedly inclusivist eclecticism of modern Hindu apologetics, which we have had occasion to consider. However, Panikkar is aware of the danger in characterizing modern Hindu eclecticism as ever and always a form of Vedantic inclusivism. He therefore advances an important distinction between what he calls the democratic and the aristocratic modes of eclecticism. While I have previously referred to this distinction in passing, it is now time to examine it more closely, both to flesh out what Panikkar means by it and to explore possible uses to which it might be put.

In Panikkar's terms, democratic eclecticism presumes "that truth lies in the common agreement and in the elimination of all particular discrepancies, so that a universal consensus (even if relative) can be brought about by adopting these incontrovertible ideas which men hold" (1975: 51). Because the criterion for selection appears to follow the logic of the least-common denominator, Panikkar calls such a view "minimalist." The example he gives is the nineteenth-century French philosopher Victor Cousin, whose eclectic attempt to build a consensus of world philosophy was an important influence upon both the American transcendentalists and Rammohun Roy's followers in the Brāhmo Samāj.

In contrast to the democratic approach, aristocratic eclecticism "picks up the best of each system so as to offer the cream, so to speak, of the different human experiences. Here the eclectic is not the minimalist but the maximalist, the man of genius who is able to offer a 'better' system based on the 'best' experiences of mankind" (Panikkar 1975: 51). The very language Panikkar uses to describe this approach reminds us of the Indian *sāragrāhī*, the one who extracts the finest essence, or *sāra*, from a variety of positions, which he then combines to produce the consummate system. Here we really have to do with Rushdie's "take the best and leave the rest." Here, too, we have to do with Vivekananda's *āptas*, those "men of genius" who have appeared throughout history and who have risen to a higher knowledge of truth. In other words, unlike its democratic cousin—which is more concerned with a pedestrian cataloging of shared human truths—aristocratic eclecticism is grounded in the mystic flights of the *yogī*, the *ṛṣi*, the Upaniṣadic sage, whose superhuman cognitions make manifest connections undreamt of by ordinary mortals. Clearly the concept of aristocratic eclecticism applies well to the Vedantic version of modern Hindu eclecticism, represented preeminently by Vivekananda and Radhakrishnan.

Indeed, such critical distinctions prove helpful when we consider the particular eclecticisms of the Indian Renaissance. Panikkar provides a tool for us to distinguish democratic Brāhmo eclecticism from its more aristocratic Vedantic cousin. Not only are we cautioned against generalizing about modern Hindu discourse, but we also are prompted to consider what might have contributed to such differences in the principles of selective borrowing. Thus the democratic eclecticism of the Brāhmos may be seen to reflect the peculiar context of religious reform in early-nineteenth-century Calcutta. This was the period when Rammohun Roy worked out his view of Hindu theism in the shadow of the Enlightenment and the French Revolution and in conscious dialogue with other democratic eclectics like the Unitarians. By contrast, Swami Vivekananda's aristocratic eclecticism appeared at the end of the century. Profound changes in the relationship between England and the Indian people—such as a century of Christian proselytizing, the solidification of the Raj after 1857, and the increasingly racist presuppositions of the imperial elite—may well have suggested to Indians that the democratic humility of Rammohun was no longer appropriate or beneficial.

In Vivekananda's day, the colonized could no longer even pretend to be an equal partner in dialogue with the colonizer. Colonial curriculum, policy, and preaching all attempted to extract from Indians the confession that in the Europeans they had met their betters, the agents of their civilization. This is what makes the message of Vivekananda so startling and so generative. With him we begin to notice the beginnings of a mission in reverse—an attempt to shout down the colonizer, to make the West listen for a change. When Vivekananda made bold to claim there were some things the West did not know, what else was he doing but attempting to one-up the imperialists? Such one-upmanship is most apparent in Vivekananda's spiritual challenge to the Occident: "When the Oriental wants to learn about machine-making, he should sit at the feet of the Occidental and learn from him. When the Occident wants to learn about the spirit, about God, about the Soul, about the meaning and the mystery of this universe, he must sit at the feet of the Orient to learn" (CW 4: 156). Clearly while granting the West its unique area of expertise—the very one that ostensibly allowed the British to rule over India—Vivekananda at the same time attempted to steal the thunder from the West by suggesting that compared to "the meaning and the mystery of this universe," such technical virtuosity was worth but little.

And between the eclecticisms of Rammohun and Vivekananda stands yet another mode of selective appropriation represented by the work of Rammohun's latter-day successor in the Brāhmo movement, Keshub Chunder Sen. Keshub is fascinating for the way he bridges, without necessarily directly connecting, the religious hermeneutics of Rammohun and of Vivekananda. I say he bridges without directly connecting because I fear that if we make the continuity appear too strong between Rammohun and Vivekananda, we will not only fail to register the profound differences between them but will also fail to give due emphasis to the particularities of Keshub's eclecticism. If bridge he is, then we must pause to examine the architecture of the bridge itself, and forget for a moment the two shorelines it connects.

For instance, if we consider the way Keshub typologizes East and West in his lectures, we may initially be inclined to see him as the direct progenitor of a worldview such as Vivekananda's. The continuity is apparent in a passage such as the following from one of Keshub's lectures: "India in her fallen condition seems destined to sit at the feet of England for many long years, to learn Western art and science. And, on the other hand, behold [that] England sits at the feet of hoary-headed India to study the ancient literature of this country" (Sen 1940: 345). For all that this might have served as the very text from which Vivekananda cribbed when making his later pronouncements, we must bear in mind that there are significant differences between what Keshub and Vivekananda are up to with such rhetoric. As I have noted, for Vivekananda such dichotomizing served the purposes of cultural one-upmanship. For Keshub, however, the goal is rather to promote something closer to a utopian world of mutual exchange and learning. Thus he goes on to say of India and the West: "Here they have met together, under an over-ruling Providence, to serve most important purposes in the Divine economy. . . . Let modern England teach hard science and fact; let ancient India teach sweet poetry and sentiment" (Sen 1940: 345). The differences between Keshub and Vivekananda in this respect can be accounted for by a number of factors, from personality, to historical context, to education and religious upbringing. Rather than viewing these factors as mere epiphenomena inflecting an essential core eclecticism, we should strive to particularize their very eclecticisms.

As I have said, Panikkar assists us in this task by suggesting that any general concept of eclecticism should be prepared to acknowledge its different modes and manifestations. One is tempted to push the matter further, however, and inquire whether it is possible to offer any general methodological principles that inform the interrelationship of democratic and aristocratic eclecticism. For instance, is it possible to view the two modes within a developmental sequence? Does one mode give birth to the other? Such questions do appear to have occurred to Eduard Zeller as he examined the philosophies of later Hellenism. In fact Zeller did ultimately propose something very like a developmental model to explain the origins of eclecticism. It may prove illuminating to consider the model he proposed.

When confronted with the eclecticism of Alexandrian thought, Zeller seems to have found himself hard-pressed to account for its origin. What he proposed was that it could be understood as the logical outgrowth from earlier forms of skepticism. To put matters only somewhat more briefly than Zeller himself does, his argument went as follows: At the end of the Aristotelian era, the cultural integrity of the classical period dissolved. Philosophy found itself paralyzed; theory was forgotten in favor of concentration on worldly matters; and the possibility of attaining certain scientific knowledge was called into question. In a word, skepticism reigned. In Zeller's terms, the crux of skepticism is that it puts all dogmas on an equal footing. With respect to all truth claims skepticism proclaims, *Weder–noch*—'neither one nor the other' (Zeller 1883: 4).

However, Zeller reasoned that such skepticism could not "rest in pure negation." Faced with inadequate conceptions of truth on all sides, the skeptic will be compelled to develop a theory of probability in matters of truth. There must be reason to expect some things to be more true than others. If not, how can the philosopher do his work? Without any ground to stand on—even if that ground is arrived at by means of the probable—how can the philosopher expect to achieve any practical results? According to Zeller, it required only a very short step to move from the skeptic's conception of probable truth to the admission that what is probable might just as well be true:

> Doubt would inevitably continue to exercise such an influence that no individual system as such would be recognised as true, but the true out of all systems would be separated according to the measure of subjective necessity and opinion. . . . Thus scepticism forms the bridge from the one-sided dogmatism of the Stoic and Epicurean philosophy to eclecticism. (Zeller 1883: 4–5)

Out of this short step eclecticism emerged. In contrast to the skeptic, the motto of the eclectic was, *Sowohl–als auch*—'one as well as the other.'

Zeller's views have recently received fairly extensive critical reconsideration and it seems safe to say that his particular model for the rise of later Greek eclecticism has been shown to have significant flaws (see Donini 1988; Dillon and Long 1988). It would therefore seem unwise to attempt to apply his model uncritically in other contexts. Nevertheless, even those working to revise Zeller's portrait of the later Greek eclectics have recognized a grain of truth within his developmental model. Thus John M. Dillon and A. A. Long have as much as acknowledged that Zeller was on to something when he contrasted the *Weder–noch* with the *Sowohl–als auch*. What Zeller's model suggested is that skepticism and eclecticism represent "alternative medicines for dealing with the same illness"; that illness was "a philosophical legacy that had become diffuse and multiform" (Dillon and Long 1988: 6). Dillon and Long suggest that rather than positing a genetic relationship between the perspectives of the skeptic and the eclectic, it makes better sense to view them as related strategies for coping with contexts in which philosophical, theological, or cultural consensus has become problematic. Viewed in this way, Ptolemy's scientific eclecticism may be called a "methodology of optimum agreement," in contrast to the skeptic's pessimistic dismissal of all doctrines as contradictory (Dillon and Long 1988: 10).

The kinds of context that Dillon and Long describe are precisely those that pertain during periods of intense and sustained cultural encounter. In this respect, there are important parallels between ancient Alexandria and nineteenth-century Calcutta. In both contexts knowledge was contested and multiform. In Calcutta, the orthodox dogmatisms of Brahmanical Hinduism, Evangelical Christianity, and government secularism competed aggressively with one another, just as the various philosophical schools did in late antiquity. In both contexts, the conflict created among these competing orthodoxies occasioned what might best be called a series of unorthodox attempts to deal with difference. As in Alexandria, in Calcutta such attempts often resulted in the adoption of skeptical and eclectic philosophical positions. Thus when looking at Calcutta one finds the eclecticism of Rammohun Roy and the Brāhmo Samāj contested by the skepticism of the group known as "Young Bengal"—a cohort of English-educated Bengali youths, who scoffed at Hindu norms, reveled in drink, and parodied the missionaries, all the while gobbling up the writings of Hume, Voltaire, and Paine (see Bose 1976: 69–91).

Certainly it will not do to construct a procrustean theoretical model that can claim to neatly explain the origins of eclecticism in widely varying contexts like Alexandria and Calcutta. And yet, when one surveys the intellectual developments of nineteenth-century Bengal it is hard not to notice patterns reminiscent of what Zeller claimed to see in the ancient world. What is more, if we were to combine Zeller's insights into the relationship between skepticism and eclecticism with Panikkar's distinction between democratic and aristocratic eclecticism, we might in fact equip ourselves with an important tool for assessing the varieties of eclectic experience in colonial India. While our goal may not be to describe a linear evolution from the democratic eclecticism of Rammohun to the aristocratic approach of Vivekananda, an overview of this historical period in Bengal would certainly equip us with a better understanding of the genealogy of eclecticism in modern Hindu discourse. Should the fruits of this endeavor suggest general conclusions about the development of eclecticism in other historical contexts, so much the better.

How closely skepticism and eclecticism were intertwined in colonial Calcutta can be seen when examining the biographies of the many young Bengali men for whom an English education served to undercut their allegiance to Hindu norms but failed to guide them into the Christian fold. One thinks of men like Tarachand Chuckerbutty, Ramtanu Lahiri, Rajnarain Bose, and Akshay Kumar Dutt (on the latter two, see Hatcher 1996). These were men who found themselves caught in a spiritual tug-of-war between rationalistic skepticism and the theological eclecticism of groups like the Brāhmo Samāj.

The missionaries—who played such a large role in educating these young men—were acutely aware of this situation. They continually reminded themselves that their educational work had been only partly successful. Since they viewed education as *praeparatio evangelicum*, they could congratulate themselves in many cases on having weaned their pupils from the putative evils of Hindu polytheism; however, when it came to introducing the same students to the solid food of Christianity, their efforts were often in vain. Having created skeptics of the educated Hindu youth, the missionaries could only sit back and sigh in frustration when they saw the same youth living out their skeptical philosophies in coteries like Young Bengal or gravitating to movements like the Brāhmo Samāj. In the eyes of the missionaries, groups and movements such as these represented nothing more than a "halfway house" for the spiritually homeless, a place where the "educated Natives" could "lay aside the gross errors of Hindooism without admitting the Divine origin of Christianity."[5] Echoing Zeller, we might say that the cultural integrity of the precolonial context had been dissolved, not only through the advent of Christian missionaries, but also by the economic policies of the East India Company, the growing trend toward secularism in the government, and the very Enlightenment legacy that informed the curriculum in many an English medium school. In this vortex of epistemological and social dissolution, the skepticism of the *Weder–noch* had its obvious appeal.

The Young Bengal group, or the "Chuckerbutty Faction"—as they were sometimes called after their spokesperson, Tarachand Chuckerbutty (the latter name being the rough Anglicization of Cakravartī)—was critical not only of so-called Hindu orthodoxy, but also of what they viewed as the more recent orthodoxy of the Brāhmo reformers. To the Chuckerbutty Faction, the same errors that plagued orthodox Hinduism were being perpetrated in the liberal Hindu theism of Rammohun. Chastened by the Enlightenment critique of sectarianism, Young Bengal could neither return to the religious customs of their forefathers nor endorse the new sectarianism of the Brāhmos. When it came to theology, they faced the same dilemma: On the one hand, the educated Bengali had read of the rise of reason in ancient Greece; for him the mythologies of Puranic Hinduism could be nothing more than irrational fantasy. On the other hand, he had also read Hume's *Dialogues Concerning Natural Religion*;

as a result, he could not accept the Brāhmo version of natural theology, with its heavy reliance on the argument from design.

Yet living in the halfway house of the *Weder–noch* proved difficult. All too often we find the very same skeptical freethinkers eventually gravitating to the Brāhmo movement—including Mr. Chuckerbutty himself! Once again, Zeller's model is thought-provoking—unable to live by the neither–nor, the young skeptics were inevitably lured by the siren song of the both–and.

Just how fine a line separates skepticism from eclecticism may be illustrated by examining the position of Ramtanu Lahiri, a paragon of Young Bengal independence and skepticism. Ramtanu was impatient with the Brāhmos, suspecting them of offering little more than a temporizing philosophy that shied away from the hard challenges of reason. Rather than give in to the false comforts of such wishful thinking, Ramtanu was prepared to live out the challenge of the neither–nor. And yet, even within his hardheaded skepticism, we detect the faintest traces of that desire to identify some probable truth that Zeller saw as the impulse leading toward eclecticism. For as Ramtanu was to write, "Let the votaries of all religions appeal to the reason of their fellow-creatures and let him who has the truth on his side prevail" (Sastri 1983: 165). It seems Ramtanu's call can be read in two ways: On the one hand, Ramtanu advances the triumphal claim of the rationalist that in the end, only one position regarding religion is tenable—namely, the one that pays due respect to the dictates of reason. But if taken to its rationalist extreme, as in the case of Ramtanu, such a position can scarcely be called religious. Thus the neither–nor response to religious truths verges on the either–or dogmatism of reason. Yet, on the other hand, Ramtanu's appeal to the members of every religion to search their religion in the light of reason seems to hold out the possibility that within every religious system some truths will in fact emerge that will be tenable. If so, it seems we might without too much difficulty slide over to the position of the *Sowohl–als auch*.

We need to avoid reading Zeller's model as unidirectional, however; if skepticism can verge into eclecticism, then surely the reverse can occur as well. A good example in the context of nineteenth-century Calcutta can be found in the case of the Sanskrit *paṇḍit*, educator, and social reformer Ishwar Chandra Vidyasagar. As I have attempted to demonstrate elsewhere, Vidyasagar had a profound involvement with Brāhmo eclecticism in the early part of his career; in particular he shared a close friendship with the leading Brāhmo rationalist, Akshay Kumar Dutt (see Hatcher 1996: chap. 9). However, if Vidyasagar is remembered today for a position on religion, it is not for any sort of Brāhmo eclecticism, but instead for a pronounced skepticism or agnosticism. In his case, at least, the uncertainty of the *Weder-noch* seemed to represent a more rationally honest position than the selective world-building of the eclectic. In this respect, having begun with close ties to Brāhmo thought, he gravitated in the end to a position more akin to the hardheaded skepticism of Ramtanu.

That in colonial Calcutta we notice more skeptics becoming eclectics than we notice eclectics becoming skeptics is perhaps due to nothing more than the need to find a point of anchorage in the shifting sands of cultural encounter. In such a fluid context, the skeptic was continually faced with the prospect of becoming culturally deracinated (Kopf 1969: 262–263). It might be said that Vidyasagar negotiated this hazard by drawing upon his family identity and personal training as a *brāhmaṇ paṇḍit*, an identity that stood apart from any dogmatic or sectarian affiliations. By contrast, the members of Young Bengal did not typically have such traditional identities to draw upon; they were a diverse, fluid, and internally conflicted group, and as such could not call upon a single cultural norm. Not surprisingly, we find that these young men frequently ended up by fleeing to firmer ground. For Tarachand Chuckerbutty it was the theological eclecticism of the Brāhmo Samāj; for others, it was the concrete rewards of comprador employment or administrative service.[6]

The case of Rajnarain Bose is illustrative here. Born in 1826, Rajnarain studied at the Hindu College when it was the fountainhead of Young Bengal iconoclasm. His faith in Hinduism was severely shaken. The sorts of movements that began to attract his interest offer a capsule summary of the diversity that nurtured colonial Hindu eclecticism. To begin with, there was the example of Rammohun Roy, with his critical rationalism, comparative perspective, and defense of Hindu theism. Then there were the Unitarians, whose influence on the tenor of reform debate in early-nineteenth-century Calcutta and on the work of Rammohun in particular was significant. In fact, Rajnarain was so attracted to the writings of William Ellery Channing that for a time he considered himself to be a Unitarian. However, at one point Rajnarain recognized that if it was a matter of affirming the unity of God, he could hardly do better than become a Muslim—which at one point he very nearly did. After all, here was an ethical monotheism that took an uncompromising stand against polytheism and idolatry, those purported evils of Hinduism so maligned by Christian missionaries. Furthermore, in Islam, Rajnarain found the same rational evidences of the creator that had been identified by Christian natural theologians like William Paley. And yet, no sooner did Rajnarain begin to contemplate the apparent strengths of natural theology than he felt the critical thrust of David Hume's skepticism (see Bose 1961: chap. 2).

One can scarcely imagine a more contested field of choices. As it turned out, Rajnarain eventually threw in his lot with the Brāhmo Samāj. Skeptical aloofness gave way to the need to find an identity within a movement that was not only rooted in the distinctive ethos of Bengal but was also oriented toward the wonders of ancient Indian culture. It was not so much that he surrendered his rationalism to the demands of faith as it was that he turned the tools of reason away from the task of upholding the destabilizing demands of the *Weder–noch* toward the more comforting task of demonstrating the claims of the *Sowohl–als auch.*

Rajnarain was initiated into Brāhmoism under the tutelage of Debendranath Tagore. It was Debendranath who had resuscitated the Brāhmo Samāj and infused it with a new vision of its theological message after it had languished in the wake of Rammohun's death. The specific changes instituted by Debendranath, with the assistance of men like Rajnarain and Akshay Kumar Dutt, need not be listed in detail here (see Hatcher 1996: chap. 9). In a nutshell, we notice a continued respect both for Rammohun's universalism and his dedication to the ancient roots of Indian religion, modified by an increasing dependence upon the arguments of natural theology—since reliance on a scriptural norm like Vedānta could no longer be reconciled with the rationalism of the group, as had been the case with Rammohun. Under Akshay Kumar's tutelage, the Brāhmos discovered that the whole world could be read as their scripture; apparently those that knew Hume's critique chose to overlook it (see Sarkar 1985: 26). In adopting Akshay Kumar's version of natural theology, Brāhmos decreed that everything one needed to know of God and God's purpose could be read off of the evidence of his design in creation. At the same time, by opening up the world to exegesis, the Brāhmos effectively admitted the possibility of deriving truths from the evidence that might be found in the record of humanity's religious experience. Brāhmos began to look at the world's scriptures. As Rajnarain was to put it: "There is no hard and fast rule regarding scriptures. Any book that speaks about the existence of God is dear and can be used" (Bose 1966: 8; cf. Bose 1861: 96).

While Brāhmoism was acclaimed as a universal religion, Rajnarain balanced this conviction with the assertion that no religion existed in a universal form. Rather, each religion needed to clothe itself in the modes of thought characteristic of its national culture. Brāhmoism, having arisen in India, took the Hindu mode. However, this did not mean Brāhmos only looked to things Indian:

> As there are various ways of illustrating religious and moral truth, those adopted by other nations in their religious writings are deserving of careful study and the beauties of those writings of transfusion into their own sermons, discourses, and hymns after casting them in national modes of thought and dressing them in national imagery and national modes of expression so as not to interfere with the Hindu aspect of the Samaj. (Bose 1870: 3)

In other words, Brāhmos recognized differences in the expression of theism around the world, and sought to translate what was usable in these various expressions into terms that would make sense within the national context of Brāhmoism. The important thing, said Rajnarain, was to bear in mind that while such differences "must naturally arise from the usual course of things" this did not mean they militated against the apprehension of shared human truths. The differences were but "adventitious, not essential—national, not sectarian." What underlay them all, and what Brāhmos at heart paid allegiance to, was what Rajnarain called *Sar Dharma*—the essential religion (Bose 1870: 2–3). Once again we return to the idea of the *sāragrāhī*, the eclectic who grasps the essence.

In Rajnarain's case it appears that the real challenge was somehow to balance the retrieval of this universally valid essence with the maintenance of an authentic sense of national identity and belonging. Reason was to be the key to this balancing act: not the skeptical reasoning of the neither–nor, but the eclectic reasoning of the both–and. In terms of the identity of the colonial subject, the real strength of Rajnarain's democratic eclecticism was that it appeared to allow for a sense of both national belonging and universal meaning. David Kopf makes note of this when he remarks that on the one hand Rajnarain retained his respect for the "universalist legacy" of Rammohun, while on the other he was "among the first to condemn Young Bengal" for the way its appeals to the universals of reason contributed to "cultural alienation" (Kopf 1979: 193). It is hardly surprising, then, to find that Rajnarain was eventually hailed as the Grandfather of Nationalism in India, since he had done so much to harness his Brāhmo eclecticism to the task of articulating a healthy response to the deracinating effects of colonial education and Christian propaganda (1979: 166–167).

The force of Rajnarain's commitment to a national ideal is best understood by contrasting it with the outlook of Keshub Chunder Sen. Keshub had begun to play a central role in the Brāhmo Samaj after 1860, chiefly through the support and encouragement of Debendranath. However, it was not long before his vision and objectives began to diverge from those of Debendranath and Rajnarain. The chief sticking points were Keshub's extreme universalism, which threatened to dilute the Brāhmos's sense of cultural pride as Indians, and his increasing appeal to the power of his own charisma.

Keshub had a fiery personality; he claimed that his tutelary deity was the Vedic god of fire, Agni, and that he had been initiated into a gospel of enthusiasm (see Sen 1940: 445; *Jīvan veda*: 15–22). He seemed to invite excitement and provoke schism at virtually every turn. Indeed, less than a decade after his emergence into prominence in the Samaj, Keshub and a group of dedicated followers broke with Debendranath's group to form the Brāhmo Samaj of India (Bhāratīya Brāhmo Samāj). Henceforth, those remaining loyal to Debendranath's vision were known as the Ādi (or original) Brāhmo Samāj. By 1879, Keshub's imprint had been so forcefully felt within the Brāhmo Samaj of India that this group itself splintered, with the secessionists forming the Sādhāraṇ Brāhmo Samāj and Keshub's followers instituting what was to be called the Church of the New Dispensation (Nava Vidhān).

In the secondary literature on the so-called Bengal Renaissance, one typically finds Keshub and the Nava Vidhān treated as examples of a mystically inspired, charismatic syncretism. In some cases, this reflects an attempt to distinguish Keshub's theological vision from that of earlier Brāhmos like Rajnarain, who are considered to be rationalistic eclectics along the lines of Rammohun (see Goblet 1885: chaps. 13–14). However, while the charges of mysticism and charisma can be adequately supported, the claim that Keshub was a syncretist is open to debate.

We may lend our support to the former charges—that Keshub opened the door to mysticism and even guru-worship—by advancing the following evidence: First of all, there is the undeniable fact of Keshub's enthusiasm and ardor, which differed markedly from the patrician sobriety of Debendranath and the austere rationalism of Akshay Kumar. Second, one must take into account the Brāhmos's increasing reliance after 1860 upon the inner voice of intuition as a means of knowing God (see Halbfass 1988: 225). One could hypothesize that this attention to an inner voice arose largely as a counterbalance to the evidentiary theology of Akshay Kumar, which left little room for spirit and emotion. Be that as it may, the problem with a theology of intuition is that once one acknowledges the possibility of an inner voice, one must also consider the possibility of inspiration and prophecy. This is what happened in the case of Keshub. We thus note with interest Keshub's increasing appeal after 1875 to what he called *ādeśa*, or the guidance of divine inspiration, which seemed to many to be an attempt to justify innovations that did not square with the rationalistic presuppositions of the movement (Damen 1988: 147–150).[7] Finally, alongside Keshub's fiery personality and appeals to inspiration, one must reckon with Keshub's relationship in the late 1870s with Sri Ramakrishna, the famous mystic who would one day become guru to Vivekananda. Keshub and Ramakrishna met frequently and the former was apparently greatly impressed by Ramakrishna's attempt to use meditative states of consciousness to plumb the truths of other religions.

That these three factors combined to give to Keshub's Brāhmoism a very different stamp is certain. However, it remains to be seen whether the New Dispensation is best called an attempt at syncretism or a variant of Brāhmo eclecticism. Despite the opinions of later commentators, it must be noted that according to Keshub himself, the New Dispensation was an exercise in eclecticism. References to eclecticism abound in his lectures and essays from around the beginning of the 1880s. Thus, in an article published in January 1880 in the *Sunday Mirror* (Keshub's chief journalistic outlet in Calcutta at the time), the Nava Vidhān is identified as an "eclectic dispensation." In September of the same year Keshub spoke of the New Dispensation being "the Church of Harmony, the Philosophy of Eclecticism" (see Sen 1940: 382, 420). Two years later, as he felt the need to guide his followers in their new religious undertaking, Keshub compiled a sort of credo entitled "Man of the New Dispensation." This credo featured the following relevant declaration:

> I value and accept truth in all sects and in all scriptures, and am above the sin of sectarianism. . . .
>
> I always cultivate the eclectic religion of the New Dispensation. (Sen 1940: 488)

Here we can see how eclecticism is both rooted in the skeptic's disdain for sectarianism and yet has transmuted the skeptic's *Weder–noch* into the eclectic's *Sowohl–als auch*. Thus, when we view Keshub in light of Zeller's categories we find a framework for appreciating the distinctly eclectic logic at work. I might likewise pause to relate Keshub's perspective to my earlier discussions of eclecticism in the West, in which case we would be able to see a distinct correlation between Keshub's antisectarianism and Diderot's ideal of eclecticism. In either case, eclecticism appears to be the appropriate category to apply.[8]

I emphasize Keshub's self-understanding as an eclectic for a number of reasons. First of all, we obviously need to avoid using a term like *syncretist* if it is going to lead some to conclude that what Keshub was about was the unjustifiable corruption of authentic religious truths. Second, and more important, if we label Keshub a syncretist we have to admit that this was obviously not the term he applied to himself or to the New Dispensation. Admittedly, it is not the job of the scholar of religion to simply repeat uncritically what his informants tell him; we have a duty not merely to describe, but also to explain, which often entails looking behind or beneath the testimony of our informants for more satisfying answers. However, it is not even simply because Keshub tells us so that we should view him as an eclectic. We have, as a third very good reason, the fact that his characterization of the eclecticism of the New Dispensation accords very well with what we have discovered about the genesis of eclectic philosophies in contexts of religious and cultural change. Eclecticism, for Keshub as for other Brāhmos, provided the best answer to a problem whose only other solution seemed to lie in becoming a skeptic. And indeed, when we look into his biography in a bit more detail, we find that he originally found his way to Brāhmoism in much the way Rajnarain had.

When Keshub first rose to prominence in the Samāj, his primary interest was to counter the skepticism of Calcutta's educated youth. This is especially clear from his 1860 address "Young Bengal: This Is for You." Recognizing the skeptics' disdain for sectarianism and metaphysics, Keshub urged them to find in the Brāhmo Samāj a nonsectarian religion based on the simple and rationally acceptable credo of love for

God and service to humanity. This was also the year in which Keshub established the Sangat Sabhā, or Society of Fellow Believers, as a special forum for spiritual exploration and critical discussion (Damen 1988: 53–54).[9] Toward this end they gathered regularly to plunge into an eclectic syllabus of readings heavily weighted with selections from contemporary Western theists and eclectics—among them, Victor Cousin (see Damen 1988: 58).

No doubt Keshub's appeal depended in large part upon his personal example. In terms of both personality and theology he was rapidly emerging within the Samāj as an important voice in favor not just of the dry logic of natural religion, but also of the impassioned feeling of a religion grounded in what he understood to be God-given intuitions.[10] In a sense, Keshub was asking Brāhmos to broaden their vision of where the knowledge of God might be found. Alongside the natural world and our innate intuitions, he argued God was also manifested in history. Thus by the mid-1860s he began to explore the impact of so-called great men on the course of history, a theme developed by his contemporaries, Carlyle and Emerson. By thus broadening the horizon of religious knowledge, Keshub could remain true to the universalism and comparative spirit inaugurated by Rammohun—a spirit longing to move beyond the manifest differences among religions to an appreciation of the religious truths shared by humans around the world and throughout history.

In an era when the world's great religions were understood according to a largely Protestant—which is to say scripturalist—paradigm, it was natural for Keshub to think of other religions in terms of their sacred books. He professed to respect all scriptures, but like Rammohun, he also felt free to selectively appropriate what he valued in other religious texts. While this was entirely in keeping with the Brāhmo spirit, Keshub once again broadened the scope of his selectivity beyond the horizons imagined by Debendranath and Rajnarain.

The latter two had worked together closely in the late 1840s compiling an eclectic compendium that was to serve as the Brāhmo's very own holy book (Bose 1961: 29). This work, known as *Brāhma Dharmaḥ*, was published in 1850, and contained a wide selection of Hindu texts on wisdom and morality, from the Upaniṣads, to the *Mahābhārata*, the *Laws of Manu*, and the *Mahānirvāṇa Tantra* (see Hatcher 1996: chap. 9). With such a precedent in place, it remained only for Keshub to wander even farther afield in his search for truths to harvest. This he had the opportunity to do in 1866 when he and his followers broke with

Debendranath and Rajnarain to form the Brāhmo Samāj of India. Among the resolutions that called the new Samāj into being was one that stipulated the publication of a "compilation of Theistic Texts from all scriptures" (Sen 1940: 118; see Damen 1988: 72). This new work was brought forth the very next month, under the title *Śloka saṃgraha*, or literally, 'a collection of verses.' Keshub had an epigram for the book composed in Sanskrit, the first lines of which read:

> The wide universe is the holy temple of God;
> the pure heart is the land of pilgrimage;
> truth is imperishable scripture.

In proclaiming the Brāhmo's religious home to be the entire universe, Keshub revealed the point at which he broke decisively with the more nativist Brāhmoism of Debendranath and Rajnarain.

In a sense Rammohun had bequeathed to the Brāhmos the age-old problem of reconciling the universal and the particular. It was a difficult task to respect and defend the nobility of Hindu religion while expanding one's vision to take in the whole world of human religious knowledge. Not surprisingly, the pendulum tended to swing to one pole or the other. In the work of Debendranath and Rajnarain, the particular was uppermost.

As Debendranath was to proclaim openly, Brāhmoism had never been intended as something new, but simply as a further development of genuine Hindu religion (Tagore 1953: 36). Rajnarain followed him in this respect, and we have seen what a boost this gave to incipient feelings of national pride. However, by linking the meaning of Brāhmoism to the heritage of Hinduism, Rajnarain might also be charged with planting the seeds of Hindu chauvinism. We see this most clearly in his famous 1872 address, *Hindudharmer śreṣṭhatā*, or "The Superiority of Hinduism." By his own account the address was delivered to a standing-room-only crowd, a good number of whom were not universalistic Brāhmos at all, but conservative *paṇḍit*s and other representatives of so-called Hindu orthodoxy. We have to marvel at the irony of a Brāhmo being heralded as the 'crest-jewel of the Hindus' (*hindu-kula-cūḍāmaṇi*) by the very *paṇḍit*s who had consistently opposed the reformist causes spearheaded by men like Rammohun and Vidyasagar (see Bose 1961: 55).

Rajnarain's 1872 defense of Hinduism was by no means unprecedented in his earlier work. Nor was it without justification in terms of Rammohun's work, one of whose poles was a defense of Hindu theism.

In both cases, the felt need for defense or apologetic was provoked by Evangelical Christian attacks on Hinduism, both as a form of social organization and as a religious philosophy.

One of the missionaries' favorite targets from early in the nineteenth century had been the philosophy of Vedānta, by which they meant the renunciant monism of Śaṅkara's Advaita Vedānta. Rammohun had internalized enough of this critique to wish to argue that the core philosophy of Hinduism was not monistic illusionism but a monotheism consistent with that found in Judaism, Christianity, and Islam. At the same time, however, Rammohun would not concede everything to the missionaries. Instead, he worked zealously to retain and redeem the name of Vedānta by publishing and commenting on his own Bengali translations of its Sanskrit sources, namely, the Upaniṣads and the *Brahma Sūtra*s (see Hatcher 1996: chap. 8). The implication of this is that from the time of Rammohun, Vedānta became what we might call the sacred cow of the modern Hindu interpreter—a cultural marker, but one which needed constant explanation and defense.

A second round of attacks on Vedānta, initiated during the early years of Debendranath's revival of the Brāhmo Samāj, only served to reinforce the sense of Vedānta as an embattled emblem. This time the assailant was Rev. Alexander Duff, a Scottish Presbyterian with an undying animus toward what he called the "stupendous" institution of Hinduism. In 1839 Duff presented a thoroughgoing and unsympathetic analysis of Hindu culture entitled *India and India Missions*. His prose was heavily freighted with the language of warfare and demolition, the dominant trope being the goal of toppling "the fortress of Hinduism" (Duff 1988: 587). His main artillery was targeted on the so-called pantheism of Hinduism, its other-worldly quest for the apparent annihilation of self in the Absolute, and the immorality that allegedly derived therefrom.

Brāhmos had viewed themselves as followers of Vedānta ever since the time of Rammohun. They were understandably wounded by Duff's assault. Rajnarain responded to Duff's book in two essays written in English for the Brāhmo journal *Tattvabodhinī Patrikā*, accusing Duff of misinterpreting Vedānta in light of his own "unsocial and uncatholic" sense of Christian superiority.[11] It is evident from Rajnarain's essays that in the mid-1840s Brāhmos sought to affirm, as Rammohun had, that their Vedantic theism was not an innovation but simply a return to the so-called unitarian, or monotheistic, religion of the ancient Vedas. However, Rajnarain's essays also appealed to modernist arguments drawn from rationalism and natural theology. Anticipating that the missionary might accuse the Brāhmos of stealing such arguments from modern Christian sources, Rajnarain protested, "Has the Baconian Philosophy a more natural connection with Christianity than with Hindooism?"[12] Interestingly, we can see here a positive legacy of Rajnarain's Hindu College education, especially his Enlightenment confidence in the universality of reason.

Rajnarain's essays triggered a second assault, this time by Duff and a young Bengali Christian named Krishnamohan Banerjee, who had chosen to convert after his life as a renegade member of Young Bengal began to prove hollow. In this second attack, Duff and Banerjee reiterated their principal complaints, this time tailoring them more specifically to address the Brāhmo position. They alleged that the God of these modern Vedantists was hardly the God of love and atoning sacrifice, and they once again indicted Vedānta on the charge that it offered no "moral standard by which actions are to be weighed."[13]

While Duff wrote in an acerbic, confrontational tone—making it easier for the Brāhmos to dismiss him as something of a fanatic—Banerjee's criticism was far more compassionate and sympathetic. As a Bengali himself, and a former member of the band of well-educated skeptics and freethinkers, he openly professed the highest regard for the Brāhmo leaders. At the same time, however, his critique was far more trenchant than Duff's; ultimately, he had little patience with what he took to be the weaknesses of the Brāhmos's interpretive strategy. With great irony he pointed out that while the "modern revivers of the Vedant" accept the Vedas as authoritative, they only refer to those texts from the Vedas that can conveniently be endorsed in "an inconveniently enlightened age like the present" (Banerjee 1845: 102–103). In other words, he criticized the Brāhmos for their selective approach to interpretation; he targeted their eclecticism. As someone who had fled the unsettling life of the skeptic's *Weder–noch* for the settled assurances of Christian orthodoxy, he found the eclectic's *Sowohl–als auch* as troubling as had Ramtanu from his position of dogmatic rationalism.

Banerjee and Duff were largely responsible for sharpening the debates over Vedānta. They certainly were not to have the last word. By the 1850s the debate was in full swing. While groups like the Brāhmos and their allied organization, the Tattvabodhinī Sabhā, furthered the propagation and defense of Vedantic doctrines, other Christians joined in the attack. Rev. James Long of the Church Missionary Society—an otherwise more sympathetic observer of Bengali culture—criticized what he called the "one-sided" Vedānta of the Brāhmos in his 1848 *Handbook of Bengal Missions*; Rev. Joseph Mullens of the London Missionary Society wrote a prize-winning essay, "Vedantism, Brahmism and Christianity Compared," which was published in Calcutta in 1852; and in the same year an anonymous essay entitled "Vedantism and Christianity" appeared in the *Calcutta Review* (vol. 17). In all of these cases, Vedantism was held up for scathing criticism on moral and soteriological grounds, while the Vedantists themselves were almost universally maligned as shameless eclectics, who borrowed from Christianity what they could not find in Hinduism.

It is to such literature and the debates out of which it grew that we may ultimately trace our current rubric of Neo-Vedānta—in fact the phrase "Neo-Vedantists" appears in the anonymous essay mentioned above. The point is, missionaries like Mullens and Long effectively concurred with the earlier verdict of Duff and Banerjee: The educated defenders of Vedānta could not be seen simply as revivalists. Instead, they were guilty of creating something new; they were in fact modern Vedantists. The prominent role played in the creation of this new Vedānta by the eclecticism of the early Brāhmos is evident. And it is clear how much that eclecticism troubled the missionaries. Long himself comments—none too generously—on the journal *Tattvabodhinī Patrikā*, edited by Akshay Kumar:

> What it *finds* not in purely native sources, . . . it borrows, *without acknowledgment*, from Christianity; adopting quite the language of European ethico-religious writers, a language hitherto wholly unknown in Hindu literature. It is at once curious, interesting, and instructive, to see how such are so far enlightened by education as to reject the absurd abominations of Pauranic idolatry, but, . . . are *compelled* to have recourse, like the equally disingenuous anti-Christian philosophers and transcendentalists of the west, to that very Christianity which they repudiate and malign, yet from which they must, after all, unconsciously *borrow*, or knowingly *filch*, all that is truly rational in principle, pure in sentiment, and good in practice. (Long 1848: 351–352)

With Long's complaint I return to a theme I noted in connection with Rammohun's debates with Joshua Marshman. For the Christian, such selective appropriation amounts to a violent act and a despicable one; it is not just borrowing, but *filching*.

Setting aside the condemnatory tone of such a passage, what Long provides us with is sure evidence of the way in which Brāhmo selectivity worked to reconfigure the meaningfulness of Vedānta in nineteenth-century Bengal. To make a long story short, debates over Vedānta continued through the century. The creative eclecticism of Vivekananda, which we have already had occasion to consider, did wonders for giving Vedānta a central place in the emerging discourse of apologetic Hinduism and Indian nationalism. The movement founded by Vivekananda in his master's name became as it were the institutional proof of the moral, social, and philosophical viability of Vedānta. Vivekananda's mantle was inherited in turn by Sarvepalli Radhakrishnan. Indeed, Radhakrishnan was to recall how as a young man he had been greatly moved by the writings of Vivekananda. As an erudite philosopher and international statesman, Radhakrishnan was able to address in numerous books the lingering suspicions and renewed accusations of Vedānta's opponents. Thanks to the work of Radhakrishnan, the twentieth-century Hindu apologist was equipped with what could finally claim to be (adopting the title of his most popular book) "the Hindu view of life."

This brief overview of the emergence of Neo-Vedānta serves to illustrate the complex interrelationship that exists between what we might call the democratic eclecticism of the Brāhmos and the aristocratic eclecticism of Vivekananda and Radhakrishnan. On the one hand, construing the emergence of Neo-Vedānta as a historical progression from Rammohun to Radhakrishnan allows us to emphasize what the twentieth-century exponents of aristocratic Neo-Vedānta owe to the democratic eclectics of the nineteenth century; on the other hand, after viewing the strange filiations and schisms among the Brāhmos—not to mention the complicated avenues through which a figure like Sri Ramakrishna came to influence individuals like Keshub and Vivekananda—it is equally important to recognize that the genealogy of Neo-Vedānta is more like a complex web of kinship relations than it is a linear historical progression. That is, we cannot simply trace the Vedantic eclecticism of Vivekananda straight back to the eclecticism of Rammohun, no matter how much the latter used Vedānta as a rallying flag. Among other things, this would require us to overlook the basic distinction we have drawn between democratic and aristocratic eclecticism. The importance of preserving this distinction can be understood with reference to Adorno's notion of reification: we must avoid reifying eclecticism because that would mean forgetting the differences among its manifestations.

Clearly we reify every time we resort to general categories. And there is something to be gained by taking eclecticism as a general category and concluding that Rammohun, Keshub, and Vivekananda are all eclectics—not to mention that they share this distinction with Voltaire, Jefferson, and Ptolemy. However, by introducing the latter examples, drawn from such widely differing historical and cultural contexts, we are led to confront the obvious limitations of our general category. At this point we remember that our general category is merely an expedient device—a device whose very expediency depends upon our forgetting (in Adorno's sense) the differences among the particular items it claims to name. When we remember this, we must in turn begin to dismember our category, breaking it apart in search of difference. Taking Vivekananda as an example, we resist the simple designation 'eclectic' and go off in search of something that better captures the distinctness of his project. Panikkar has already assisted us in this respect. In his terms Vivekananda becomes an aristocratic eclectic. The question is, Are there further ways we can account for the distinctive character of Vivekananda's eclecticism? Certainly one could advance a myriad of historical particulars, but among these, there do appear to be three general developments in the latter part of the nineteenth century that work in concert to create the possibility of a Vivekananda: first, Rajnarain's 1872 lecture on the superiority of Hinduism; second, the fiery example of Keshub; and third, the teaching and example of Sri Ramakrishna.

An important shift in Brāhmo interpretive practice took place when Rajnarain delivered his 1872 address. By advancing the superiority of Hinduism, Rajnarain departed from the democratic eclecticism of his Brāhmo forebears. It had certainly never been Rammohun's goal to argue the inherent superiority of Vedic theism. His agenda, in a more democratic fashion, was consensus. It was enough that Hindu theism might be granted the same rational credibility as Unitarian theology or Muslim monotheism. No doubt the subsequent half century of defending Hindu theology from Christian attacks, coupled with the Brāhmos's gradual slide into conservative spirituality under Debendranath, prepared the way for Rajnarain's eventual decision to advance his aristocratic claim. At the same time, Rajnarain may well have had Keshub in mind, since the latter seemed all too willing to dilute the Hindu content of Brāhmoism with the truths of other religions. In this respect Rajnarain's address appears to be a defensive move, a near-desperate attempt to cling to Indianness as a mark of authenticity.

Even taking all of this into account, the striking thing about Vivekananda's aristocratic eclecticism is its offensive thrust—something largely absent even from the cultural flag-waving of Rajnarain's 1872 address. In Vivekananda's works Vedānta is not reeling back on its heels, trying to regain its balance; rather, it is up on its toes, ready to plunge forward into the world. Thus while we must certainly register the import of Rajnarain's claims of Hindu superiority, something else is needed to account for Vivekananda's confident posture. That something else could well be the example of Keshub. Psychologically, Vivekananda seems to owe a great deal to Keshub: his fiery personality, his bold and unceasing attempts at self-fashioning, and his desire to come to terms with an increasingly complex world situation. In this latter connection it is at least suggestive that among the figures I have been discussing, Rammohun, Keshub, and Vivekananda all traveled beyond India, while Debendranath and Rajnarain did not. If nothing else, there is a profound symbolic message here, since the former three thinkers made it their task to encounter, appropriate, and interpret the entire religious universe.

We could even go one step further and say that both Keshub and Vivekananda got a push in this direction from Sri Ramakrishna. The life and teachings of Ramakrishna occasioned a profound set of shifts in colonial Hindu consciousness, and these must be taken to represent the third development that prepared the way for the aristocratic eclecticism of Vivekananda. What Keshub dignified through his appeals to intuition, inspiration, and prophecy, Ramakrishna highlighted with the practice of meditative absorption. (Just how the two might have influenced one another in this regard is itself an intriguing and disputed question). Together these two delivered into Vivekananda's hands the central key of his religious hermeneutic—the concept of experience. I have already had an opportunity to dwell upon the significance of this concept within Vivekananda's interpretive strategy. It only needs mentioning here that for Vivekananda (and Radhakrishnan after him), experience, or *anubhava*, was the essentialistic canon by which one could proceed to select truths from among the world's religions. The aristocratic character of their eclecticism is ensured by the fact that for them, as for many Neo-Vedantins subsequently, *anubhava* is defined ultimately in Vedantic terms: it is the self-validating and blissful experience of *brahman*.

One way that Vivekananda elaborated this view of experience into an eclectic method, as we have seen, was by appeal to the category of the *āpta*, or reliable witness. We can now see the ways in which Vivekananda's views in this matter—quite apart from their roots in the epistemological discussions of classical Indian philosophy—were also rooted in the theological developments associated with the Brāhmo movement.

Recall that Rammohun had begun by validating the Vedānta perspective and by arguing, somewhat against the traditional grain, that knowledge of *brahman* was accessible to everyone (see Hatcher 1996: chap. 8). This claim was expanded under Debendranath and Akshay Kumar, who worked together to create the new Brāhmo scripture, *Brāhma Dharmaḥ*. Tellingly, that book opens with the words *oṃ, brahmavādino vadanti*, or, 'Those who proclaim God say . . .' The important concept here is that of the *brahmavādī*, someone who knows Brahman (i.e., a *brahmavit*) and who in turn teaches others. In Debendranath's terms, the *brahmavit* is a great and blessed individual who is righteous, sinless, and diligent (Tagore 1975: 1).

In other words, the *brahmavit* who becomes a *brahmavādī* looks a great deal like Vivekananda's *āpta*. What's more, a *brahmavādī*, like Vivekananda's *āpta*, can appear anywhere, anytime. In India the greatest *brahmavādī*s were the *ṛṣi*s who composed the Upaniṣads, but the implication is that one might find *brahmavādī*s in ancient Israel or medieval Europe. Thus as Indocentric as Debendranath's *Brāhma Dharmaḥ* is as a text, it clearly opened the interpretive door through which Keshub could sally forth into the world. Over that door were inscribed the words "The knowledge of God is hidden in your heart" (Tagore 1975: 1). By its own logic, *Brāhma Dharmaḥ* seemed to beg for the creation of Keshub's more globally inclusive *Śloka saṃgraha*. And once Keshub had discovered his scripture within the wide world of religious experience, it remained only for Vivekananda to give that experience its definitive Vedantic stamp.

There were thus two paths for the eclectic to follow. The one, adopted by Brāhmos, as by Unitarians, was the democratic search for the various ways God had been revealed to human hearts. The hope was that out of such difference a comforting grid of familiarity could be created that would finally reconcile fractious religious differences. However, as Zeller himself noted, by limiting themselves to "those doctrines in which all were agreed," democratic eclectics tended to leave for themselves only "a very few propositions of indefinite universality" (Zeller 1883: 17). Agreement, in other words, has not always seemed enough for the eclectic; another standard has sometimes been perceived as necessary. That standard is unity itself.

And so we arrive at the other path open to the eclectic, the path of aristocratic eclecticism, whose other name is inclusivism. This has been the path of the Neo-Vedantins since the time of Vivekananda. We might follow Zeller and say that, like the later Greeks, the Neo-Vedantins choose to take the experiential evidence of "immediate consciousness" as their sole criterion of philosophic truth. Each group claims to discover the key for reconciling difference in the experience of the soul's union with God. Where such an interpretive decision leads is made all too clear if we examine the bold and inclusive eclecticism of Radhakrishnan: "We do not then so much *think* reality as *live* it, do not so much *know* it as *become* it. Such an extreme monism . . . we meet with in some Upaniṣads, Nāgārjuna and Śaṃkara in his ultra-philosophical moods, Śrī Harṣa and the Advaita Vedāntins, and echoes of it are heard in Parmenides and Plato, Spinoza and Plotinus, Bradley and Bergson, not to speak of the mystics, in the West" (Radhakrishnan 1970: 81).

Surely this is one of those assertions of modern Hindu inclusivism that have driven commentators like Bharati up the wall. Radhakrishnan apparently has no compunction against taking a bulldozer to intellectual history; he levels the world's philosophy down to a neat, Neo-Vedantic playing field. We can scarcely avoid siding with Bharati; are we really prepared to abandon the particulars of history in favor of the commodious inclusivism of such universalism?

If not, then we ought to be careful how we attempt to resuscitate Zeller's model as a key to understanding eclecticism. Do we really want to say that what Plotinus did in late antiquity is what Emerson did in nineteenth-century America and is what Radhakrishnan did in twentieth-century India?[14] If we do, we run the risk of sounding every bit as inclusivist as Radhakrishnan himself. We run the risk of reifying eclecticism, of forgetting about difference.

A better option is to use Zeller—and Panikkar, for that matter—to help us identify and characterize moments of eclecticism in religious history, but then to abandon them when we detect our categories beginning to gobble up the phenomena we wish to explain. As we have seen, this is the methodological rule of thumb endorsed by Doniger in her reflections on balancing archetype and manifestation in the study of myth (see O'Flaherty 1988). Adopting such a method, we may find that Zeller helps us begin to understand the emergence of eclectic religiosity out of the vortex of skepticism in Bengal. And in tandem with Panikkar, Zeller's model may also help us make sense of developments within eclectic thought, as one moves from the probabilistic truths of the democratic eclectic to the essentializing truths of the aristocratic eclectic. And so we come a long way in unraveling the complicated kinship among Brāhmos and Vedantins. But it is precisely here that we must remind ourselves that such a model cannot possibly exhaust the many permutations of eclecticism in world history. To the contrary, there remain a myriad of eclecticisms. Thus, while the global spread of modern ideology can certainly account for some important parallels among Rammohun, Jefferson, and Voltaire, global modernism cannot explain any of them in particular.

In keeping with the spirit of this cautionary remark, I would like now to attempt to muddy the very waters I have attempted to clear. Adopting another metaphor, I would like to take the map I have developed of the genealogy of eclecticism in Bengal and blur its clean lines. What would become of my neat cartography if I were to superimpose upon it two more images of modern eclecticism? The examples I have in mind are both drawn from the nineteenth century, a century fully worthy of Charles Jencks's characterization of it as the "age of eclecticism" (as cited in Docherty 1993: 294). Each example also represents what amounted to an extremely influential force in nineteenth-century thought. Finally, each of these examples can be said to have played a prominent role in shaping the character of modern Hindu eclecticism. Having added these layers to our map, will we be forced to return once again to the theoretical drawing board?

The first example I wish to highlight in closing this chapter is the eclecticism of the comparativist, by which I mean the scholar of comparative religion. Max Müller serves as an excellent case in point, inasmuch as he may nearly be reckoned the father of comparative religion. Müller's work is relevant for at least three reasons: First of all, like so much other nineteenth-century Indology, Müller's work demonstrated to the colonial Hindu that in the eyes of the West the heritage of Indian civilization was not only long-standing but also spiritually profound. In this respect, Müller might almost be called a primary player in the so-called Indian Renaissance (see Sharpe 1975: 38). Second, Müller's work seemed to many to confirm that Rammohun's efforts to contrast the present status of Hinduism with its ancient glories was in fact justified; Müller could advance what he took to be objective evidence supporting the idea that contemporary Hinduism represented the degradation and stagnation of a once-vital religion. In this sense Müller, no less than Rammohun, served as a guide to groups like the Brāhmos. In fact, one can find evidence of the Brāhmos's adopting Müller's conclusions in their own attempts to define a more reformed and rational religion. Thus none other than Akshay Kumar makes approving note of Müller's claim that the ancient Hindus were originally monotheists (Datta 1987: 74). Third, and finally, when a scholar like Müller delivered a series of lectures at Cambridge University that was entitled "India: What Can It Teach Us?," he made it clear that in many cases the Indian heritage was one the West was willing to draw upon in reconfiguring its own understanding of religion and philosophy.[15]

Müller's eclecticism is part democratic, part aristocratic. In his quest to uncover "the origin of religion in the heart and mind of man" he has been reckoned "a true son of the Enlightenment, and a genuine disciple of Kant" (Sharpe 1975: 39). Clearly this also places him in the same camp as the transcendentalists, who owed much to Kant. At his aristocratic best, Müller sensed behind the manifest diversity of religion a single essential religion that originated from the experience of God within every human soul. In this universalist vein we find Müller musing upon "The Real Significance of the Parliament of Religions":

> Let theologians pile up volume upon volume of what they call theology; religion is a very simple matter, and that which is so simple and yet so all-important to us, the living kernel of religion, can be found, I believe, in almost every creed, however much the husk may vary. And think what that means! It means that above and beneath and behind all religions there is one eternal, one universal religion, a religion to which every man, whether black or white or yellow or red, belongs or may belong. (Cited in Ziolkowski 1993: 159)

However, while Müller was inspired by the prospect of a "universal religion," he also backed off from this grand and inclusive idea to admit we might better speak of "a union of different religions, resting on a recognition of the truths shared in common by all of them, and on a respectful toleration of what is peculiar to each."

> In this way it would be possible to discover a number of fundamental doctrines, shared in common by the great religions of the world, clothed in slightly varying phraseology. Nay, I believe it would have been possible, even at Chicago, to draw up a small number of articles of faith, not, of course, thirty-nine [as in Müller's own Anglican tradition], to which all who were present could have honestly subscribed. (Cited in Ziolkowski 1993: 155)

Here we detect a more democratic spirit reminiscent of Rammohun. No doubt the tension between this democratic desire to provide an inventory of beliefs and the aristocratic urge to encapsulate all beliefs within a single idealist norm reflects the tension within Müller's work between Kantian idealism and empirical scholarship. In any case, the fact that for Müller the job of studying the world's religions went hand in hand with advancing the cause of a more rational religion for humanity, based on the data of such scholarship, indicates the degree to which his work shows clear affinities with the eclecticism of Rammohun and Keshub. Indeed, the fact that comparative religion has often merged its goal of objective scholarship with the normative attempt to develop more satisfactory forms of religious life has led Thomas Bryson to suggest that the historian of religion is in fact an agent of religious change. Accordingly, a scholar like Müller is not much different from an apologist like Vivekananda. Both "select, simplify, and re-contextualize" in an attempt to bring about new forms of religious life (see Bryson 1992: 355). Needless to say, while Bryson views this as syncretism, I prefer to emphasize the eclectic's program of choice and appropriation.

The second and final example of nineteenth-century eclecticism I would like to highlight is a man whose name I have already invoked in more than one context: Victor Cousin. Cousin's name is writ large across the face of modern eclecticism. We have already seen that Keshub's Saṅgat Sabhā had Cousin in its syllabus; it turns out Debendranath was familiar with his work as well. A world away in New England, Unitarians like Orestes Brownson were raving about Cousin's work as early as 1836 (see Hutchison 1976: 26). And it is well known that Emerson read Cousin's *Cours de philosophie* of 1828 with great relish. In fact, it was through reading *Cours* that he came to develop a profound respect for the *Bhagavad-gītā*, as we can tell from the evidence of his letters (see Rusk 1966: 322–323). Considering the widespread appeal of his writings, it is hard not to view Cousin as the very fountainhead of modern eclecticism. However, what mapping of eclecticism I have done so far should caution me against making so bold a claim. I might more appropriately concur with the verdict that while Cousin did not invent eclecticism, he certainly baptized it.[16] That baptism began with the lectures he commenced in 1816 and proceeded to deliver—with a certain degree of modification and adjustment—over the next half century.

It was in 1816 that Cousin noted how interesting and instructive it would be to expose what he referred to as the "vices" of the modern schools of philosophy. This could be done most effectively, he suggested, by ranging their teachings in juxtaposition. He went on to propose that this critical maneuver should be matched by a more creative and constructive attempt to reunite the collective merits of these competing philosophies in *le centre d'un vaste eclecticisme.*[17] This eclectic focal point would both contain and complete the doctrines of modern philosophy. So was Cousin's eclectic method presented to the world.

In the beginning, at least, it appears that Cousin was prompted toward eclecticism by two facts, one philosophical, the other political. First, he noticed a growing conflict between what he called the two "exclusive" schools of philosophy—the empiricism or sensualism of Locke, and the idealism or spiritualism of Kant. The problem of mediating this difference intrigued him. The need seemed especially urgent to him, since he claimed the French were turning from sensualism toward idealism, while the Germans were abandoing the idealism of Kant and Fichte for the natural philosophy of Hegel and Schelling. The second fact that struck Cousin was a political one: He claimed to see in the French Charter adopted after the battle of Waterloo a curious amalgam of the politics of the *l'ancien régime* and revolutionary democracy. It was precisely these "contrarities" that led him to praise the charter as an emblem of a "true eclecticism" (Cousin 1872: 270). Like contemporary French literature, Cousin noted, the charter represented the juxtaposition of "two elements which may and ought to go together, classic legitimacy and romantic innovation"; in this respect, the charter, like the suggested merger of sensualism and idealism, represented to him the ideal of "moderation," and such moderation was "the necessary philosophy" in an age that sought understanding rather than confrontation (1872: 270–271).

Cousin's eclecticism represents his own philosophical response to these circumstances. That response is conciliatory, broad-minded, and optimistic. As he notes:

> Our philosophy is not a melancholy and fanatical philosophy which, preoccupied with a few exclusive ideas, undertakes to reform all others upon them; no, it is a philosophy essentially optimistic, the aim of which is to comprehend all things; its unity is not a systematic and artificial unity, it is a harmony, the living harmony of all truths, even when they appear opposed. (Cousin 1872: 257)

This apology for eclecticism makes it difficult to say whether Cousin is an eclectic in the democratic or the aristocratic mode. In consciously objecting to the imposition of an arbitrary notion of systematic unity, he seems decidedly antiaristocratic. Indeed, his willingness to include even opposing truths within his eclectic system lends a decidedly democratic tone to the project. This seems to be the way Panikkar understands Cousin.

However, at the same time there is a synthetic and universalizing side to Cousin's eclecticism as well. This is especially apparent in his attempt to define and defend the systematic character of eclecticism. Cousin envisions his eclecticism as a kind of scientific method. As he puts it, "If we would collect and combine the truths scattered in different systems, we must first separate them from the errors with which they are mingled; and in order to do this, we must know how to ascertain and distinguish them" (Cousin 1839: 105). In other words, we need a criterion. Cousin claims to have this criterion, and he calls it simply "truth." As cryptic and contested as such a criterion turns out to be in the end, it is Cousin's confidence in possessing it that lends to his program the decidedly "essentialistic" character of aristocratic eclecticism, to borrow Panikkar's term. Furthermore, because it might also be said of Cousin's eclectic method that "the process is always decided from the start," such eclecticism—like Vivekananda's—betrays a totalitarian impulse to forget the very differences in which it claims to delight (see Horkheimer and Adorno 1972: 24).

In this sense, we might describe Cousin's system as a form of Hegelian eclecticism. This would have to be a somewhat ironic designation, since we have already encountered Hegel's putative disdain for the superficiality of eclecticism. Still, the mask of irony can also be the face of truth. Recall that while Hegel criticized eclecticism for its patchwork inconsistency, he also praised it when he found it used to good effect by the Alexandrian philosophers. What he liked about them was precisely what Zeller had called the *Sowohl–als auch*. It is precisely this both–and that Charles Jencks has dubbed the "Hegelian injunction" (as quoted in Docherty 1993: 288). It is this decidedly Hegelian drive for reconciliation that we find in Cousin, as when he explains how one might finally reconcile Locke and Kant:

> Having avoided these two vicious solutions of the problem, namely, the adoption of one or the other of these two systems, or the troublesome effort of seeking a new one, which would only be the one or the other more or less modified, we arrive at the only solution that is left, the abandonment of all the exclusive sides by which the two systems repel each other, the adoption of all the truths which they contain, and

> by which they are established, and the conciliation of all these truths in a point of view more elevated and more extended than either system, capable of containing them, of explaining them, and of completing them both. (Cousin 1872: 255–256)

The echoes of Hegel's *Aufhebung* are strong here, especially when Cousin speaks of developing a position "more elevated" and more comprehensive than the two original positions. These echoes should not surprise us, since Cousin visited Germany more than once, where he became acquainted with Hegel personally. In fact, it was Hegel who bailed Cousin out of jail in Dresden in 1824 after Cousin was arrested under the suspicion of being a liberal agitator![18]

To invoke Hegel, however, in explaining Cousin's eclecticism may lead us somewhat prematurely to view the latter as a synthetic or syncretistic attempt at ultimate reconciliation on a par with Hegel's grand philosophy. This was in fact a charge Cousin was on the alert for. He protested strenuously that his eclecticism was not a "blind syncretism":

> Eclecticism does not mingle together all systems; for it leaves no system entire; it decomposes every system into two parts, the one false, the other true; it destroys the first, and admits only the second in the work of reconstruction. It is the true portion of each system which it adds to the true portion of another system, that is to say, truth to truth, in order to form a true whole. It never mingles one entire system with another entire system; therefore it does not mingle all systems. Eclecticism, therefore, is not Syncretism; the one is indeed the opposite of the other; philosophically and etymologically, they resemble each other like choice and mixture, discrimination and confusion. (Cousin 1839: 41–42)

Does he protest too much? Perhaps, but Cousin's very defensiveness allows me to underscore once more a point I have been at pains to make: Eclecticism is not syncretism, at least not in the minds of those who practice it as a self-conscious method. It differs from syncretism as choice differs from mixture.

The problem with the category of syncretism is not, as Cousin suggests, that syncretism promotes confusion; that is only to perpetuate the hackneyed pejorative sense of the term. Rather, the problem with syncretism is that it refers to the production of something new; it purports to describe the merger and subsequent transformation of disparate elements within a harmonious system. When defined in this way, syncretism necessarily implies a departure from, or violation of, the presumed authenticity of an earlier tradition. As one contemporary advocate of the category of syncretism himself notes, "Syncretism presupposes a context to which it must be contrasted for study" (Bryson 1991: 11). Eclecticism, on the other hand—while it can be and has been used to create new systems—may also serve simply as a method for gathering the evidence to demonstrate the meaning or truth of an already existing tradition.

Consider again the case of Rammohun and Keshub. What if we labeled them syncretists? In the case of Rammohun the label simply makes no sense. He compared, collated, and tried to revive; he did not attempt to mix, harmonize, or synthesize. Suppose, then, that we agree to call him an eclectic, but insist on calling Keshub a syncretist. Now we run the risk of establishing what looks to be an imposing and rigid distinction that obscures from the very start the significant affinities that we know to exist between their work. What is more, we have deliberately turned a deaf ear to Keshub's own use of the language of eclecticism. This being the case, why not agree to call Rammohun and Keshub both eclectics? In doing so, we not only suggest something important about the dynamics of their interpretive work, but we also open the way for us to compare and contrast their religious worldviews. We might thus say that Rammohun was an eclectic who gathered evidence to demonstrate the particular truths of what he took to be the hoary tradition of Hindu theism, while Keshub was an eclectic who gathered evidence to demonstrate the universality of religious truth.

For the same reasons, I prefer to view Vivekananda and Radhakrishnan as eclectics, however much their goals of Vedantic inclusivism seem to suggest the will to syncretize.[19] To illustrate this point, consider Vivekananda's lecture "The Way to the Realization of the Universal Religion," which he delivered in Pasadena in 1900 (see CW 2: 359–374). In this lecture Vivekananda makes the somewhat surprising claim that the way to universal religion lies not through focusing on commonalities, but through highlighting difference. As a modern *uddhāraka* or *sāragrahī*, he proposes taking the best and leaving the rest. In effect he urges us to select the best that each religion has to offer, while bearing in mind that religious insights and doctrinal assertions differ markedly from one tradition to another. Thus from Islam we might choose to accept the basic postulate of the brotherhood of man. From Hinduism we might adopt the wisdom of yogic spirituality. And from Christianity we might choose to recognize the action of God in history.

The point is, Vivekananda does not propose combining these various truths to create a new religion that would render the separate traditions obsolete. Quite the contrary, he tells us, every religion "has a soul behind it" and these souls may well differ one from the other; "variation," he says, "is the sign of life" (CW 2: 364). Clearly difference is not Vivekananda's worry; he is in no hurry to homogenize or to blend away the lumps that give the world's religions their texture. If anything troubles him, it is exclusivism. His eclecticism becomes all the more significant for us because of his suggestion that the way to counter exclusivism is not by abolishing difference, but by learning to be at home in a world that is religiously plural. Like Gandhi after him, Vivekananda seems to suggest that the goal is to find amid this plurality of truths the particular insights that can help one to become a better Hindu, Christian, Muslim.

As Cousin put it, the key to eclecticism is discrimination; to be eclectic is to be selective. The goal of the selective attempt to create new connections out of the shattered remains of prior systems is to reconcile opposition. This, as Cousin asserts, is nothing particularly new:

> Eclecticism is not of yesterday. It was born the moment that a sound head and a feeling heart undertook to reconcile two passionate adversaries, by showing them that the opinions for which they combated were not irreconcilable in themselves, and that, with a few mutual sacrifices, they might be brought together. Eclecticism was long ago in the mind of Plato; it was the professed enterprise, whether legitimate or not, of the school of Alexandria. (1839: 105)

Cousin thus traces the roots of his project back to the ancient eclectics, while betraying a bit of hesitancy in pronouncing whether Diderot or Hegel had the better view of their work.

In the end, Cousin's system serves less as a model for something we might like to implement and more as a reminder of the complex interpretive possibilities within the eclectic search for connections. I have already weighed the pros and cons of applying the rubrics of Zeller and Panikkar. I now return to the significance of the tension I identified between Diderot and Hegel. For Diderot, as we have seen, the connections posited by the eclectic must not be predetermined or we risk forfeiting our autonomy as agents of connection-making. For Hegel, the eclectic's connections make sense only by virtue of a prior logos, an overarching reason that drives the system toward final unity. One might return from here to the Vedic ritual, where one is faced with the challenge of constructing relationships in which identity is strong enough to suggest resemblance, but not so strong as to culminate in identity. There is a broad spectrum here within which the eclectic might attempt to construct his or her world. We can, if we wish, reduce this spectrum to a series of bipolar reifications: the skeptic and the eclectic, Diderot and Hegel, the Many and the One, the democratic and the aristocratic, the particular and the universal. However, the point is that these dichotomies do not fit neatly on top of one another; by superimposing them we cannot reduce the problem to a single, more manageable dichotomy. Instead, what we must confront is the need to negotiate between the options of either–or and both–and. To borrow the language of Jim Collins, who has given much thought to the eclectic process of self-fashioning in postmodern culture, I am attempting to think about eclecticism as a strategy for negotiating a realm of "excess," a realm within which actors must play out the "dramas of choice" that allow them to envision themselves and their world (see Collins 1995: 88–89).

If this is the realm in which the eclectic constructs his home, the question for many will be: Is this any place to live? What kind of home could I possibly construct in such a vertiginous space? In the preceding chapters I have invoked the writing of Salman Rushdie as proof that the dynamics of eclecticism do afford ample scope to construct homes for ourselves. However, the time has come to reflect more intensively on this problem as it applies to the construction of modern Hindu self-understanding. In the next chapter I would like to consider the metaphor of the home as a means for investigating the forces at work in the colonial and postcolonial Hindu search for identity.

6

My Own Private Bungalow

The Dynamics of Eclectic Home-Building

Even now the older houses just outside the concrete city centers look like slums, and the new bungalows on the outskirts are at one with the flimsy structures of world fairs in their praise of technical progress and their built-in demand to be discarded after a short while like empty food cans.

—Horkheimer and Adorno

I would like to begin this chapter with an exercise in visualization. I ask the reader to form a mental image of a typical bourgeois homeowner from the recent American past. To assist us in our endeavor we might invoke the following suggestive passage from Walter Kidney's study of eclecticism in American architecture:

> Imagine a well-to-do American businessman, motoring home some time around 1928. Pausing before a Tudor archway, stone in stucco, he opens garage doors of a standard pattern, then drives his car into a space lined with terracotta block and lighted with a single naked bulb. He walks up two steps into a kitchen area of cream-painted nonarchitecture, then into a rather diminutive great hall, with diamond-paned windows, massive beams of varnished boards, and a baronial fireplace of painted cement; then up the stairs to a bathroom of tile and porcelain and nickel plating. (Kidney 1974: 1)

Provided Kidney has assisted you with your visualization, you are now inside our businessman's house. I would like to suggest that you are now also staring the problem of eclecticism in the face.

As far as architecture is concerned, we might say that eclecticism involves the deliberate combination of stylistically diverse elements within a single design. But behind this rather straightforward definition lurk several critical problems. For instance, there will be some who will view such combination as a form of historical reference; there will be others who will angrily reject it as nonhistorical—even antihistorical—pastiche, what with its apparently random juxtaposition of motifs and styles. According to this latter view, such eclecticism amounts to the "trivialization of history" (Collins 1995: 138). Critics may likewise differ over whether the driving force behind the architect's *bricolage* is profound nostalgia, an attempt to invent tradition, or simple pragmatism. To raise these interpretive disagreements is to revisit the debates over eclecticism that have haunted its intellectual history.

My immediate goal is to return to these debates, but along a somewhat different route suggested by the case of eclecticism in architecture. I venture onto this tack for three basic reasons: First, in the medium of architecture the creative dynamics of eclecticism are made visible—whether it is in the modernist eclecticism of a Louis Sullivan, the postmodern selectivity of a Michael Graves, or the juxtapositions of colonial Indian architecture (to which I shall turn presently). As with Kidney's well-to-do home, a building allows us to visualize what is at work, as well as what is at stake, in eclecticism. Second, architecture (and the visual arts more generally) offer another avenue for investigating the theoretical fault lines fracturing modernism and postmodernism. As we discovered in chapter 2, there is no easy way to categorize the tensions operating here. The fault lines appear within both modernism and postmodernism, as much as they separate them. In any case, to go in search of these fissures is to rejoin this century's debates over themes like appropriation, history, and truth. Third, and finally, I am particularly interested in exploring architecture for what it suggests about the metaphorics of home-building. That is, what can architecture tell us about the eclectic's attempt at creative world construction, be it through philosophy, literature, or religion?

To illustrate what I mean by this third point, I would return to the very point made by Kidney after he pictured for us the home of our businessman. Of this home and the businessman's relationship to it,

Kidney writes: "*No sense of incongruity or shock* for our businessman in his passage from space to space, no feeling that something of the great hall need be brought into the bathroom or, for that matter, that the bathroom should dictate to the great hall: *each of them he finds good in its way and in its place, and indeed he is proud of both*" (1974: 1; emphasis added). Though our businessman is clearly surrounded by a welter of architectural motifs, Kidney wants us to appreciate that this pastiche occasions no discomfort on the part of its owner. Even though—when viewed in terms of its architectural and historical referents—our businessman's home seems to be little else than an exercise in confusion, for the businessman it is nothing if not a cheerful confusion; it is his *home*.

It is precisely this nexus between eclecticism and the comforts of home that I would like to emphasize. After all, it has been said that one of the appeals of eclecticism is that it provides for a "homely philosophy" (see Michel 1984: 45). There is a wonderful double entendre here, which we can put to good use.[1] If we return to our businessman's eclectic home, it may indeed appear to be nothing if not homely—if we use the adjective in its most colloquial sense. As Kidney himself suggests, it looks odd, jumbled, and somewhat awkward. On the other hand, when we imagine our businessman dropping his briefcase by the door, slipping out of his wing tips, and plopping down in front of his huge fireplace, we have to marvel at how homely he feels; he really has made himself at home. With its awkward comforts, his eclectic home is a homely home indeed!

I take the irony of the homely home to be a powerful metaphor for what we see being constructed through the discourse of modern Hindu eclecticism. No matter how awkward, strained, or naive such eclecticism may appear to the likes of a Bharati, it must also be said to fulfill one fundamental and all-important purpose: it provides for a comfortable home. As J. M. Kitagawa pointed out with respect to the so-called new religions in Japan, though "eclectic and not well systematized," these religious movements offered people a "home" amid the otherwise confusing welter of Confucianism, Buddhism, Shinto, and Christianity in contemporary Japan (1990: 333). Similarly, if the cumulative discourse of modern Hinduism has produced a home in which stucco archways clash with baronial fireplaces and nickel-plated kitchen fixtures, this does not make that home unlivable. Far from it—like our American businessman, the modern Hindu considers each of the elements in his worldview to be "good in its way and in its place."

More than simply a place that offers comfort, security, and shelter, however, the eclectic's home is also a matter of pride. A homely philosophy is not just a comfortable way of viewing things; it is also a way of thinking deeply imbued with a sense of the local, the indigenous, the national. Here a quick glance at the related German words *heimisch* (national) and *Heimat* (nation) allows us to see how much national identity is connected to a sense of being at home (*sich heimisch fühlen*). When we consider the significant role played by modern Hindu discourse—from Rammohun to Radhakrishnan—in shaping the ideology of Indian nationalism, we come to recognize how the homely home being constructed by these modern Indians represents a national home. To adopt the central idiom of Indian nationalist discourse, what the modern Hindu eclectic seeks is *svarāj*, a term literally bespeaking the independence gained through self-rule, but most tellingly rendered as 'home rule.'[2]

As Partha Chatterjee has recently pointed out, when the colonizers' dominating knowledge and material interests forced their way into Indians' lives, the response of the colonized was to construct a home untouched and undefined by the colonizer. As we have seen in the case of Keshub and Vivekananda, this home was defined in terms of Indian spirituality, which could then be contrasted with the material world of the colonizer.

> The world was where the European power had challenged the non-European peoples and, by virtue of its superior material culture, had subjugated them. But, the nationalists asserted, it had failed to colonize the inner, essential identity of the East, which lay in its distinctive, and superior, spiritual culture. Here the East was undominated, sovereign, master of its own fate. (Chatterjee 1993: 121)

Both Keshub and Vivekananda claim that when it came to spirituality the Europeans would have to sit at the feet of the Indians. We can now recognize that in helping to construct what would become a defining trope of modern Hindu discourse—that is, the materiality of the West, the spirituality of the East—Keshub and Vivekananda were laying the foundation for a new Indian home. Chatterjee rightly notes that the creation of this home was a discursive act based upon "an ideological principle of *selection*" (1993: 121). Selection and construction—these define the eclectic project of national home-building. We might well speak of "appropriation as self-construction" (Collins 1995: 18).

Neither nations nor houses fall from the sky—despite the evidence of Dorothy's flight to Oz and of the opening footage in Gus Van Sant's film *My Own Private Idaho*. Both must be imagined before they can be constructed (see Anderson 1991). Houses, and even house plans, have to be constructed—a fact which places them squarely in the realm of human agency and history rather than in the ethereal realms of the ideal form. In a way it is like the view of the cosmos that we find in the ancient Vedas. As Brian Smith has pointed out, for the Vedic ritualists, not even divine creation was conceived as ushering into being a fully formed and well-ordered cosmos. Rather, the cosmos—like the human person and the sacrifice—had to be constructed. In the job of construction the ritualist made use of a system of resemblances. However, Smith warned us not to view the positing of resemblances as the ritualists' attempt at creating a symbolic counterpart (*pratirūpa*) to some ideal or Platonic form (*rūpa*). Rather, the *pratirūpa* is "made as well as discovered, a phenomenon that tends to distinguish this conception from the Platonic one."[3] It is not a matter simply of finding a material symbol that shares an essence with its ideal form; it is a matter both of finding and making a relationship of resemblance. As Smith puts it, "All form in Vedism is constructed rather than given" (1989: 76–77).

The dynamics of finding and making—the methods, if such there are, of the *bricoleur*—are particularly apropos when considering eclecticism. The eclectic certainly displays a penchant for working with *objects trouvés* (O'Flaherty 1984: 212). In the remainder of this chapter I would like to reflect on the dynamics of such finding and making in colonial and postcolonial India. In particular, I would like to expand upon the metaphor of the homely home, aided by concrete examples drawn from the history of architecture in India. Not only is architecture a vocation whose very raison d'être is to help us construct homes and worlds in which to live, but also, India offers countless monuments that graphically illustrate the ways colonial power/knowledge and indigenous culture were implicated in processes of finding and making identity. The two examples I would like to explore are Calcutta's Victoria Memorial Hall (see Fig. 3) and the far more humble, yet now nearly ubiquitous, bungalow.

Like the Statue of Liberty, Victoria Memorial Hall has come to stand metonymically for its city. This dazzling white edifice has been given almost iconographic status. It is prized as Calcutta's glistening gem,

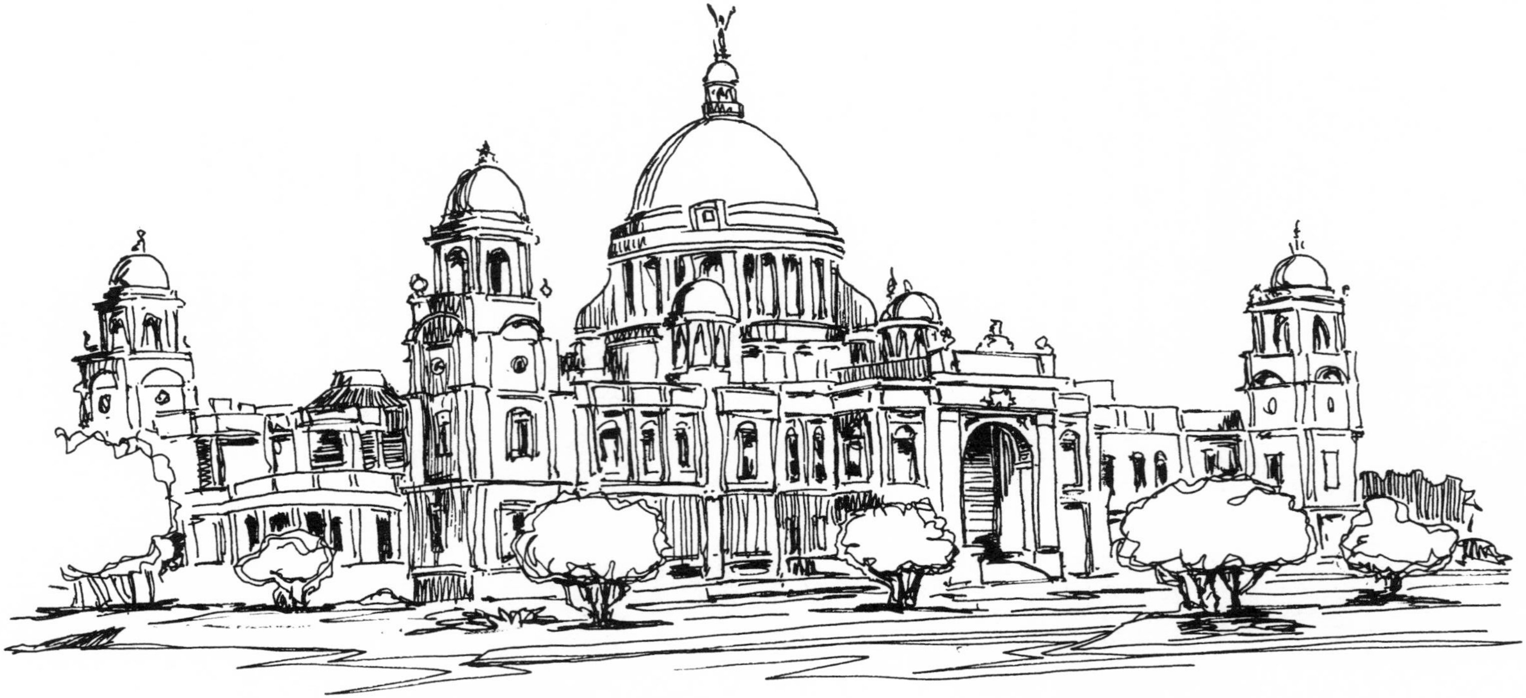

Figure 3 Victoria Memorial Hall, Calcutta. Drawing by Selden Richardson. Used by permission of the artist.

which dissolves in its pristine rays the stereotypical grey-green decay of the much-maligned city of darkness. In this regard, it is rather like the buildings of the White City, which served to distract the visitor's eye from the industrial haze and troubling poverty of turn-of-the-century Chicago.

In a city like Calcutta, whose history extends back no further than the arrival of the colonizer, the symbolic centrality of a Raj monument-cum-museum is telling. Ironies—colonial and postcolonial—abound. Take for instance the memorial's patron, Lord Curzon, viceroy of India. Curzon arranged for the cornerstone to be laid by the then Prince of Wales, who visited India in 1906. This was just after the first partition of Bengal, when the Swadeshi agitation opposing partition was at its peak. The incendiary character of the agitation apparently did little to dull Curzon's imperial enthusiasm; in fact, he was confident that nationalist activity was on its last legs. He therefore dedicated the memorial not just to Victoria, empress of India, but also *ad maiorem gloriaram imperii*. His monumental museum would enshrine the relics of the Raj and bring glory to the great imperial capital.

Of course, Curzon could not have foreseen that the Prince of Wales would return to India five years later as King George V, only to announce that the seat of the government of India was to be moved from Calcutta to Delhi. (Curzon's dismay at this move may have been as much personal as it was political, since he had arranged to have a commanding statue of himself installed at the memorial; see Irving 1981: 32.) Surely Curzon could have done a better job of assessing the role of the Indian National Congress and of the Swadeshi movement in advancing the cause of nationalism. That he failed to do so only serves to heighten the monumental irony of the memorial's postcolonial presence. Today, Curzon's glorious Raj museum exists as little more than an antiquarian relic-box, housing "a volume of Raj memorabilia" (Chaliha and Gupta 1989: 180). What's more, independent India has cut its imperial pretensions down to size through the clever—if heavy-handed—addition of an enormous bronze statue of the Swadeshi leader, Aurobindo Ghose, immediately opposite the memorial's main entrance. Empire is outflanked by resistance, while irony is heaped on irony.

Ironies continue as we ponder appraisals of the architectural significance of the memorial. In an effort at what might be called colonial double-coding, the style that Curzon chose for the building was part Renaissance, part Mughal—a style known as Indo-Saracenic.[4] There is no part Bengal, interestingly enough, presumably because Bengal offered no style the British could identify as suitably imperial. At any rate, the idea was to convey an appreciation for India's architectural heritage, while leaving no doubt that that same heritage had been claimed and completed by the civilizing traditions of Western culture.

One postindependence guidebook describes this "enormous but symmetrical pile of white marble" in no uncertain terms as "one of the great buildings of the modern world" (Barry, n.d.: 119). Intemperate hyperbole, surely. And yet, since the memorial looks exactly like a replica of a foreigner's idea of what a native ruler would build, it is not all that surprising to hear it praised as one of India's architectural wonders. In Jean Baudrillard's terms, the memorial is a simulacrum—the generation by a model of an image of reality. As for the memorial's relationship to an Indian empire, what Baudrillard says of the simulacrum holds true: "The territory no longer precedes the map, nor survives it. . . . It is the map that precedes the territory" (Baudrillard 1983: 2).

We witness the incredible power of the simulacrum in the comment registered by W. H. Auden when he visited the memorial. "Some enthusiastic guide informed him that the monument had been built by the same man who designed the Taj Mahal" (Moorhouse 1986: 231). In the face of such a declaration it would hardly do to point out that Calcutta did not even exist when the Taj Mahal was built. It is far more helpful to recall what Baudrillard says about the relationship between another well-known map and its engendered territory: Disneyland and America (Baudrillard 1983: 23–26). The same process of signification that grants to Walt Disney the power to create the reality of America itself ensures that Victoria Memorial Hall will create the reality of British India, endowing it as well with an imperial aura that extends into the distant past. To paraphrase Baudrillard, the Raj plagiarizes itself and makes retroactive its original myths—remakes Indian architecture so that it is more perfect than the originals.[5] In a sense, then, Auden's guide was right. The Victoria Memorial Hall is supposed to look like it belongs to the same imperial line as the Taj Mahal.

But Auden's guide was right in another sense as well. There is a curious validity to the claim that the Taj and the memorial were built by the same person, at least if we take that person to be the burra sahib—the big man, the mighty ruler, the imperial patron. Waxing Hindu, we might say, "Same patron, different avatars." Whether it was as Shah Jahan or Lord Curzon, the burra sahib was the power behind the symbol. He was the one who found an architect to memorialize his rule. He was also the one who subscribed (or extracted) from his subjects the enormous funds necessary to finance the job. And, finally, he was the one who marshaled the labor.

All of this suggests that in at least one sense both the Taj and the memorial were built by the same man. But when we consider the question of the patron's relationship to his architect or designers, we notice one important difference. This concerns the burra sahib's relationship with the *mistri*, or local craftsman. In the case of Shah Jahan and Lord Curzon, the levels of dependence and the degree of cooperation between patron and craftsman differ markedly. The Mughal ruler was, like Akbar, a "cultural pluralist," someone who could place his trust in the local traditions of architecture (Tillotson 1989: 102). He was willing to learn from the local mistri, to allow the craftsman's ideas and skills to inform and inflect his design. By contrast, the British patron tended to be a cultural chauvinist who looked upon the mistri as an uneducated laborer at best and an incompetent nuisance at worst. Thus in Curzon's case he sought guidance not from local architects but from Sir William Emerson, one-time president of the British Institute of Architects.[6] If the mistri was involved, it was only to assist in copying the colonizer's designs.

It should be noted that this model did have its critics, even among the British. Thus the art historian E. B. Havell, who was an advocate of Indian art and architecture in the first decades of this century, pointed out to his imperial colleagues how sad it was that the Mughals could appreciate the "Indian master-builder" (as he called the mistri), while British architects could see in him nothing more than "an instrument for creating a make-believe Anglo-Indian style" (quoted in Tillotson 1989: 61). Havell and a few others, like F. S. Growse, were able to exert something of a corrective influence in their quest to spark a revival of the indigenous traditions of architecture. However, "they could not wash out the distaste for Indian civilization felt by the generality of the British in India; they could not expunge the Macaulayite assumptions that India was essentially barbarous, that its traditions were worthless, and that British imperialism was civilizing" (Tillotson 1989: 102). As G. H. R. Tillotson has suggested, the few design battles won by the likes of Havell and Growse pale in comparison to the monumental battle they lost when Raj architects chose to exclude the mistri from an active part in their greatest twentieth-century endeavor: the design for their new capital in Delhi (102). I will return to the "new" Delhi shortly. For now it is enough to note that while the burra sahib may have been trying manfully to take over the Mughal's seat of honor, he was not necessarily going to adopt his cultural policies.

All of the issues raised by this consideration of Victoria Memorial Hall can be reconsidered in the case of the Anglo-Indian bungalow (and its international progeny): the merger of indigenous style with imperial designs, the power differential between patron and local craftsman, and the curious dynamics of the simulacrum. In fact it is only when we take up the latter idea, explored so suggestively by Baudrillard, that we are able to join together things that might otherwise seem to have very little to do with one another, such as Disneyland, Victoria Memorial Hall, the White Palace buildings of the 1893 World's Fair, and the bungalow. In order to introduce the homely bungalow into the company of these grand icons of simulation, let us consider the pronouncement of Horkheimer and Adorno which serves as epigram to this chapter: "Even now the older houses just outside the concrete city centers look like slums, and the new bungalows on the outskirts are at one with the flimsy structures of world fairs in their praise of technical progress and their built-in demand to be discarded after a short while like empty food cans" (1972: 120).

The immediate problem here seems to be the bungalow as the representative structure of modernization and mass consumption, with its relentless program of planned obsolescence and disposability. However, with the reference to the World's Fair, our perspective on the dilemma of modernization is expanded to include the problem of simulation.[7] Or perhaps we had better say "dissimulation," since this evokes the title of the essay in which the above passage appears: "Enlightenment as Mass Deception." Without going into their essay in depth, I would simply call attention to the way Horkheimer and Adorno expose the fundamental logic of repetition that underlies what they refer to as the "culture industry." Repetition, mass production, simulation—the end result of the business of popular culture, entertainment, and amusement is that people are presented with "a model of their culture" (Horkheimer and Adorno 1972: 121). The culture industry produces, controls, and disciplines our needs and wants, all the while glorifying our freedom to choose what we want (144). Individuation is the ideology, but it does not describe what is in fact the complete submission of the individual to the general; the "peculiarity of the self" is "falsely represented as natural" (154). Simulation reigns: "Because of his ubiquity, the film star with whom one is meant to fall in love is from the outset a copy of himself" (140).

Within this ideological framework, the ubiquitous suburban bungalow is one more model of our culture, not essentially different from the World's Fair or Disneyland. It ostensibly stands for one set of values—the independence of the individual in the free market of democracy—but in fact betrays the utter subservience of the individual to the culture of capitalism. In other words, there is a disturbing irony to the bungalow, as there is to Disneyland; it is this irony that Horkheimer and Adorno wish to expose with their dialectical critique of Enlightenment rationality and capitalist culture. Behind their essay looms the shadow of fascism and Hitler, in whose dark silhouette we are asked to bear witness to the other side of the Enlightenment.

We notice the same dark truths in the spectre of colonialism as well. That is, in a monument like Victoria Memorial Hall we confront the dark ironies of colonialism. The memorial, which Indians purchased through their own subscriptions, exists to represent to Indians the glory of their subservience. One has to stretch even to use the word irony in such a case, since with respect to the memorial the words of Horkheimer and Adorno seem apposite: "The lines of its artificial framework begin to show through" (1972: 121).

Taken in this sense, despite its humble and homely facade, the bungalow too enshrines the darker history of capitalism and colonialism, those geminal players in the drama of modernity. At the same time, however, the bungalow can be read as an ongoing experiment in eclectic home-building, expressing the colonial and postcolonial desire to construct an identity. For these reasons, the bungalow calls out to be included in our dialectical analysis. In what follows I would like to attempt to honor that call, by focusing briefly on the bungalow both as evidence of the "artificial framework" of colonial ideology and as a manifestation of the Indian quest for a homely home during and after colonial rule.

There are certainly more-inspiring architectural forms in India than the bungalow, but few with a history that so closely mirrors the changing dynamics of cultural encounter in the colonial and postcolonial world. Like a handful of other curious monuments dotting the postcolonial landscape, the bungalow is, as it were, a visible reminder of the processes at work in the construction of modern Hindu discourse. What makes the bungalow doubly fascinating is the fact that it can be found all around us, whether we wander the lanes of Santiniketan, the streets of Sydney, the downs of Sussex, or the suburbs of Southern California. I think this makes it particularly apropos for a study of eclecticism as a mode of modernist universalism. Who knows—it may even prompt us to reconsider the significance of eclecticism as a mode of postmodern particularism. After all, it has been suggested that the eclecticism of postmodern architecture is emblematic of our inability to map our position in the contemporary world, which appears to us as a bewildering and decentered, multinational, global network.[8] And yet, for all its openness to diversity and its opposition to universalism, postmodern architecture can now be found everywhere (Connor 1990). Such may be the revenge of modernity, which has bequeathed to us our global culture, and which—postmodernism notwithstanding—may in the end have to be dealt with on its own terms (see Berman 1988). But I digress; before we can contemplate the theoretical implications of the global ubiquity of the bungalow, we should give some thought to where this homely home came from. To do this we must explore the dynamics behind its development in the earliest years of its colonial incubation.

When European traders first began to set up factories and establish trade centers in India, they were attracted to a type of dwelling indigenous to the region of Bengal. This dwelling was described by Francis Buchanan in 1810 in the following terms:

> The style of private ediface [*sic*] that is proper and peculiar to Bengal, consists of a hut with a pent roof constructed of two sloping sides which meet in a ridge forming the segment of a circle so that it has a resemblance to a boat when overturned. . . . This kind of hut, it is said, from being peculiar to Bengal, is called by the native Banggolo. (Quoted in King 1984: 18)

By the end of the eighteenth century this type of structure was being widely adopted for use by the British, who preserved in Anglicized form its original Bengali name, *bāṅglā*. Yet from its very inception, the colonial appropriation of this found object showed the telltale signs of *bricolage*. For instance, the most prominent and characteristic feature of the emerging Anglo-Indian bungalow—the veranda—was in fact a motif that had been introduced into India by the Portuguese in the sixteenth century (King 1984: 30; see Meade 1988: 134).[9]

The chief virtues of the bungalow were its "simplicity, cheapness and flexibility" (Meade 1988: 142). Of these virtues, flexibility has perhaps accounted most directly for the long and protean career of the bungalow. The British in India quickly became enamored of the bungalow because it could be set up quickly like a tent, while at the same time offering a bit more substance. Thanks to its adaptability of scale and function, the bungalow proved to be "suitable for nearly all the practical and representational requirements of the [East India] Company's service and the manifold gradations of its hierarchy" (Meade 1988: 148). It was soon doing duty in a number of roles—as an outbuilding, military barracks, or an up-country way station (the ubiquitous Dak bungalow). We shall see that flexibility will continue to be the defining characteristic of the bungalow long after it has departed Bengal. Indeed, by the time it reaches Southern California in the early twentieth century the bungalow will have—in the words of its great American exponent, Gustav Stickley—"departed considerably from the original Indian model" (see Stickley 1988: vi). Thus on the American scene alone one finds the bungalow inflected according to California, Japanese, Spanish, ranch, forest, and mountain styles; and let's not forget the "barnacle," a kind of barn-bungalow hybrid (see Stickley 1988).

Bearing in mind the early appreciation and appropriation of the bungalow by the colonial British, one must not lose sight of the fact that it was not typically their first choice for a primary residence. For this purpose, those settling in India around 1800 preferred the so-called garden house. The basic features of the garden house were not Indian in origin at all, but derived from neoclassical models. Especially popular at this time were Palladian-style buildings. Understandably, however, the exigencies of climate argued against the direct transplanting of this style. Thus at the time of its introduction into India, the Palladian garden house began to undergo a transformation. One notices, for instance, the deepening of the porticos, in the hope of gaining more shade throughout the day; likewise the characteristically massive columns become thinner to make more room for ventilation; at the same time the same columns are spaced farther apart—both for the sake of better ventilation and to facilitate the hanging of rattan blinds, known among the British as tatties (see Meade 1988: 138). Despite these changes, the British still recognized in their garden house the familiar lineaments of a neo-classical European home. As Martin Meade has noted, the garden house thus served as something like a "cultural sheet anchor" helping the Englishman keep his bearings in the emotional currents of self-imposed exile (146).[10]

Having said this—and having noted that the bungalow was not typically the first choice for a colonizer's home—we do notice some important early attempts to appropriate the bungalow style as the basis for an Englishman's main residence. Notable in this respect is the mention of a certain "lower-roomed house" along the lines of a bungalow that was listed among the many items auctioned from the Bengal estate of Warren Hastings in 1785 (Meade 1988: 141). This suggests that well before the nineteenth century the bungalow had begun to undergo a process of Anglicization. It is out of the Indianizing of the garden house and the Anglicizing of the bungalow that the Anglo-Indian bungalow emerged (141). As we shall see, it is a thoroughly hybrid structure, whose genesis is highly suggestive for our thinking about the discursive homes constructed by Hindu apologists.

That such a combination was sometimes awkward and forced is suggested by a satirical cartoon from the nineteenth century that has been reproduced by Anthony King, which depicts an Englishman attempting to create his vision of a landed English gentry home using the expertise of the local mistri. The result is an odd sort of hybrid that proceeds to collapse during the first rainy season. King comments succinctly that such an outcome represented the inevitable result of "the application of an inappropriate technology to a culturally unfamiliar design" (1984: 33). Putting it another way, we have returned to the problem of the relative power and hierarchical roles of the sahib and the mistri. The colonizer insists that the local craftsman use his skills not to create a native dwelling, but to participate in the ruse of creating a simulacrum of an Englishman's estate. The structural failure of the house—for which the English cartoonist seemed to blame the status-seeking foreigner as much as the incompetent mistri—is due to what we might call (adopting a phrase from Horkheimer and Adorno 1972) its artificial framework.

The humorous example cited by King raises an important point about the practice of architecture in early colonial India. Like the Englishman in the cartoon, the men who designed and built the full range of the East India Company's buildings—from Dak bungalows to governor's residences—were not professionally trained architects; at best they were civil and military engineers. When venturing into architectural design they were often guided by nothing more than the ideas and plans they could derive from books of architectural drawings or manuals of design available to them in India. We should hardly be surprised, therefore, if their designs didn't run the risk of either collapsing in the first rains or ending up looking like awkward, if sturdy, renderings of vaguely familiar styles. Not the most inspiring way to begin constructing an imperial legacy—and yet these were the professional circumstances in which the tradition of British building in India took its start. It is precisely these rather humble origins that explain the subsequent importance within imperial architectural history of a kind of engineering vernacular that was promulgated through the building projects of the Public Works Department (PWD). The PWD style—as it came to be known—was to place an indelible stamp on colonial architecture across all of India. As a colonial vernacular, the PWD style amounted to the attempt to create a style of building that could preserve the colonizer's sense of national identity and colonial mission, while articulating that sense through forms inflected by the local context. Viewed in these terms, the tension between the garden house and the bungalow was a dynamic one.

Throughout the first half of the nineteenth century the demands of local context may have swung the balance toward the appropriation of indigenous architectural norms; the demands of climate and the need for practical and adaptable structures recommended a structural form like the bungalow. Things began to change, however, following the Mutiny of 1857. For one thing, when rule over India was transferred from Company to Crown, the British were led to ponder more seriously the imperial consequences of their architectural endeavors in India. Suddenly the concessions made to local context by the PWD style seemed problematic. This was no longer the era of nabobs and Englishmen-gone-native like Hindoo Stewart, with their hookahs and Indian wives.[11] An empire needed building; and the empire's buildings needed to announce their European heritage. It would no longer do to allow the PWD bungalow to neglect its British inheritance. If the PWD was to continue building bungalows, these buildings would nevertheless need to provide the British in India with a "visible assurance of their own cultural identity" (King 1984: 48).

The bungalow wasn't abandoned; rather, in the spirit of an ongoing process of selection and self-definition, it was recruited for a more serious mission: symbolizing the increasing hold of the British over India. Through its ubiquitous employment by Raj builders, the once-Indian bungalow could ironically be made to promote the monolithic cultural and political identity of the British. As an imperial structure, it came to map a territory the British were fast claiming to control. Thus, by the end of the nineteenth century the bungalow had, in the words of Anthony King, "spread throughout the land": "From Bangalore to Bombay, though frequently differing in style, the plan and structure of the bungalow was more or less the same. For the official and his family who used it, moving at the end of each 'tour,' it provided continuity through the process of a colonial career" (King 1984: 49). Through its very ubiquity the bungalow attested not only to the colonizer's hold over the length and breadth of India, but also offered to the colonizer—no matter his posting or billet—a reassurance of his cultural origins.

King makes the further point, however, that even while the bungalow bespoke this monolithic symbolic identity, it continued to evolve into a diversity of styles, as it took root "from Bangalore to Bombay." In one sense, the "chameleon-like" character of the bungalow speaks of the ways it continued to be inflected by its Indian context, a cultural milieu long known for its gift of "assimilation and reinterpretation" (Meade 1988: 133, 156). To put it differently, while the British burra sahib was busy staking out the boundary markers of his rule, the Indian mistri was subtly reappropriating those very markers for his own purposes. It may not be necessary to appeal, as Meade does, to India's ancient penchant for eclectic appropriation. Rather, we might simply say that the particularities of local context and the antagonistic need of colonizer and colonized for self-definition worked toward the eclectic evolution of the bungalow. The manifold hybridity of the colonial bungalow may well be viewed in terms of the concept of "hybridity" developed by Homi Bhabha—a hybridity which is the very "*problematic* of colonial representation," but which we must not view as a kind of syncretistic resolution, or *tertium quid*. Rather than resolution, this eclectic hybridity is all about difference; it is about appropriation and resistance (see Bhabha 1985: 156, 162).

The hybrid extremes to which the bungalow could evolve—and we have already seen the selective appropriation behind the original merger of the Bengali thatched hut, the Iberian veranda, and the English garden house—are perhaps nowhere more manifest than in the peculiar case of the Hill Station bungalow. The latter was a style of resort home built by and for the British on the cooler mountaintops of places like Simla and Ootacamund. It was to these mountain resorts that officials and civilians gravitated during the hot season to escape the discomforts of life in cities like Delhi, Madras, and Mysore.

Several factors encouraged a greater freedom on the part of the architect or designer working in a Hill Station. To begin with, the Hill Stations were less encumbered by the "hierarchical formalities and architectural pretensions of colonial power" than were imperial centers like Delhi (Meade 1988: 149). Here the colonizer was more free to evoke Europe and his longed-for home. This greater freedom manifested itself in attempts to evoke the architecture and emotional landscapes of places like Scotland or the Lake District. The temperate weather of the hills came to the colonizer's aid in this respect, since it obviated the need to tailor design to the concerns of climate. Windows, eaves, columns, and verandas could be articulated with far more latitude. Finally, this greater range of expression was additionally aided by the presence in the Hill Stations of a wide range of craft styles not found in the plains. Thus, as Meade notes, the "individualism of local craftsmanship and woodcarving" exerted its influence on the design of the Hill Station bungalow; here in the mountains, one might even find a craftsman who could re-create the gables of a Swiss cottage (1988: 150).

Designing and building their homes under such circumstances, the residents of the Hill Stations transformed the bungalow into "an exuberantly eclectic architectural hybrid" (Meade 1988: 150). So hybridized did the Hill Station bungalow become that it is difficult for the architectural historian to find words to categorize it. Meade comments wryly that one scholar has proposed that the style of the Hill Station bungalow be dubbed "Himalayan Swiss Gothic" (1988: 150). For all its absurdity, such a label is curiously apposite. First of all, it speaks of nothing if not eclecticism and difference. But second, the presence of the "exuberantly eclectic architectural hybrid" serves well to suggest the inevitable, if reluctant, reappropriation of the bungalow by its Indian context. No matter how hard the colonizer attempted to simulate his European home, he was undone by the fact that this new home was in fact a home away from home. The Anglo-Indian bungalow, the once-and-former *bāṅglā*, thus introduced a term of difference into his relationship with his European home that could not be overcome. There is, in Bhabha's terms, an unavoidable separation from origins and essences precisely at the heart of the colonizer's attempt to appeal to such essences (see Bhabha 1985: 162).

Of course, the same predicament of hybridity applies to the colonial Indian as well. The same dynamics that apply in the case of the colonizer's attempt to create an imperial home apply to the Indian's attempt to make the colonial home his own. There is appropriation and there is resistance. I can only allude very briefly to this (re)appropriation of the bungalow by the colonized Indian. One waits for a more in-depth study of the ways in which the colonized Indian elites adopted the architectural markers of style and status from their colonial overlords. Certainly one sees this process beginning very early in a city like Calcutta, where the educated Babu adopted everything from the coat and top hat to the food and entertainments of the colonizer. It only follows that in such a context the Babu's home, too, should come to reflect his idea of the British idea of what a suitable Indian dwelling should be. Since the educated Indian's interests, entertainments, and domestic affairs were expected to revolve around the parlor tastes of the colonizer—rather than the customs of the Indian street or village—it was incumbent upon the Babu to construct for himself a home that featured a proper parlor (see Banerjee 1989). This tension between the norms of the colonizer's parlor and indigenous culture is illustrated nicely by an account of a visit made by Sri Ramakrishna to the home of Vidyasagar. The latter, despite his status as a great *brāhmaṇ paṇḍit*, lived in an impressive two-story European-style house in North Calcutta—complete with an impressive book-lined parlor on the second floor. When Ramakrishna pulled up in front of the house, the otherwise unselfconscious, even rustic, holy man made a point of asking his devotees if it mattered that his shirt was unbuttoned! (see Ramakrishna 1988: vol. 3, 3).[12] And what was true for Vidyasagar and Ramakrishna was no less true for the wealthy Indian princes, for whom the cost of participating in the empire was the adoption of the colonizer's notion of hearth and home, not to mention palace (see Meade 1988: 149).

And as much as this appropriation by Indians of the colonizer's tastes worked eventually toward a nationalist program defined in terms of expelling the colonizer, that very program—hybrid as it was—incorporated profound ironies and points of internal resistance. This is a theme that has been explored with great insight by Ashis Nandy, to whom I shall return shortly. But for now let me offer an example of such conflicted appropriation, again drawn from the realm of architecture. I have in mind the development of modern theaters in Calcutta. As Sudipto Chatterjee has pointed out, at the very time when educated Bengalis began to work for the creation of their own so-called national theater in the late nineteenth century, the model they chose for the design of their theaters was that of the European proscenium stage; what is more, they chose names for their theaters like Minerva and Lyceum.[13] To relate this to themes I have already developed, we see here a striking example of the way the very appropriation that is at the heart of the attempt to build a homely home is necessarily preconstrained; like the *bricoleur*, it must operate through and with the categories it has received.

We might interpret this process in terms of what C. A. Bayly has called the "colonisation of taste," which he sees accelerating after 1860 (see Bayly 1983: 429). However, it would be wrong to conclude, as Anthony King seems to, that what Indians inherited with the Anglo-Indian bungalow was an entirely European legacy (see King 1984: 49ff.). Without a doubt, the adoption of the Anglicized building style has deeply and irrevocably shaped Indian cultural practice—influencing everything from the way Indians envision the basic family unit to the way they construct and use bathrooms. Yet, by focusing largely on the bungalow as an index of the way the Indian city became implicated in global capitalism, King fails to give adequate weight to what Martin Meade chooses to call the Indian reinterpretation of the bungalow. It is precisely such reinterpretation—with all the tensions that come with such hybridity—that one finds in abundant evidence when wandering through recent Indian suburban enclaves like New Delhi's Defense Colony or Santiniketan's Purvapalli. As Meade notes:

> Early adopted by the Indian middle classes, personal taste and the vagaries of fashion all found individual expression in the bungalow and have continued to do so since Independence. Art Deco styling appears in the 1930's, modernist concrete forms predominate by the late 1950's and 60's . . . and these are now being overlaid once more by an eclectic collage of stylistic references. Invariably however these designs display uniquely Indian traits of form and function—the bungalow has been completely assimilated and re-absorbed into the culture of its origins. (1988: 156)

As Meade sees it, reinterpretation is a form of reappropriation, which is itself put at the service of self-construction. However, we should be equally cautious about adopting Meade's language of *complete* reabsorption. What could "complete" mean in this case? Surely not a return to some essentially Indian bungalow; surely not the erasure of the Anglo-Indian bungalow's colonial hybridity.

In the end, we find ourselves hovering between postulating a complete colonization of Indian taste by European norms and asserting the return of the bungalow to its Indian roots. Neither pole alone can capture the tensions and differences that animate the bungalow's history.

Applying Bhabha's reflections on the English book in a colonial context, we might say the bungalow "retains its presence, but it is no longer a representation of an essence; it is now a partial presence, a (strategic) device in a specific colonial engagement, an appurtenance of authority" (Bhabha 1985: 157). Only an ironic stance seems capable of grasping the bungalow in these terms. For as Indians appropriated the bungalow for their own purposes they acknowledged the colonizer's culture of taste and power and simultaneously called that culture into question; they resisted it. In Bhabha's terms there is mimicry and mockery, the mere "*ruse* of recognition" (157).

We can illustrate this double move by examining what is perhaps the grandest example of a bungalow on Indian soil, namely, Government House, in New Delhi. Intended to be the home of the imperial viceroy, it is now the official residence of India's president and is known as Rashtrapati Bhavan (see Fig. 4). Designed by Edwin Landseer Lutyens to be the centerpiece of Lutyens's and Herbert Baker's design for imperial New Delhi, this massive sandstone bungalow was intended to be "a vision of authority made manifest" (Irving 1981: 190). Or shall we say, "a (strategic) device in a specific colonial engagement, an appurtenance of authority"? And just what is it we see when we look at Rashtrapati Bhavan today? The legacy of imperial authority? The reclaimed authority of independent India? Or only a ruse?

But let me back up a bit to consider the genesis of the viceregal residence, which served to anchor the planning for the new imperial capital that was inaugurated with the grand Durbar of 1911. We are hardly surprised to learn that our principal player, Lutyens, was rather notorious for his outspoken denial of an architectural tradition in India. We are no less surprised to hear that he liked to joke about the inferiority of Indian building techniques. In fact, it turns out Lutyens had scarcely much good to say even of the widespread use of the Indo-Saracenic style in British public buildings in India (Irving 1981: 101–102). As for the ubiquitous Anglo-Indian bungalows, Lutyens had his own technical term: he called them "bungle-ohs" (Meade 1988: 152).

Lutyens's self-proclaimed preference in terms of method was to approach his work in India "as an Englishman dressed for the climate" (as quoted in Irving 1981: 170). He swore by what we might call the comforting and (to him) apparently universal grid of classical architecture. He demanded that this grid form the logic and backbone of an architecture in India. If there were to be a need to provide exotic decora-

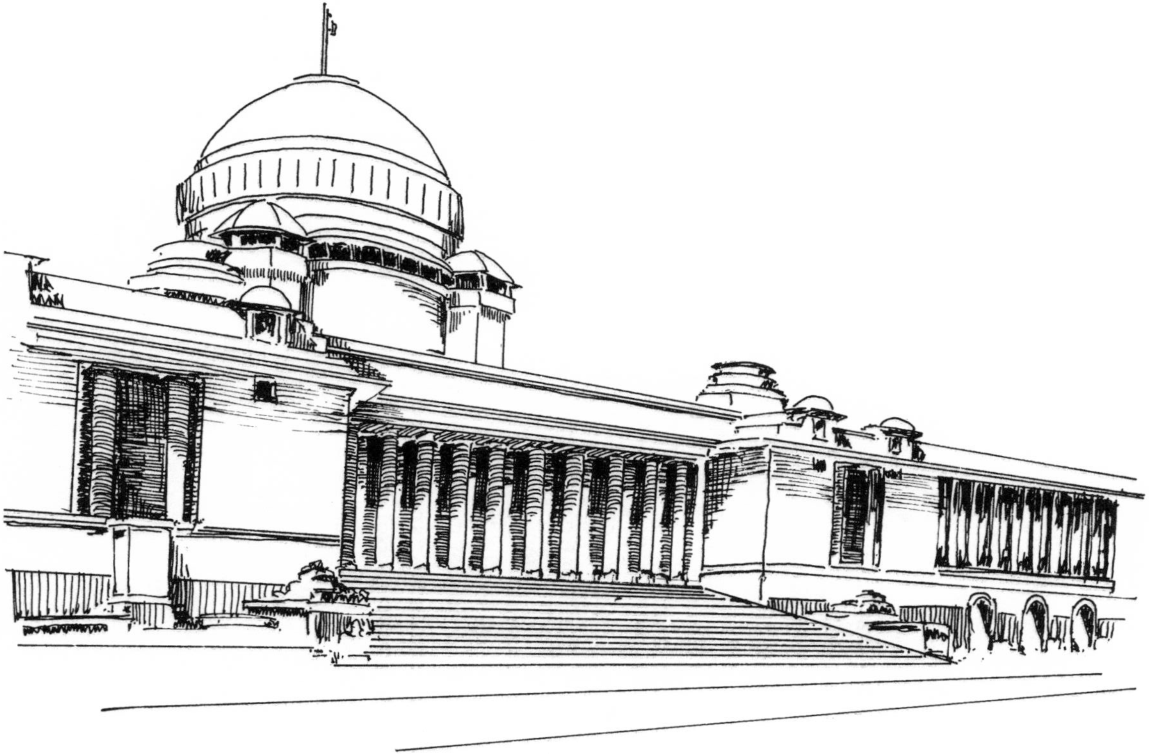

Figure 4 Rashtrapati Bhavan, New Delhi. Drawing by Selden Richardson. Used by permission of the artist.

tion to suit the Indian context, it would only amount to a superficial veneer on the sound framework of the classical grid. As one scholar has put it:

> Emblematic ornament was acceptable if discreetly subsumed within the controlling geometric system. Universal classical principles were quite capable of comprehending within their framework the exoticism of Indian ornament. But such decoration could not be allowed to seize command and actually determine the architectural outline and profile, as in the popular Indo-Saracenic style. . . . Rather, in the manner of the Palladians, decoration had to be "within reason." (Irving 1981: 170)

This method was, in Lutyens's own words, "better, wiser, saner, and more gentlemanlike" than superficial attempts at hybridizing (as quoted in Irving 1981: 170).

Such principled methodological strictures notwithstanding, even Lutyens found it necessary to heed the political imperative. The government required of him that he work within its stated goal of creating buildings that would be symbolic of modern India rather than merely of Western Europe; after all, it was the Indian people who were going to have to foot the bill for their new cityscape (Irving 1981: 102). As a result, one of the most striking ironies of the viceregal residence in New Delhi is that for all of Lutyens's arrogant classicism, it ended up by succumbing to the dynamics of colonial hybridization. Lutyens's Government House can on many accounts be reckoned a marvelous pastiche of architectural motifs. Indeed, it has been said that at first glance this viceregal residence strikes the visitor as "at once a giant Indian bungalow, embattled Rajput fortress, and Mughal tomb" (Irving 1981: 174).

Apart from its hybridity, the most striking aspect of the viceregal residence is its reference to the colonial bungalow. Indeed, if one concentrates on its "one principal storey, outspreading wings, portico-loggias and defining horizontal of the chujja-cornice," one discovers that this imperial mansion is in fact the "most palatial sublimation of the Anglo-Indian concept of the bungalow" (Meade 1988: 154). And this building sprang from the drawing board of the sworn enemy of "bungle-ohs," from the man who had early on objected to the idea of having Indian draftsmen brought in to help "Orientalize" the government's designs! This is surely a delicious irony, although Martin Meade, in his study of the Anglo-Indian bungalow, chooses not to dwell on it. Instead, Meade prefers to see in Government House a testament to Lutyens's ability to rise above his earlier antipathy to Indian architecture. Surely it is not this simple. Robert Irving's judgment that "Lutyens's august, supremely ordered Viceregal palace at New Delhi not only expressed the 'ideal and fact of British rule in India,' but achieved that fusion of traditions which both politics and climate dictated" seems closer to the mark (Irving 1981: 170). It is not that Lutyens had come to love Indian architecture, but that he was constrained by the colonial context into certain choices. But we might go even further still and suggest that in Lutyens's hybrid Government House we have a monumental version of the homely bungalow: a vision of authority and irony.

The irony does not stop here, of course, since Lutyens's viceregal residence lives on as the first home of the independent Indian nation. In pausing to mark this transition from Government House to Rashtrapati Bhavan we capture, almost in a snapshot, the symbolic and emotive complexity of the Indian eclectic's homely home. Here (as in so many other sites) postcolonial Indians have inherited a home of their own that they were never intended to occupy. Likewise, in reappropriating the bungalow, they ironically reclaim what was never really their own, since the Anglo-Indian bungalow lives only as mimic and not as original. Finally, here in Rashtrapati Bhavan is a national symbol suitable for tourism posters, yet one that nevertheless bears the inerasable stigma of its colonial past. Rushdie says that only a madman would prefer someone else's version of a story to his own, but the case of Rashtrapati Bhavan clearly demonstrates that even the sanest of people sometimes end up living in someone else's idea of a house.

Psychologically we can interpret the significance of this fact in terms of what Ashis Nandy has called "the second form of colonization." That is, even after the colonizing West has left India, "the West is now everywhere, . . . in structures and in minds" (Nandy 1983: xi). Nandy's work has allowed us to recognize the invidious and ongoing process of colonialism, whereby to overcome the colonizer, the colonized first had to learn to speak the colonizer's language and play the colonizer's game. The colonized, to paraphrase Nandy, had to become intimate with his enemy. But even acknowledging this fact is not enough. We must remember that even now, after the colonizer is gone, the intimacy and the tortured game persists. This is why Nandy says that "colonialism is an indigenous process released by external forces" (1983: 3). After those external forces have been removed, the momentum of the process continues to drive the dynamics of postcolonial life. In any case, Nandy seems to suggest that Bayly's notion of the colonization of taste is not strong enough; we need to speak of the colonization of psychology, practice, and material culture.

It is tempting to look back over the history of colonialism in a romantic mode. When one does so, the process seems purely tragic. That is, the cherished and once-noble authenticity of the Indian people has been forever banished to some precolonial past that can never again be retrieved. Nandy reminds us, however, that there is a danger in pursuing such a reading of colonial and postcolonial history. The danger is that by falling prey to such a reading one adopts the very notion of rationality that had all along been used by the colonizer to explain (away) Indian culture; one commits the error of reifying the "standard stereotypes" of the colonizer's dominant ideology (Nandy 1983: 113). Such stereotypes serve to perpetuate—among other things—the view of India as spiritual, parochial, and effeminate. Even for the anticolonial Indian these become the only terms available for expressing dissent. By construing India as an Other to a West it desires not to be, the nationalist unwittingly makes of India the Other the West always wanted it to be.

Nandy's approach is to resist such dichotomizing altogether, since it seems to emerge from the colonization of rationality itself (1983: 113). His model for this is the quintessential modern Hindu, Mahatma Gandhi, who in his almost laughable ordinariness is the "archetypal survivor":

> Seemingly he makes all-round compromises, but he refuses to be psychologically swamped, co-opted or penetrated. Defeat, his response seems to say, is a disaster and so are the imposed ways of the victor. But worse is the loss of one's "soul" and the internalization of one's victor, because it forces one to fight the victor according to the victor's values, within his model of dissent. Better to be a comical dissenter than to be a powerful, serious but acceptable opponent. (Nandy 1983: 111)

The idea of "comical" dissent is a powerful one, suggesting not just the arch humor of Gandhi, but also the clever strategems of Vivekananda and the outrageous eclecticism of Keshub. While the temptation has been, and still is, to view all of these men through the lens of the heroic—and nationalist panegyrics of such leaders have performed their task of resistance, after all—we realize that if viewed as comic figures, the voices of Keshub and Vivekananda and Gandhi are liberated to attest to the paradoxical hope that "the insane may often have a higher chance of achieving their civilizational goal of freedom and autonomy without mortgaging their sanity" (Nandy 1983: 113). To return to Rushdie, it turns out the madman is not the "irrational" Hindu eclectic, but the one who chooses to live by the colonizer's weather reports.

In *Gandhi*, Richard Attenborough's 1982 film, Gandhi makes his way up the steps of Government House after completing his famous Salt March of 1930. He looks comical against the backdrop of Lutyens's enormous and authoritarian steps. The problem is, so do the British sentries who stand guard over this glorified bungalow. As Robert Irving has noted, the building seems sadly comic; the "magnified scale" of its dome "may signify not so much boundless self-assurance as insecurity" (1981: 186). Unfortunately for them, the British could not or would not admit this.[14] Gandhi, however, who had the nerve to visit the viceroy's parlor in his dhoti, had a flair for comic annoyance—which is captured nicely by Ben Kingsley (in the title role) in his exchanges with Sir John Gielgud. As Gandhi undoes the Edwardian sternness of the viceroy, he announces with a smile his moral victory; political victory is only a matter of time. In this sense, the Mahatma's comic march up the steps of Government House amounts to an act of occupation. Henceforth—even if it will take another decade and a half—this will be Rashtrapati Bhavan. In this comic moment, Lutyens's imperial mansion becomes the Indian's homely home.

Bringing this rather lengthy meditation on the bungalow back into direct relation with the problem of eclecticism, let me propose one lesson I see in all this: Whether one examines the character of the Anglo-Indian bungalow or the strategies of modern Hindu discourse, one must reckon with the process of *bricolage*. Like all *bricolage*, this process is an eclectic one; recalling Lévi-Strauss, it is preconstrained. When it came to advancing an apologetic Hinduism, modern Hindus were confronted with the task of working in, through, and against a variety of traditions, discourses, and styles bequeathed to them by the colonial context. Some of this repertoire was indigenous, some of it was not, but all of it was reconfigured and revalued through the very dynamics of colonial hybridity and excess. As Jim Collins has pointed out with respect to another world of excess, "The imageability of any cultural space is not simply the residue of structural and economic determinism operating in a semiotic vacuum"; rather, "the development of a sense of self-location . . . depends upon the negotiation of cultural landscapes that come to us already imaged" (1995: 37).

The history of the bungalow may not provide a perfect analogy to the formation of modern Hindu discourse, but it does at least suggest how complex and cobbled together all colonial artifacts can be—how they attempt to appropriate what has already been imaged as a means both of pronouncing their own authority and resisting the authority of the already-imaged. Certainly there is an analogy between the homely ironies of Rashtrapati Bhavan and those expressed in the discourse of modern Hindu eclecticism. In both we find the sublime and the ironic, the disharmonious and the comic. But in neither can we sensibly speak of the corruption of some authentic essence or original meaning.

7

Conclusion

In a complex enigma the greatest ingenuity is not always shown by him who first gives the complete solution.

—Samuel Taylor Coleridge

In the preceding chapters I have tried to raise a number of questions regarding the phenomenon of eclecticism. Is it possible to devise a general model of eclecticism that can do justice to its various historical manifestations? What are the differing valuations of eclecticism within modernist and postmodernist discourse? Can an awareness of the shifting verdicts on eclecticism within the Western intellectual tradition help us revisit or revise dominant Indological attitudes toward the eclectic dimensions of South Asian religious life and literature? If so, how might we formulate an alternate interpretation of modern Hindu eclecticism?

At the outset of this undertaking, I made Agehananda Bharati the foil with which to raise these problems. I questioned the presuppositions of scientific rationality and confident historicism that he brought to bear on the apologetic strategies of Renaissance Hinduism. I called into question his posture as the scholar who knew better than to be taken in by what he viewed as a species of sloppy thinking unsupported by the higher traditions of Sanskritic or Brahmanical Hinduism. One of the ways I went about challenging Bharati's authority was by juxtaposing his hard-nosed analysis of modernist Hinduism with the more playfully eclectic imagination of Salman Rushdie. Over against Bharati's scholar-Indologist I juxtaposed Rushdie's Saleem Sinai, who survived the upheavals of postcolonial India by living eclectically. In this fashion, Bharati and Rushdie became the poles between which I attempted to situate a dialectical consideration of modern Hindu eclecticism. The time has come to ask whether there is, in fact, somewhere we can safely land between these poles.

Scholars like Bharati are tempted to ask, and then conclusively answer, the question, What is authentic? It is the paramount temptation for a scholar who claims to "know better." If this book serves no other purpose, I would like it to issue a gentle reminder that when we feel this temptation overtaking us, we would do well to remember Rushdie's Zeeny Vakil, "champion of the eclectic *impure* bricolage artist" (Dayal 1992: 444). Zeeny realized that to begin to talk about authenticity was to strap oneself into a straitjacket:

> She was an art critic whose book on the confining myth of authenticity, that folkloristic straitjacket which she sought to replace by an ethic of historically validated eclecticism, for was not the entire national culture based on the principle of borrowing whatever clothes seemed to fit, Aryan, Mughal, British, take-the-best-and-leave-the-rest?—had created a predictable stink. (Rushdie 1989: 52)

Who wants to wear a straitjacket? They're for madmen. Notice how Zeeny deftly turns the tables, by construing the Indologist as the madman and the modern Indian eclectic as the voice of sanity. That Indology is madness may be more than we care to say, and yet Zeeny would have us at least admit that neither is she mad. Granted, her version of truth tends to upset those who like to decide such matters.

Like Gandhi, Zeeny has the nerve to cause a stink. She risks scandal and absurdity by asking such uncomfortable questions as, "Why should there be a good, right way of being a wog?" (Rushdie 1989: 52). Zeeny sees only too clearly that to essentialize a lost authenticity for her culture is to play right back into the very imperial matrix that gave us that ugly word, *wog*. Of course what makes her argument so persuasive is that according to it, Hindu fundamentalism is as guilty as modern Indology. Both fall victim to the appeal to authenticity. To prove one's Hindu-ness is to play the same game of authentication and essentializing that guides the hand of Western imperialism. Zeeny, for her part, was not going to don such a straitjacket.

A reading of Ashis Nandy tends to support Zeeny's more in-your-face analysis. In Nandy's terms, imperialists and Hindu apologists alike get caught in the same dichotomizing web of the colonizer's rationality when they set off in search of authenticity. To see this is to see why the interpretive fate of modern Hindu eclecticism seems to be batted back and forth between the high-minded historicism of scholars like Bharati and the earnest apologetic of groups like the Vedanta Society (not to mention the politicized Hinduism of groups like the Vishwa Hindu Parisad and the Rashtriya Swayamsevak Sangh). It appears as if one must choose between saying that Vivekananda's practical Vedanta does not correlate with anything in the Hindu tradition, or that Vivekananda is the very prophet of Hindu-ness. Thankfully, Nandy offers another option—we could choose to transcend the dichotomies altogether, or at least attempt to stand them "on their head" (Nandy 1983: 113). I would suggest that one way to do this is simply to live up to the fact of *bricolage*, as Zeeny does, by situating the eclectic *bricoleur* within the vortex of colonial hybridity.

This is not to issue a blanket apology for eclecticism. To adopt the metaphor from the preceding chapter, for all that we might be prepared to view modern Hindu eclecticism as the *bricoleur*'s attempt to construct a homely home, we should also be prepared to admit that this metaphor also suggests an ideological shadow side to eclecticism. That shadow side is visible in the silhouettes of individualism, totalitarianism, and nationalism. To put it very succinctly, modern expressions of eclecticism have often involved it in the quest to take possession of, or lay a claim to, the world—in the name of one's religion or one's nation. This is the same aspect of eclecticism that allows it to shade so quickly into inclusivism, as it so often does in the work of Vivekananda and Radhakrishnan. We have seen that the eclectic's attempt to selectively manipulate diversity in the interests of constructing a personal and/or national identity leads all too often to the suppression of difference (see McGowan 1991: 20).

Once again, the bungalow can help us make this point more concrete, by allowing us to see just what is at stake in the modern attempt to construct personal and national identity. In the preceding chapter we considered the bungalow primarily in terms of its origins as a found object in the villages of colonial Bengal; we followed its eclectic evolution amid the matrix of colonial knowledge and power, noting its postcolonial persistence as a preferred middle-class Indian building style. But the bungalow has traveled well beyond India. By charting its global wanderings we stand to learn much about modernity and bourgeois capitalism, about nationalism and democracy, about urban and suburban planning, but most important, about the fundamental ideological significance of owning a home of one's own.[1] In the bungalow we find all that is promising and problematic about eclecticism as a homely philosophy: appropriation, imperialism, individualism, nationalism, inclusivism.

To see this better, we might step back in time again and consider what is thought to have been the first statement of an "eclectic theory of architecture" in the modern West. The theory was advanced by Thomas Hope in 1835 in his "An Historical Essay on Architecture":

> No one seems yet to have conceived the smallest wish or idea of only borrowing of every former style of architecture whatever it might present of useful or ornamental, of scientific or tasteful; of adding thereto whatever other new dispositions or forms might afford conveniences or elegancies not yet possessed; of making the new discoveries, the new conquests, of natural productions unknown to former ages, the models of new imitations more beautiful and more varied; and thus of composing an architecture which, born in our country, grown on our soil, and in harmony with our climate, institutions and habits, at once elegant, appropriate and original, should truly deserve the appellation of "our own." (Quoted in Collins 1965: 119)

Hope is calling for a homely architecture—one that is rooted in the very soil, and expressive of the very "institutions and habits," of his native land. But notice how he thinks such a national architecture can be created: by "borrowing," by the selectivity of the eclectic; the homely home will be built by picking and choosing from among the wealth of knowledge pouring into England along with the spoils of colonial expansion. In this way, the British will be able to create an "elegant" and "original" expression of themselves, their culture, and their era.[2]

This nationalistic sense of possession via eclecticism finds its mirror likeness in the bourgeois conception of the individual, the subject who defines himself through his freedom and autonomy. The ideology of capitalism and the astounding energy of the middle class have worked together to guarantee the expression and preservation of such individuality. Perhaps nowhere is this more evident than in the capitalist dream of owning a home of one's own. In fact, this is one of the prevailing winds that blew the humble Anglo-Indian bungalow so far from its original moorings, eventually washing it ashore in places as far flung as Europe, North America, and Australia.

Ironically, as the bungalow shifted continents and climes, it demonstrated a remarkable ability both to confirm the vision of Thomas Hope and to make a mockery of it. By becoming the most "elegant" and "original" expression of the "institutions and habits" found in its several new environs, the bungalow called into question the very uniqueness of these supposedly homely values. This can only be explained, as Anthony King has suggested, by understanding the way the spread of modern capitalism and the spread of the bungalow went hand in hand. The principal values the bungalow came to stand for were those of a rapidly globalizing ideology of capitalism and modernity.

If we move from England to the United States, we can illustrate this point by examining the work of Gustav Stickley. Stickley was the early-twentieth-century pioneer of the so-called craftsman style in American design. He aggressively promoted every imaginable variety of bungalow. And in words that provide an almost comic counterpart to Hope's, he eulogized the uniquely American character of the California bungalow:

> And this dwelling, which at the first blush seems but a cross between an East Indian house and a Mission adobe house, in reality proves to be *the most genuine expression of American feeling in domestic architecture that has yet appeared.* Built to suit the needs of one great section of our country, it has developed a beauty and a charm of its own. *It is original because it is like the country it has grown out of*; it is becoming a definite style because it has met a definite demand, and because it is genuine it will be permanent. (Stickley 1988: 24; emphasis added)[3]

The paradox of asserting the hybrid origins of the bungalow and its uniquely American character does not seem to have struck Stickley. Unlike Hope, he does not appear to have recognized the interplay between eclectic borrowing and homely self-assertion. He does, however, demonstrate that he understood what drove this history of appropriation and reconfiguration: it was the demands urged by capitalist democracy. For as Stickley noted earlier in the same essay, "The new architecture that is so rapidly and steadily developing in America is . . . a general expression of that spirit of individuality and freedom which is especially characteristic of this country" (1988: 12).

The point I wish to make is that when we peel back the ideological skin that masks the eclectic quest for individual and national self-definition—the search for a homely home of one's own—we frequently find a disturbing core of inclusivity. To define oneself is always to define the other as well; to construct a self, one must take care to suppress anything that might "threaten the self's sense of unity" (McGowan 1991: 21). This can be done by exclusion or encompassment, the two in fact being but opposite sides of the same coin. The eclectic, the advocate of the *Sowohl–als auch*, claims to avoid the error of exclusivity. Of course, in doing so, he often falls victim to the temptation of benevolent inclusivity: by putting all the pieces together in one's homely philosophy, one claims—more or less openly—to have put everything else in its place as well. The American bungalow encompasses the Anglo-Indian bungalow, which itself encompasses a world of forms, from Spain through England to Bengal. Similarly, Vedānta becomes the essence of religion and Hinduism the religion of Vedānta. Thus, as Radhakrishnan puts it, "The Vedānta is not a religion, but religion itself in its most universal and deepest significance" (1927: 18).[4] Such a pronouncement surely marks an important moment in the enunciation of Indian nationalism's homely philosophy; however, it represents a highly problematic position as well. For while the *uddhāraka* may have reconciliation as a goal, we are reminded of the poor lamb in the stomach of the lion. The business of extracting truths to define essentials can be a violent one.

If "the post-colonial desire is the desire of decolonized communities for an identity" (During, quoted in Docherty 1993: 458), then in the discourse of modern Hinduism—as in the inflections of the postcolonial bungalow—one discerns this desire coming to expression. Simon During's comment that the desire to determine such an identity is "closely connected to nationalism" (1993: 458) only serves to reinforce what I have tried to communicate using the semantics of the homely home. The genesis of modern Hindu discourse is complex, marked at every juncture by hybridity, resistance, and irony. By attending to this complex genesis we hopefully become more sensitive to the idioms and strategies employed by the Hindu apologist, as well as more suspicious of our own canons of authenticity and tradition. We need not sign off on the eclectic's homely home, but we at least may be less quick to write it off as a piece of clumsy engineering. In the end, our goal may be less to develop criteria for assessing the authenticity of the modern Hindu's homely home than to wrestle with the cultural, epistemological, and ethical dynamics that are associated with the construction and ongoing maintenance of such a dwelling.

Is it possible, then, to have it both ways? Can we affirm the important role played by the apologist's homely home as an antidote to colonial subjugation, while retaining our suspicion of the viability of this homely home, especially in the postcolonial world? If Rushdie's call to take-the-best-and-leave-the-rest has helped us appreciate some of the positive dynamics within eclectic borrowing, must we not still acknowledge with Bharati that (to use the words of Horkheimer and Adorno 1972: 121) the "lines of its artificial framework" still show through? Ironically, in Rushdie's Zeeny Vakil we see the tension between these two verdicts. On the one hand, Zeeny is all in favor of the eclectic; on the other hand, she is only too aware of the danger faced by colonized subjects, who, in order to defend themselves from the colonizer's grasp, end up defining themselves back into that grasp. Zeeny might thus exclaim that Vivekananda's eclectic vision of a spiritual India served to bolster Indian national pride and resistance to European hegemony. However, she might also remind us (in her less-than-gentle fashion) that Vivekananda accomplished this end by agreeing to play the wog.

Recently a similar position has been advanced by Partha Chatterjee, who argues that while Hindu apologetic discourse helped to produce a "nationalist discourse which is different from that of colonialism," it did so by tacitly agreeing to remain trapped within a framework of "false essentialisms" bequeathed to it by the colonizer (1993: 134). Following Chatterjee, we must ask what good these false essentialisms are, particularly when the time of their strategic utility—namely, the nationalist period—has passed. More important, we must ask if there are dangers in making continued appeals to such essentialisms.

As Chatterjee makes explicit, the development of the apologist's essentializing discourse was based on a pattern of selective appropriation of the idioms and norms of Western modernity. By constructing such dichotomies as inner/outer, home/world, spiritual/material, feminine/masculine, the nationalist attempted to apply "difference as a principle of selection" (1993: 121). The deployment of such criteria not only allowed the Hindu eclectic to map the world of colonial excess—a vortex of competing meanings, values, and desires—but it also allowed the eclectic to construct a homely home that could be called his own. As we have seen, the thrust of the eclectic is precisely in this direction, toward a homely philosophy and a nation-as-home. We might choose to admit that this is all well and good. We might, as many have done, applaud the vigorous attempts by the likes of Keshub, Vivekananda, and Radhakrishnan to appropriate a world of India's own. However, having seen the ironies and violence such appropriation involves, we might choose instead to speak, with Chatterjee, of the "failure of the Indian nation" (134). What is this failure? It is a failure occasioned by the nation's attempt to create a homely culture that is all too clearly (in hindsight, at least) "defined by a system of exclusions" (134). In other words, we are back to the shadow side of eclecticism: the totalitarian or inclusivistic urge that necessarily suppresses difference, rather than celebrating it.

This is where we stand, then, when we set out to evaluate modern Hindu eclecticism. We are faced with an enigma that we should perhaps not be too eager to resolve. Instead, our solutions may need to be partial, contextual, tentative. I want to say "pragmatic," but the vision of pragmatics I have in mind may seem anything but practical to some. What I want to suggest is that we may need to get used to the vertigo we feel when confronted by eclecticism. Notice that I don't say that we should get used to the errors committed in the name of eclecticism, but simply that we should not commit the further error of thinking we can overcome our vertigo by providing an answer up front to the question of its truth or error. I say this because even to begin to assess a fairly well delimited case like modern Hindu eclecticism—and a beginning is about all I have provided here—we are going to find ourselves necessarily having to move constantly between (and within) the interpretive worlds of modernism and postmodernism, between the options of historicism and endless textuality, between choices favoring the One or the Many, between the comforts of the uniform grid and the ambiguities of heterotopia.

Since this must be our intellectual practice, and since vertigo is scarcely an appealing way to construe it, perhaps I might better appeal to the wisdom of the Zen master, who tells us the key to enlightenment is to be "ever shuttling from beginning to end" (Sekida 1975: 230). However, in the present case the emphasis should be placed squarely on the act of shuttling, rather than on the notion of a beginning or an end. What we are faced with is the necessity for constant movement in-between. The question is, Can we live like this?

My understanding of what a life of shuttling in-between might require has been significantly shaped by the so-called neopragmatism of Richard Rorty. I have been drawn to Rorty because he is one thinker who has demonstrated a willingness to recast philosophy in light of the very crises of reason and history we have encountered in our overview of eclecticism. What is more, Rorty has given special attention in his philosophy to the discourse of postmodernism, which we have found has its own contribution to make toward our understanding of eclecticism. While Rorty is suspicious of some of the intellectual and moral conclusions drawn by the postmodernists, he nevertheless demonstrates ways in which pragmatism can be shown to be congenial to the basic tenets of postmodernism. It is precisely because Rorty seeks to "split the difference" between modernist project and postmodern critique that I think he may be in a position to offer us the hand we need in negotiating the aporias and intellectual vertigo occasioned by the eclectics (see Rorty 1985).

Along with Jean-François Lyotard, Michel Foucault, and a range of other postmodernists, Rorty abjures modernity's so-called grand narratives as well as the intolerance of its homotopic grid toward diversity. At the same time, however, he is not ready or willing to give up on Enlightenment ideals, most particularly the liberal dream of community and social solidarity. His own position is worth quoting in extenso, since it represents an attempt to negotiate between the postmodernism of a Lyotard and the Enlightenment ideals of a Habermas:

> We could agree with Lyotard that studies of the communicative competence of a transhistorical subject [e.g., Habermas's attempt at furthering the Enlightenment project] are of little use in reinforcing our sense of identification with our community, while still insisting on the importance of that sense. . . .
>
> If one had such a de-theoreticized sense of community, one could accept the claim that valuing "undistorted communication" was of the essence of liberal politics without needing a theory of communicative competence as backup. Attention would be turned instead to some concrete examples of what was presently distorting our communication—e.g., to the sort of "shock" we get when, reading Foucault, we realize that the jargon we liberal intellectuals developed has played into the hands of the bureaucrats. Detailed historical narratives of the sort Foucault offers us would take the place of philosophical metanarratives. Such narratives would not unmask something created by power called "ideology" in the name of something not created by power called "validity" or "emancipation." They would just explain who was currently getting and using power for what purposes, and then (unlike Foucault) suggest how some other people might get it and use it for other purposes. (Rorty 1985: 173)

Pursuing this mediating approach, Rorty goes on to develop a position that calls for us to be thoroughgoing ironists. That is, he asks us to continually doubt the validity of the stories and metaphors we use to explain our world. This, he suggests, does not lead to a failure of seriousness when it comes to committing ourselves to the liberal dream of creating communities free of cruelty and the humiliation of other human beings (see Rorty 1989). It is just that Rorty wishes us to be aware of the historical contingency of our communities, our languages, our very identities. In fact, what he has to say about the contingency of language is of direct relevance to my own attempt to arrive at a mediating position with respect to eclecticism.

Rorty suggests we must begin by recognizing that all our language games and vocabularies are contingent; they are developed, employed, and discarded through the innumerable chance developments of history and circumstance. Once we recognize this, we must confess that no single vocabulary can claim an exclusive hold on truth. Your biblical narrative, my scientific rationalism, her aboriginal stories only have meaning (as Wittgenstein would say) insofar as they work. Do they allow us to cope with our world? When she and I try to communicate about time, for instance, success will not be measured in terms of whose word most closely represents some independently-existing thing called time. Success will come when we have arrived at a vocabulary that helps us communicate with one another. There can be no rules in advance for what words will figure in this vocabulary. Languages do not fit the world, nor do they stand outside us, such that we need to put ourselves in right relation to them.

Consequently, it can make no sense categorically to say that one may not juxtapose the wisdom of Lao-Tzu and the admonitions of Amos; the words of the Prophet and the wisdom of the Buddha. That would be to presume that one language game matches an independently existing reality better than another; it would be to presume that if I introduce Hindu concepts into Christian theology I run the risk of relaxing the fit between Christian discourse and the way things really are. But there is no fit to relax; there is only more- or less-successful communication. Consider, for instance, the wildly eclectic religious views voiced at the 1993 World's Parliament of Religions in Chicago. If we give up our assumption that among the many religious positions represented at the parliament, one alone necessarily achieves the best fit with the way things really are, we can perhaps acknowledge that the best way to talk about community and solidarity may be to work out—or piece together—new vocabularies that draw from a variety of religious traditions. Rather than asking whether these new vocabularies are true, we might—following the pragmatism of William James—refer to the scriptural adage, "By their fruits ye shall know them." (James 1961: 34). The problem is, of course, that to determine the value produced by any vocabulary, one must have some notion of what constitutes the good.

Rorty approaches this problem by contrasting what he calls the attitudes of the liberal ironist and the liberal metaphysician. For the latter, there must finally be some right language that can make us free; such language will be good language. The liberal ironist, however, makes no such assertion. Rather than laying claim to knowledge of the true subject or real self espoused by humanism's liberal metaphysics, the liberal ironist acknowledges that "our chances of freedom depend on historical contingencies," which are only sometimes shaped by the language game we play (Rorty 1989: 90). The liberal ironist does not need to know why she should avoid humiliating others (which is a question that raises the need for a foundational metaphysic); she only needs to know what humiliates. Needing no final argument for kindness, the liberal ironist "just wants our *chances of being kind*, of avoiding the humiliation of others, to be expanded. . . . Her sense of human solidarity is based on a sense of common danger, not on a common possession or a shared power" (Rorty 1989: 91).

Can this pragmatic approach help us arrive at a way for coping with our conflicting views of modern Hindu eclecticism? As a test case let's use the example of the essentializing Neo-Vedānta so closely associated with Vivekananda and Radhakrishnan. No one will deny that the fruits of Vedantic eclecticism have included an increase in Indian self-esteem, a rejection of the colonizer's claim to represent true civilization, an increase among Indians in interest in the Western world, and an increase among Westerners in respect for the religions of Asia. Few will deny that this brief list represents some good fruit. And it should be noted that it is not simply among Indians that the likes of Vivekananda and Radhakrishnan are admired; these figures have represented to the world—and continue to represent—positive and ennobling ways to combat cultural arrogance, economic and political imperialism, and theological exclusivism. This is to say nothing of the obvious appeal of their spiritual vision to countless people around the world.

Vivekananda and Radhakrishnan have helped us imagine new worlds in which to live. This they could do because, in Rorty's terms, they looked upon the world and imagined the world as poets. By a "poet," Rorty means someone who is "the maker of new words, the shaper of new languages" (Rorty 1989: 20). In this he follows the lead of Harold Bloom, who reminds us that the root meaning of *poesis* is "the act of creating." Poets are the ones who come along from time to time and by redescribing our world, re-create it for us. Like Nietzsche's free spirits, they give us a new set of metaphors through which to view our world and our experience (see Nehamas 1985: 61–62). Thus, not just Homer, Yeats, and Shakespeare, but Copernicus, Kant, Nietzsche, and Einstein are all poets. And, so too, are Vivekananda, Radhakrishnan, Gandhi, Rammohun, and Keshub.[5]

It is certainly illuminating to think of Vivekananda in this light. As one American newspaper reporter said of him: "He is an artist in thought, an idealist in belief and a dramatist on the platform" (CW 3: 485).[6] Here was someone with the savvy not just to re-create himself, but also to re-create the image of his spiritual preceptor, his homeland, and the entire colonial paradigm. That is, his poetry amounted to a profoundly unsettling and ultimately liberating redescription of India's world during the high noon of imperial rule. His poetry included such metaphors and redescriptions as "man-making religion," the "don't touch me-ism" of caste, God as incarnate in the lowest of the low (*daridra nārāyaṇa*), Raja Yoga, and practical Vedanta. As a poet he creatively appropriated—and reenvisioned—scriptures and philosophies. In his hands the recondite wisdom of the Upaniṣads became the stuff of energizing slogans. By creatively mistranslating Kaṭha Upaniṣad 3.14 as, "Arise, awake, and stop not till the goal is reached," Vivekananda provided for generations of nationalist and postcolonial Indians a mantra of pride, determination, and success.[7] At the same time, he redescribed for Americans and Europeans the spiritual geography of a world besotted with evangelical fervor, imperial hubris, and industrial megalomania. In the end, it is hard not to credit the poetry of Vivekananda—and that of the other great modern Hindu eclectics—with producing some very fine fruit, indeed.

The problem is, as we grow accustomed to the poets' metaphors, we also become increasingly complacent about the way they have redescribed things; we turn their metaphors into literal truths. As Rorty reminds us, the poets' redescriptions all too quickly become for us descriptions plain and simple; we forget that they are not meant to be taken literally. In Adorno's terms, we reify them, thereby effectively forgetting what is important in them. We forget to take our poet's vocabularies with a healthy dose of irony and start to prescribe them as final solutions. It is at this point that we lose what Rorty says is essential for the public purposes of the liberal ironist: "imaginative acquaintance with alternative final vocabularies . . . in order to understand the actual and possible humiliation of the people who use these alternative final vocabularies" (Rorty 1989: 92).

We can certainly see this happening in the case of the postcolonial afterlife of the Hindu eclectic's defense of Indian spirituality. In fact, the essentialized Vedānta of a Vivekananda or a Radhakrishnan can become all too dangerous in this regard. Because of its shadow side of inclusivity, such Neo-Vedānta can give no place to non-Hindu or nonelite Indian groups save what they are prepared to accept through a suppression of their differences; the Neo-Vedantic redescription, so powerful a device against the humiliating effects of colonial rule, becomes itself an agent of humiliation. This is the point Partha Chatterjee has attempted to stress. If you build the Indian nation solely in terms of one species of modern Hinduism, you achieve not solidarity, but its opposite: fragmentation and cruelty.

In the postcolonial world, when the strategic moment of the eclectic's resistance has largely (if by no means entirely) passed, it is easy for us to forget the poetry of their words and to begin to take those words as something more like gospel truth. In the hands of metaphysicians, the redescriptions of modern Hindu discourse may be called upon to validate the suspect political programs of groups espousing various forms of Hindu particularism, such as the Shiv Sena, the Bharatiya Janata Party, or the Vishwa Hindu Parishad. Such groups would all-too-willingly reify Neo-Hindu metaphors, effectively transmuting poetic anticolonial eclecticism into postcolonial chauvinism. In their nonironic use of the rubric of Hindutva (i.e., Hindu-ness), these groups demonstrate none of that sympathy for "alternative vocabularies," which, in a multireligious, multilinguistic region like South Asia, would seem to be the very key to community. When we consider that the destruction of the Babri Mosque in Ayodhya in 1992 was carried out in the name of Hinduism, Rorty's pragmatic calculus allows us to see how sour such fruit really is.

Nor can we entirely absolve the Renaissance eclectic from responsibility for where nationalist Hindu discourse has tended after independence. As we have seen, there are dangers implicit in the very eclectic exuberance of a Gandhi or a Radhakrishnan. These become apparent even within the colonial context. But this is precisely where Rorty's view of irony is so helpful. As he acknowledges, redescriptions can themselves be humiliating, notably by undercutting someone else's final vocabulary. However, as he points out, there is no more fundamental connection between humiliation and irony than there is between humiliation and metaphysics (Rorty 1989: 90). Because redescription is an intellectual activity, it is bound to be unsettling. The crucial thing is that we must be thoroughgoing ironists rather than scripture-quoting metaphysicians. We should look to modern Hindu discourse not for the final answer, but for yet one more possible vocabulary—which may itself be just as quickly rejected or revised in the light of yet another vocabulary. As Rorty puts it, a dialectic is called for in which one attempts constantly to play vocabularies off one another (1989: 78). Needless to say, this is precisely what I have tried to model by contrasting the likes of Bharati and Rushdie.

Clearly we need to maintain some critical distance from the eclectic spirit if we hope to be able to discern its logic as well as indicate its strengths and weaknesses. But it may also be wise to consider the kinds of assumptions we harbor about authenticity, history, rationality, and system that prevent us from acknowledging the interpretive strengths of the eclectic mode. In other words, rather than dismissing modern Hindu eclecticism out of hand, or turning it into something it is not—such as syncretism—we ought to consider the following sorts of questions: What does eclecticism share with and/or contest about the modernist temper? The postmodernist? What makes for the practical strength of eclecticism? What particular resources does the eclectic mode offer during times of disorienting cultural encounter and religious change? Bearing such questions in mind, the relentless experimentation and self-construction apparent in the work of a Rammohun or a Keshub or a Vivekananda merit not our scorn, but our respect and careful consideration. If nothing else, they may provide us with an excellent occasion for thinking through what it is like to live the ironist life.

As Rorty puts it, ironists cook up special systems of general ideas precisely to attack the notion of general ideas. It is just that the ironist's special system—unlike that of its literalist inheritors, be they in the Vedanta Society or the Vishwa Hindu Parishad—is meant to be expendable. Perhaps once the eclectic's system has completed its task, it can be discarded. One thinks in this connection of the example of Sakyamuni Buddha, whose wisdom figures prominently in the work of modern Hindu eclectics like Vivekananda. The Buddha was surely one of the world's great pragmatists, or ironists, if you will. He viewed his teaching as a raft. Its purpose is to get you across the river. Once you're across, you have no further need for it; only a fool would strap the raft on his back and stagger off down the road![8]

Modern Hindu apologists show a particular fascination for the Buddha; typically this is grounded in the Buddha's purported humanism, egalitarianism, and rationalism. However, does the modern Hindu also have a special insight into the pragmatics of the Buddha's teaching? Despite the fact that Vivekananda (to take an example we are by now familiar with) was responsible for creating the institutions that were to embody and propagate his vision of Hinduism both in India and abroad, one wonders if he was also moved by the Buddha's pragmatism or imbued with enough of Rorty's sense of irony to view his own message as an expedient device. The question becomes all the more poignant when one considers that the institutions Vivekananda brought into being—the Ramakrishna Math and Mission in India and the Vedanta Society worldwide—are among the most guilty in terms of transforming his poetry into literal truth. Thanks to the work of such organizations, Vivekananda's metaphors have today become "axiomatic features" in the presentation of Hinduism (Rambachan 1994: 4). The question is, Did the swami sanction such a shift from metaphor to gospel? Was his paramount mission really one of reviving interest in Advaita Vedānta? Or have his followers merely latched onto the particular raft he used to cross a particular river? Would he have preferred that they drop the raft and go off in other directions? It may be difficult to say. Still, could he have foreseen that his poetic vocabulary of Hindu spirituality and Indian pride would in time be canonized, we might imagine him responding with yet another strategic redescription.

In the same spirit we might consider anew many of the poetic redescriptions of modern Hindu discourse, granting them a greater measure of respect than they have received from the likes of Bharati. We may be less quick to attribute their homely philosophy to a poor grasp of history or a lazy approach to truth, and more willing to find therein the sort of unreliable narratives that have been shown by Rushdie to prove so valuable for living. It is not that we can "neither challenge nor criticize the diction of the Indian apologetic" (Bharati 1970: 268). Bharati was troubled by the tendency to make the discourse of modern Hinduism sacrosanct. We should be too. We should continue to ask why this happens and with what consequences. But wherever possible we should, following Zeeny, appreciate the stink caused by modern Hindu eclecticism, rather than merely reducing its discourse to our madness.

Notes

CHAPTER 1

1. One may find passing references to one or more aspects of Hindu eclecticism in works such as the following: Bose 1884; Goblet 1885; Dimmitt and van Buitenen 1978; O'Flaherty 1980; Bailey 1987; Dalton 1993.

2. Useful discussions of this evidence can be found in Carman 1964; Panikkar 1975; and Bryson 1992.

3. Both of these possibilities are mentioned by Gustav Mensching in his essay on syncretism in *Die Religion in Geschichte und Gegenwart* (see Carman 1964: 32).

4. For a critique of such a concept of syncretism, see Baird 1971: 142–152. For an attempt to redeem the category for use in a "less controversial" sense, see Bryson 1992.

5. Reconciliation is a clear feature of Judith Berling's definition of syncretism, which Bryson finds attractive (see Bryson 1992: 12). Hendrik Kraemer proposed "amalgamation" as a nonjudgmental substitute for syncretism (see Carman 1964: 37).

6. Interestingly, Kraemer took the paradigm of Ryobu-Shinto in Japan as an example of a "truly gigantic paradigm of consciously and systematically developed syncretism in doctrine, cultus and rites" (as cited in Carman 1964: 36).

7. I am grateful to Matt Dusek for calling this passage to my attention.

8. We shall see in chapter 5 that this is precisely the tenor of criticism advanced against the nineteenth-century Bengali reformers by some missionaries and Hindus (such as Bose 1884).

9. I remain indebted to several anonymous readers who expressed concern that I was lavishing attention on Bharati that would be better directed elsewhere. I trust the remarks in this paragraph answer such concerns. This book is by no means a referendum on the work of Bharati, which is a task I shall leave to others.

10. For a more recent example of a work written within the same matrix that also calls attention to the problem of modern Hindu eclecticism, see Madan 1987. In this book Madan sets off on what he calls a "quest for Hinduism" in the modern world. It was apparently no easy matter to hunt down such a beast, for the quest ends on a despairing note. Madan concludes that as a result of their exposure to Western culture, modern Hindus have no choice but to live amid what he calls "the ruins of a once-living religious faith" (1987: 164). Authentic Hindu faith is thus a thing of the past. If Hindus once lived by it, they don't anymore. Instead, they live solely by means of "strategies." Like Bharati, Madan characterizes these strategies as "a vaunted tradition of eclecticism," which he traces back to the Hindu reformers' well-meaning but hopeless attempt to preserve the vitality of the Hindu ethos. For Madan, as for Bharati, eclecticism is a kind of false consciousness that should be met with the objective suspicion of the historian and the sociologist.

11. In speaking of a scholarly paradigm here, I realize I run the risk of oversimplifying, most notably by caricaturing Indology as a species of empirical, social-scientific discourse. For a far more nuanced reading of the varieties of hegemonic discourse in Indology and related fields, see Inden 1990.

12. The difference between the Bharati of 1970 and the Rushdie of 1991 can in part be explained by the reflexive turn in comparative studies prompted by Edward Said's critique of Orientalism (see Said 1978). It is common now to find studies of Hinduism that open with apologies for the history of Western constructions of India, constructions that "reveal an attitude that is communicated together with the very idea of 'science' and 'scientific.' Basically it consists of the assumption that the 'scientist' knows better and, eventually, will know it all" (Klostermaier 1994: 10).

13. One is reminded of the apology (of sorts) offered by Michael Ondaatje in the acknowledgments he cites in his family memoir: "While all these names may give an air of authenticity, I must confess that the book is not a history but a portrait or 'gesture.' And if those listed above disapprove of the fictional air I apologize and can only say that in Sri Lanka a well-told lie is worth a thousand facts" (Ondaatje 1993: 206).

14. It was Matt Dusek, with his training in epistemology, who helped me see the matter in these terms.

15. Bharati concluded his essay by noting that it was the delicacy of the ego that accounted for the lack of any self-criticism or irony among Indians regarding their modernist ideology. One might have referred him to the scatological traditions of nineteenth-century street humor or to the evidence of Calcutta folk painting, both of which repeatedly send up the deracinated Babu (see Banerjee 1989). From the early-nineteenth-century satire of Bhavanīcaraṇ Bandyopādhyāy to the critical literature of Rabindranath Tagore, Bengali literature (to take but one vernacular) certainly testifies to a healthy sense of self-criticism. Rushdie was by no means the first to offer a parody of the stresses of the colonial experience.

16. My reading of Adorno has been greatly influenced by the work of Martin Jay, to whose book on Adorno I was directed by Martin Srajek.

CHAPTER 2

1. For Kant's essay, "What Is Enlightenment?," see Beck 1963.

2. Lucien Braun has pointed out that many of the articles on the history of philosophy that are found in the *Encyclopedie* of the *philosophes* were based upon Brucker's work, being at times little more than translations from the Latin (see Braun 1973: 153).

3. It was Martin Srajek who initially helped me to see this point.

4. Zeller's great work was *Die Philosophie der Griechen in ihrer geschichtlichen Entwicklung*, 4th rev. ed. (Leipzig: O. R. Reisland, 1909). For the portion dedicated to later Greek eclecticism, see Zeller 1883.

5. Raimundo Panikkar has attempted to give a quasi-etymological justification for such a train of thought, by suggesting that to be eclectic is to be *ek-logos*, or removed from the guiding light of reason (see Panikkar 1975).

6. For good discussions of the problem of treating postmodernity as a matter of historical periodization, see Jameson 1984; Huyssen 1984; Turner 1990.

7. We find Zeller's charge that eclecticism represents the exhaustion of thought echoed in the article on "Eclecticism" found in the 14th edition of the *Encyclopaedia Britannica*, where we are told the eclectic lacks "the capacity for original work" (Dillon and Long 1988: 3). The charge is a perennial one, as evidenced by the reception given to Patrick Suskind's novel *Das Parfum*, with its pastiche of "citations, near-citations, and imitations" (Ryan 1990: 399).

8. For his part, Hegel thought that the decision to view the Alexandrians as eclectics was due to Brucker's mistaken interpretation of Diogenes' reference to Potamo (Hegel 1955: 400; see Zeller 1883: 110).

9. The Bhāgavata Purāṇa (1.4.20) speaks of the Vedas as *catvāra uddhṛtāḥ*, or 'divided into four.' Likewise, when the poet Bharavi refers in his *Kirātārjunīya* (10.10) to Vasiṣṭha's compilation of the Vedas, the commentator Mallinātha glosses this as *mantra-uddhāra*, or the 'division of the mantras.'

10. As is the case with so many Sanskrit words, the semantic range of *uddhāra* is broad, including as it does the supreme goal of liberation and the uprooting of criminals, as well as the more specialized legal meanings of a portion of inheritance or the booty allowed to a king during war. The connection of *uddhāra* with salvation (*uddhāraṇa*) is clear enough, given the root sense of 'lifting up.' In the Hindu view humans are mired in ignorance and desire, struggling (at times) to get free from the quicksand of *karma* and the clinging tendrils of attachment. What is needed is either the saving knowledge of the eternal self or the intervention of God's grace. The great philosopher of nonduality, Śaṅkara, whom we shall meet in the next chapter, uses such language in his commentaries on the Bhagavad-gītā (2.11) and the Bṛhadāraṇyaka Upaniṣad (6.2.16).

In the modern period the word *uddhāra* came to be used in the sense of 'reform' and 'improvement' (*unnati*). These concepts, which were central to bourgeois discourse during the nineteenth century, played a prominent role in the discourse of the Indian Renaissance (see Hatcher 1996). Thus we find the selective strategies of the *uddhāraka* linked to the goals of social *uddhāra*—as in the case of Rammohun's arguments against *suttee* and that of Gandhi's opposition to untouchability. For a view of *uddhāra* as 'reform' in premodern and modern Jainism, see Cort 1995.

11. For an excellent overview of some dominant paradigms of knowledge in the Upaniṣads, see Brereton 1990.

12. I would like to thank John Cort for calling my attention to Hemacandra and furthering my understanding of Jain theories of meaning more generally.

13. I draw upon a distinction developed in Eck 1985: 22.

14. If need be, a piece of wisdom may be attributed to the Vedas even if it is not actually found there, as has been done in the case of yet another popular apologetic slogan, *vasudhaiva kuṭumbakam* (see Hatcher 1994).

15. Le Corbusier once wrote that "number is the base of all beauty" (quoted in Taylor 1992: 108). For more on his purifying view of modernist urban planning, see Berman (1988: 164–171.). In a related context, the modernist foundations of Peter I's St. Petersburg are suggested nicely by a fragment of poetry written by a contemporary Russian official: "geometry has appeared/land surveying encompasses everything" (quoted in Berman 1988: 177).

16. For the Unitarian Universalist hymnbook, see *Singing the Living Tradition* (Boston: Beacon Press/Unitarian Universalist Association, 1993).

17. I was led to Chopra's work by the kind suggestion of my colleague, Bobbie Silk.

18. It is interesting to think through the genealogical relationship between modern and postmodern eclecticism. A comparison between the eclecticism of the two parliaments—of 1893 and 1993—might be a good place to begin. That postmodern pastiche is not entirely new certainly gives one reason to consider "the powerful alternative position that postmodernism is itself little more than one more stage of modernism proper"—the notion, that is, that when one has modernists like Gustave Flaubert, Stéphane Mallarmé, Gertrude Stein, and Marcel Duchamp there seems to be little need for the category of *post* modernism (Jameson 1984: 56).

19. For Jameson, at least, the fact that we no longer have an Archimedean point means we have lost any way of getting the critical distance necessary to challenge the economic and political realities of late capitalism. Even purported revolts—like punk rock—are merely reabsorbed and thereby defused (see Jameson 1984: 87).

20. Certainly when one considers postmodernism's avoidance of closure—not to mention its openness toward the fact of heterogeneity—one is struck by how much Adorno anticipated the claims of deconstruction (see Jay 1984: 21–22).

21. The problem of the relationship that pertains between postmodernism and capitalist consumerism is an intriguing one that cannot adequately be explored here (see Borgmann 1992 and Harvey 1989). Jameson's characterization of postmodernism as the cultural logic of late capitalism remains a compelling one (see Jameson 1984).

CHAPTER 3

1. CW = *The Complete Works of Swami Vivekananda*, 8 vols. (Calcutta: Advaita Ashrama, 1985). The third volume of Vivekananda's collected writings contains extensive selections from American newspapers regarding his lectures and travels in the United States.

2. For references to other studies that consider the ideological relationship between the parliament and the larger Columbian Exposition, see Seager 1995: 181–182, n. 3.

3. Quoting my colleague Tim Garvey, from a personal communication, March 18, 1993.

4. All was not rosy, however. A reporter for a contemporary newspaper noted that "sharp acerbities" were developing at the parliament, where a "thin veil of courtesy was maintained." This correspondent detected, behind the veneer of tolerance, the traces of "ill feeling" (CW 3: 473).

5. The effect of Vivekananda's striking illustration and equally striking lesson upon his audience may be inferred by considering the response of the Rev. Joseph Cook to one of Vivekananda's presentations to the parliament:

"To speak of a universe that was not created is almost unpardonable nonsense" (CW 3: 473).

6. I am thinking of the remarks of K. R. Sundararajan, in his paper, "Reflections on Hindu-Muslim Encounters," presented to the Midwest American Academy of Religion, at Indiana State University, in March 1997.

7. The importance of Jesus Christ to Vivekananda is apparent throughout his writings, which repeatedly incorporate New Testament allusions into discussions of Hindu spiritual practice. Consider the following letter to a friend from 1891: "Are you diligent in your Shiva Puja? If not, try to be so. 'Seek ye first the Kingdom of God and all good things will be added to you.' Follow God and you shall have whatever you desire. . . . My children, the secret of religion lies not in theories but in practice. . . . 'Not he that crieth, "Lord, Lord," but he that doeth the will of the Father'" (*Life of Vivekananda* 1: 272–273). That these were more than empty allusions is demonstrated by the fact that when faced with convincing the disciples of Ramakrishna to adopt the life of celibate renouncers after their guru's death, Vivekananda made reference not to the norms of Hindu practice but to the renunciation and passion of Jesus Christ (see Rolland 1970: 277).

8. Valid knowledge is known as *pramā*. According to the *Vedānta-paribhāṣā* (I.3), *pramākaraṇaṃ pramāṇam*, which is to say '*pramāṇa* is that which causes valid knowledge [*pramā*].'

9. In the *Tarka-saṃgraha* (sect. 59), a reliable person is defined as 'someone who speaks the truth' (*āptastu yathārthavaktā*).

10. According to one reading, the "earlier" in Pūrva Mīmāṃsā indicates that this school is interested solely in the earlier portions of Vedic revelation that deal with the specific actions of ritual and sacrifice—the so-called *karmakaṇḍa*. By contrast, "later" Mīmāṃsā takes as its focus the portions of the Vedas associated with knowledge and liberation—the so-called *jñānakaṇḍa*.

11. The skeptic of course replies by saying Vivekananda was an actor, a dramatist, a man for whom the audience was possibly more important than the message (see Sil 1995).

CHAPTER 4

1. For a modern Hindu variant of this parable, consider Sri Ramakrishna's story of the chameleon, as cited in Chatterjee 1993: 44.

2. Until recently, medical eclecticism found little sympathy from practitioners of modern Western allopathy. But this has begun to change, with the resurgence of nature cures, health food regimens, and the adoption of non-Western practices like acupuncture. Thus today we read with a fair amount of amusement a work like Morris Fishbein's 1927 assault on medical eclecticism,

The New Medical Follies: An Encyclopedia of Cultism and Quackery in these United States—especially when he turns up his nose at whole-wheat bread!

3. For the persistence of Oldenberg's language in current scholarship, see Heesterman 1993: 53. For his part, Smith is at times guilty of tarring all Indologists with the same brush. Thus he accuses G. U. Thite of sharing the largely unsympathetic view of Vedic homologic thinking (Smith 1989: 33). But surely Thite is a long way from the likes of Leopold von Schroeder, who viewed the making of homologies as a sign of imbecility, and who compared the words of the Vedic priests with psychiatric accounts of lunatics (see Winternitz 1987: 169).

4. For classic examples, see Dahlmann 1899 and Otto 1934.

5. On the varieties of historical discourse in the modern West, see White 1973.

6. For an attempt to think through the ways history has "worked to secure the mystique of the nation," see Duara 1995.

7. Compare Nietzsche: "As certainly as no one leaf is exactly similar to any other, so certain is it that the idea 'leaf' has been formed through an arbitrary omission of these individuated differences, through *a forgetting of the differentiating qualities*" (as cited in McGowan 1991: 73; emphasis added).

8. Deussen's view is questioned in Keith 1976: 440–441. As for making parallels with the Enlightenment, we might note Max Müller's comment that more editions of the Upaniṣads were being published in nineteenth-century India than were editions of Descartes in Europe (see Hume 1931: 2–3).

9. Quoting from her essay, "Unité et distinction dans les spéculations rituelles vedique" (as cited in Smith 1989: 51).

10. Smith's use of "resemblance" to replace the earlier standard usage of "identification" or "equivalence"—and particularly as a translation of the term *sāmānya* (lit., 'sameness')—has been questioned by J. C. Heesterman in his review of Smith's book (see Heesterman 1991).

11. This is the point at which Smith's view of resemblance—as refreshing as it is for its critical revisionism—encounters difficulties. Having deliberately avoided treating the *bandhu* as a kind of identification, Smith is left with two alternatives: either he must deny that the *ātman-brahman* relationship is in fact an identification, or he must deny that such an identification arose orthogenetically from the Vedic logic of resemblance. The first option, as he recognizes, is untenable because the monism of the Upaniṣadic discovery is based upon a clear case of identification: *ātman* really is *brahman*. Therefore, Smith is left to take up the second alternative and to argue that the logic of resemblance could never have yielded such a conclusion, since the ritualist viewed all such identifications as subject to the fault of *jāmi*. If such an identification arose, it was therefore not as an extension of ritual logic, but as its

inversion or collapse. Unfortunately, this leaves us wondering precisely how such an inversion came about.

For Smith, the true continuation of ritualistic logic is found not in the speculations of the Upaniṣadic sages, but in the domestic rituals of sacrifice, or *gṛhya* rites, which amount to a "condensed representation" of the solemn, or *śrauta*, rites of sacrifice (Smith 1989: 195).

12. See the definitions of eclecticism in *The New Encyclopaedia Britannica*, 15th ed., vol. 4: *Micropaedia* (New York: Encyclopaedia Britannica, 1990), p. 352, and in *The Encyclopaedia Britannica*, 11th ed., vol. 8 (New York: Cambridge University Press, 1910), p. 887.

13. Hacker concludes his essay on inclusivism by suggesting that the phenomenon is restricted to the Indian cultural context (Hacker 1983: 28). However, Halbfass has adduced evidence, from antiquity down to the modern West, that serves to undermine such a conclusion (see Halbfass 1988: 415–417). Certainly in the modern era we have had many examples beyond India, from the fulfillment theology of John Nicol Farquhar, to Karl Rahner's anonymous Christianity, to the Zen Orientalism of D. T. Suzuki (on the latter, see Faure 1993).

14. The actual patterns of arrangement within Purāṇic and other Indian forms of narrative offer a fascinating case for examining yet another way in which the ritualism of the Vedas lived on after the Vedic period. I am thinking in particular of the ubiquitous frame-story device and its possible roots in the inclusivistic logic of ritual interpretation: "In this way, the technique of the Brāhmaṇa authors becomes more discernable. They take whatever mythical, pseudo-historical matter they have at hand. They do not tell stories for the sake of story-telling. . . , but they arrange their stories according to their (ritual) purpose, adding whatever they think necessary" (Witzel 1987: 410).

15. I am indebted to Sudipto Chatterjee, who first introduced me to this wonderful passage, which occurs in one of the poet's letters (see Gupta 1967: li).

CHAPTER 5

1. See the selection from his essay "Eclectisme," from vol. 5 of *Encyclopedie* (1755), as cited in Mason 1982: 103.

2. Adopting the insights of Fritz Schumacher's *Strömungen in deutsche Baukunst seit 1800* (see Götz 1970: 204, n. 62), Wolfgang Götz has suggested that if eclecticism is a method, it is one whose rules and character cannot be explained without reference to the concept, agenda, worldview, or aesthetic canon it serves (1970: 211).

3. Whether in fact one could have a purely unconstrained eclecticism, without it simply becoming a hodgepodge of pure randomness, is doubtful. Since play itself is a rule-governed activity, a playful eclecticism may in fact

be a manifestation of a critical program aimed at contesting someone else's notion of beauty, reason, order, sobriety. Of course, whether postmodernism has a critical function at all has been questioned by the likes of Jameson (1984). Those who do recognize such a dimension, like Andreas Huyssen, are inclined to locate it in postmodernism's "radical questioning of those presuppositions which linked modernism and the avant-garde to the mind-set of modernization" (Huyssen 1984: 11).

4. I am uncomfortable with the way Panikkar contrasts the essentialistic character of eclecticism with what he calls "the existentialist character" of syncretism. By using the latter term he hopes to emphasize that syncretism arises out of practical decisions of daily life, whereby (for instance) Buddhism gradually incorporates elaborate cultic forms not in accord with the Buddha's original teaching (1975: 54). For one thing, this comes close to perpetuating the error of assuming that "participants lack a true understanding of the ancestral systems from which they have borrowed symbols, beliefs, and rituals . . . [and] that they have entered a regressive state in religion" ("Syncretism," in Smith 1995: 1043). But furthermore, such a distinction makes it seem as if practical decision-making applies only to syncretism, when in fact it is the element of *choice* that is so central to eclecticism.

5. Excerpt from a communication to the Church Missionary Society from Rev. James Long, as cited in *The Church Missionary Record* XVII (London, 1846), p. 84.

6. The complexity of the constituency, projects, and historical legacy of Young Bengal is noted in Sarkar 1985.

7. The most egregious example of such a tactic, in the eyes of Keshub's detractors, was when he appealed to *ādeśa* to justify his decision to marry his fourteen-year-old daughter to the Maharaja of Cooch Behar, thereby disregarding Brāhmo views about marriage (see Bose 1976: 161). Subsequently, when Keshub and his disciple, Protap Chunder Mazoomdar, began to preach about inspired prophecy, rationalist Brāhmos cried: "Beware, ye brethren, of this false doctrine. Cast off the idea of a religious interpreter between God and man as you would a venomous reptile." (Quoted in an article in *Brahmo Public Opinion*, as found in Ghosh 1978: 34.)

8. On another occasion, Keshub published an article in the *Sunday Mirror* directly addressing the question, "What Is the Eclecticism of the New Dispensation?" While the query itself is telling, his reply is even more fascinating, since it amounts to what must be the first enunciation of the centerpiece of modern Hindu apologetics, namely, the claim that all religions are true. In making this claim—which precedes Gandhi's famous restatement by nearly half a century—Keshub went beyond the probabilistic assertion that all religions must contain germs of truth, to the essentialist conviction that at their heart all religions are true.

9. The name itself, which had been proposed by Debendranath, pointed to the group's eclecticism, since the idea of the *saṅgat* was not a part of local Bengali culture but stemmed from the north Indian religious milieu, especially that of the Sikhs.

10. See his addresses "Basis of Brahmoism" (1860) and "Revelation" (1861) in Sen 1940.

11. The first essay was given the Bengali title "*Dāpher prativād*" [A Reply to Duff], while the second was entitled, "Vaidantic Doctrines Vindicated." They first appeared in *Tattvabodhinī Patrikā*, nos. 14 and 19 (1845). They have been reprinted in Ghosh 1981.

12. See "Vaidantic Doctrines Vindicated," in Ghosh 1981: 107–108.

13. See the article "Vedantism, What is it?," in *Calcutta Review* 4/7 (1845), pp. 52–54.

14. Some have been prepared to go this route. For example, we find a nineteenth-century observer of modern religious thought, Goblet d'Alviella, saying of Emerson: "Some of his poetical productions and indeed of his prose dissertations on the eternal One, on the universal Spirit, of which Nature is simply the product and the symbol, and on the ineffable union of the individual soul with the universal or over-soul, suggest the latest philosophers of the Alexandrian school and even certain mystics of India" (Goblet d'Alviella 1885: 170).

15. That Müller was at one in this instinct with figures like Schopenhauer and Goethe is of course well known. Interestingly, in the 1870s Garcin de Tassy was keeping track, albeit in a scornful way, of the incidences of Europeans who were drawn to 'convert' to Hindu ideas and practices, including the case of an Englishman who became a yogī under the spiritual guidance of an Indian guru (see Goblet d'Alviella 1885: 308).

16. See the entry "Victor Cousin" in *Dictionnaire de biographie francaise*, edited by Roman D'Amat, vol. 9 (Paris: Librairie Letouzey et Ane, 1961), p. 1070.

17. As quoted in ibid.

18. See ibid. At one point Cousin refers to Hegel and Schelling as "my masters and my friends, and the leaders of the philosophy of the present age" (Cousin 1839: 93).

19. For a recent attempt to argue that Vivekananda was a syncretist, see Bryson 1992.

CHAPTER 6

1. While almost any English dictionary will tell you the most basic meaning of the word *homely* is 'pertaining to or characteristic of the home,' Americans don't typically use the adjective in this way. Instead, they use it to de-

scribe either something that is plain or unpretentious or else a person who is unfortunately, but not hopelessly, unattractive. In India, by contrast, the adjective is used in the sense of 'pertaining to the home.' It is also often used in offering a cordial greeting, such as, "Make yourself homely." (One might hear this when entering someone's home or read it on placards on the walls of retail establishments.) While Americans will perhaps balk at the idea of making themselves homely, Indians use this expression to convey a sincere wish—"make yourself at home."

2. As in Gandhi's influential tract from 1909, *Hind Swaraj, or Indian Home Rule*.

3. Smith is responding to the interpretation of resemblance favored by Asko Parpola (echoing the nineteenth-century Indologist Hermann Oldenberg) in his essay "On the Symbol Concept," in *Religious Symbols and Their Functions*, edited by H. Biezais (Stockholm: Almquist and Wiksell, 1979).

4. G. H. R. Tillotson has written amusingly of the so-called Indo-Saracenic style in British imperial architecture, a phrase he concedes is worth keeping if only because of its stupidity. He notes: "The phrase was originally adopted by scholars such as Fergusson to describe the country's Islamic architecture, which is generally characterized by a blend of Indian and Islamic design ideas. For this purpose, the term was poorly chosen, for the Islamic element in the buildings concerned is not strictly Saracenic: India's Muslim conquerors were not Arabs but Afghans and Central Asians who drew many of their cultural ideas from Persia. But given the nineteenth-century association of the Islamic with the Saracenic, the term was clear, even if inexact, in its application to the architecture of the Mughals and their predecessors. And it was just that architecture which the British Victorian architects supposed they were reviving; seeing no need to distinguish their revival from its models, they gave it the same name. In fact, the revived style was far from authentic, and its distinct character ought to have had a distinct term" (Tillotson 1989: 46).

5. See the passage from Baudrillard in Docherty (1993: 196), where his topic is not the Raj but contemporary cinema.

6. As a matter of fact, it was Curzon who began the practice of appointing British architects to the government of India. In yet another irony, it was this very policy that would bring Edwin Landseer Lutyens to India in 1912 to oversee the design of the new imperial capital in Delhi (see Meade 1988: 152).

7. For a brief exploration of how Baudrillard can be tied to Adorno, see McGowan (1991: 17–19).

8. This interpretation of postmodernism as symptomatic of the "unimageablity" of our complex world—associated with the likes of Frederic Jameson—has been creatively countered by Jim Collins in his book *Architectures of Excess* (1995: chap. 1).

9. The term *veranda* itself, which is now found in Hindi and Bengali, "ap-

pears to be an adoption of Pg. [Portuguese] and older Sp. [Spanish] *varanda, baranda*, 'railing, balustrade, balcony'" (see Lewis 1991: 244).

10. Interestingly enough, while the Englishman in India clung to his neoclassical moorings, during the same period builders in England began turning to Indian architectural styles as a way to capture what was for them the picturesque. One of the earliest and most notable examples of this selective appropriation of Indian motifs in English architecture is the famous Brighton Pavillion, which underwent successive Indianizing makeovers from 1803 to 1815 (Meade 1988: 146). Hybridity, which had to be borne as a necessary evil among British builders in India, could thus emerge as an exotic curiosity back home.

11. For a nineteenth-century Bengali evocation of the early days of British colonialism, with reference to men like Hindoo Stewart, see Bose 1976.

12. I want to thank Narasingha Sil for calling this incident to my attention.

13. I draw upon material included by Sudipto Chatterjee in his paper "Performing (Domi-)nation: Aspects of Nationalism in Nineteenth-century Bengali Theatre," which was presented at the Thirtieth Anniversary Bengal Studies Conference at the University of Chicago, on April 28, 1995.

14. The "folly" of the structure had been commented on by contemporary British critics (see Irving 1981: 170–174).

CHAPTER 7

1. That the bungalow can usefully be taken as a lens through which to view such a range of issues is suggested by Anthony D. King's encyclopedic work, in which he states: "What this study has assumed, though not systematically explored, is the emergence of a capitalist world economy *and* culture which has been responsible, at different times and in different places, for the development of the bungalow in its various guises. It has been concerned with the conditions which have produced the bungalow as a cultural phenomenon—as a term, as a form of dwelling and as a particular kind of urban settlement, economy and way of life" (1984: 259). As he notes, "The bungalow is both a product, and symbol, of a complex yet inter-related world" (263).

2. Despite Hope's stirring words, it would be twenty years before architects in England began to give attention to the role of eclecticism in their profession. The event that seems to have triggered things was, appropriately enough, a contest for the design of the Foreign Office building in London. The year was 1857, the fateful year of the Indian Mutiny—the last year of East India Company rule in India and the very dawn of Victoria's rule as empress of India.

3. This passage is taken from Stickley's 1907 essay "The California Bungalow: A Style of Architecture which Expresses the Individuality and Freedom Characteristic of our Western Coast."

4. One finds a near-perfect parallel to this logic of encompassment in Christian fulfillment theology, notably that of the early-twentieth-century theologian and scholar John Nicol Farquhar (see Halbfass 1988: 415–417). For Farquhar, as for Panikkar and Rahner after him, the revelation in Christ gathers up and fulfills all the partial and imperfect religions of the world.

5. There are those who argue that Rorty's neopragmatism fails to confront the contradiction between endorsing both the modernist idiom of private freedom (bourgeois individualism) and the postmodernist preference for forms of holism. John McGowan, for instance, has asked how "the private forging of an autonomous identity" can be expected to go hand in hand with the "communal act of creation" (1991: 194). I am sympathetic to McGowan's critique of Rorty's too-handy dichotomy between private and public, as well as to his goal of construing a more positive view of liberty that would allow the individual and the communal to interpenetrate (see McGowan 1991: 180–280). For my part, while I see no reason why the tension in Rorty's position between modernist and postmodernist idioms must necessarily amount to a form of confusion, neither am I prepared to grant no role to irony in the public task of creating community—even if that role is largely critical and unsettling.

6. Admittedly, there are those for whom the poet—or, shall we say, actor—in Vivekananda proves far too problematic (see Sil 1995). However, such critics may all too often be lured into the dangerous quest for that phantom, authenticity.

7. The original reads: *uttiṣṭhata jāgrata prāpya varān nibodhata*. It has been rendered by Hume as: "Arise ye! / Awake ye! / Obtain your boons and understand them!" (Hume 1931: 353). On Vivekananda's understanding of the relationship of this phrase to the larger context of Kaṭha Upaniṣad, see CW 3:318–320.

8. The subsequent development of Buddhist philosophy retains this sense of almost deconstructionist irony. See, for instance, Malcolm David Eckel's treatment of the Madhyamaka dialectic (1992: 44–48).

Bibliography

Ahmed, Akbar. 1992. *Postmodernism and Islam: Predicament and Promise*. London: Routledge.

Anderson, Benedict. 1991. *Imagined Communities: Reflections on the Origin and Spread of Nationalism*. Rev. ed. New York: Verso.

Applebaum, Stanley. 1980. *The Chicago World's Fair of 1893: A Photographic Record*. New York: Dover.

Badger, Reid. 1979. *The Great American Fair: The World's Columbian Exposition and American Culture*. Chicago: Nelson Hall.

Bailey, Greg. 1987. "On the Object of Study in Purāṇic Research: Three Recent Books on the Purāṇas." *Review of the Asian Studies Association of Australia* 10: 106–114.

Baird, Robert D. 1971. *Category Formation and the History of Religions*. The Hague: Mouton.

Bandyopādhyāy, Brajendranāth. 1972. "Rāmmohun Rāy." In *Sāhitya-sādhak-caritmālā*, no. 16, 6th ed. Calcutta: Baṅgīya Sāhitya Pariṣat.

Banerjee, Krishnamohan. 1845. "Transition States of the Hindu Mind." *Calcutta Review* 3: 102–147.

Banerjee, Sumanta. 1989. *The Parlour and the Streets: Elite and Popular Culture in Nineteenth Century Calcutta*. Calcutta: Seagull Books.

Bardhan, Kalpana, ed. 1990. *Of Women, Outcastes, Peasants, and Rebels: A Selection of Bengali Short Stories*. Berkeley: University of California Press.

Barrows, John Henry. 1893. *The World's Parliament of Religions*. 2 Vols. Chicago: Parliament Publishing.

Barry, John. N. d. *Calcutta Illustrated*. Calcutta: Central Press.

Baudelaire, Charles. 1968. *Oeuvres completes*. Edited by Marcel Ruff. Paris: Editions du seuil.

Baudrillard, Jean. 1983. *Simulations*. Translated by Paul Foss, Paul Patton, and Philip Beitchman. New York: Semiotexte.

Bauman, Zygmunt. 1993. *Postmodern Ethics*. Malden, Mass.: Basil Blackwell.

Baumer, Franklin L. 1977. *Modern European Thought*. New York: Macmillan.

Bayly, C. A. 1983. *Rulers, Townsmen and Bazaars: North Indian Society in the Age of British Expansion, 1770–1870*. New York: Cambridge University Press.

Beck, Lewis White, ed. 1963. *Kant on History*. Indianapolis: Bobbs-Merrill.

Bell, Daniel. 1996. *The Cultural Contradictions of Capitalism*. San Francisco: Basic Books.

Berman, Marshall. 1988. *All that is Solid Melts into Air: The Experience of Modernity*. New ed. New York: Penguin Books.

Bhabha, Homi K. 1985. "Signs Taken for Wonders: Questions of Ambivalence and Authority under a Tree outside Delhi, 1817." *Critical Inquiry* 12: 144–165.

Bharati, Agehananda. 1970. "The Hindu Renaissance and Its Apologetic Patterns." *Journal of Asian Studies* 39/2: 267–287.

Bhattacherje, M. M. 1944. "Keats and Spenser." Benares Hindu University Lectures. Calcutta: University of Calcutta.

Borgmann, Albert. 1992. *Crossing the Postmodern Divide*. Chicago: University of Chicago Press.

Bose, Nemai Sadhan. 1976. *Indian Awakening and Bengal*. 3rd rev. ed. Calcutta: Firma K. L. Mukhopadhyay.

Bose, Rajnarain. 1861. *Ekamevādvitīyaṃ: Brāhmo Samājer Vaktṛtā*. Calcutta: Brāhmo Samāj.

———. 1870. *The Adi Brahma Samaj: Its Views and Principles*. Calcutta: Adi Brahmo Samaj Press.

———. 1961. *Rājnārāyaṇ Basur ātmacarit*. Edited by Harihar Śeṭh. Calcutta: Orient Book.

———. 1966. *Who Is a Brahmo*? Translated by Satikumar Chatterjee. Simla: Himalaya Brahma Samaj.

———. 1976. Reprint. *Se kāl ār e kāl*. Edited by B. Bandyopādhyāy and S. K. Dās. Calcutta: Baṅgīya Sāhitya Pariṣat.

Bose, Ram Chandra. 1884. *Hindu Philosophy Popularly Explained: The Orthodox Systems*. New York: Funk and Wagnalls.

Braun, Lucien. 1973. *Histoire de l'histoire de la philosophie*. Paris: Editions Ophrys.

Brereton, Joel. 1990. "The Upanishads." In *Eastern Canons: Approaches to the Asian Classics*. Edited by Wm. Theodore de Bary and Irene Bloom. New York: Columbia University Press.

Bryson, Thomas L. 1991. "Calcutta and Cultural Convergence: Swami Vivekananda as Syncretist." In *Calcutta, Bangladesh, and Bengal Studies: 1990 Bengal Studies Conference Proceedings*. Edited by Clinton B. Seely. South Asia Series Occasional Paper No. 40. Lansing: Michigan State University.

———. 1992. "The Hermeneutics of Religious Syncretism: Swami Vivekananda's Practical Vedanta." Ph.D. diss., University of Chicago.

Burg, David F. 1976. *Chicago's White City of 1893*. Louisville: University Press of Kentucky.

Carman, John B. 1964. "Syncretism: Historical Phenomenon and Theological Judgment." *Andover-Newton Quarterly* 64/4: 30–43.

Carroll, John. 1993. *Humanism: The Wreck of Western Culture*. London: Fontana.

Chaliha, Jaya and Bunny Gupta. 1989. "Just a Museum Piece." *Taj Magazine* 18/2: 178–181.

Chatterjee, Partha. 1993. *The Nation and Its Fragments*. Princeton: Princeton University Press.

Coburn, Thomas. 1984. *Devī-Māhātmya: The Crystallization of the Goddess Tradition*. Delhi: Motilal Banarsidass.

Collins, Jim. 1995. *Architectures of Excess: Cultural Life in the Information Age*. New York: Routledge.

Collins, Peter. 1965. *Changing Ideals in Modern Architecture*. London: Faber and Faber.

Connor, Steven. 1990. *Postmodernist Culture: An Introduction to Theories of the Contemporary*. Malden, Mass.: Basil Blackwell.

Cort, John E. 1995. "Defining Jainism: Reform in the Jain Tradition," The 1994 Roop Lal Jain Lecture, Center for South Asian Studies, University of Toronto.

Cousin, Victor. 1839. *Philosophical Essays*. Translated by George Ripley. Edinburgh: Thomas Clark.

———. 1872. *Course of the History of Modern Philosophy*. Translated by O. W. Wright. Vol. 1. New York: Appleton.

Culler, Jonathan. 1982. *On Deconstruction: Theory and Criticism after Structuralism*. Ithaca, N.Y.: Cornell University Press.

Dahlmann, Joseph. 1899. *Das Mahābhārata als Epos und Rechtsbuch*. Berlin: F. L. Dames.

Dalton, Dennis. 1993. *Mahatma Gandhi: Non-violent Power in Action*. New York: Columbia University Press.

Damen, Frans L. 1893. *Crisis and Religious Renewal in the Brahmo Samaj (1860–1884)*. Louvain: Catholic University.

Datta, Akṣaykumār. 1987 Reprint. *Bhāratvarṣīya upāsak-saṃpradāy*. Pt. 1. Calcutta: Karuṇā Prakāśanī.

Dayal, Samir. 1992. "Talking Dirty." *College English* 54/4. 431–435.

Dillon, John M. 1988. "'Orthodoxy' and 'Eclecticism': Middle Platonists and Neo-Pythagoreans." In Dillon and Long 1988.

Dillon, John M., and A. A. Long, ed. 1988. *The Question of "Eclecticism": Studies in Later Greek Philosophy*. Hellenistic Culture and Society No. 3. Berkeley: University of California Press.

Dimmitt, Cornelia, and J. A. B. van Buitenen. 1978. *Classical Hindu Mythology: A Reader in the Sanskrit Puranas*. Philadelphia: Temple University Press.

Docherty, Thomas, ed. 1993. *Postmodernism: A Reader*. New York: Columbia University Press.

Donini, Pierluigi. 1988. "The History of the Concept of Eclecticism." In Dillon and Long 1988.

Duara, Prasenjit. 1995. *Rescuing History from the Nation: Questioning Narratives of Modern China*. Chicago: University of Chicago Press.

Duff, Alexander. 1988 Reprint. *India and India Missions*. Delhi: Swati Publications.

Dumont, Louis. 1980. *Homo Hierarchicus: The Caste System and Its Implications*. Rev. Eng. ed. Translated by Mark Sainsbury, Louis Dumont, and Basia Gulati. Chicago: University of Chicago Press.

Dutta, Krishna and Andrew Robinson, eds. 1992. *Noon in Calcutta*. New Delhi: Penguin Books.

Eck, Diana. 1985. *Darśan: Seeing the Divine Image in India*. 2d ed. Chambersburg: Anima.

Eckel, Malcolm David. 1992. *To See the Buddha: A Philosopher's Quest for the Meaning of Emptiness*. Princeton: Princeton University Press.

Emerson, Ralph Waldo. N.d. *The Works of Ralph Waldo Emerson*. Vol. 4. Library Society.

Faure, Bernard. 1993. *Chan Insights and Oversights: An Epistemological Critique of the Chan Tradition*. Princeton: Princeton University Press.

Fish, Stanley. 1989. "Commentary: The Young and the Restless." In Veeser 1989.

Flood, Gavin. 1996. *An Introduction to Hinduism*. Cambridge: Cambridge University Press.

Foster, Hal. Editor. 1983. *The Anti-Aesthetic: Essays on Postmodern Culture*. Port Townsend, Wash.: Bay Press.

Foucault, Michel. 1973. *The Order of Things: An Archaeology of the Human Sciences*. Translation of *Les mots et les choses*. New York: Vintage.

Gandhi, M. K. 1962. *All Religions Are True*. Edited by Anand T. Hingorani. Bombay: Bharatiya Vidya Bhavan.

Ghosh, Benoy, ed. 1978. *Selections from English Periodicals of 19th Century Bengal*. Vol. 7. Calcutta: Papyrus.

———, ed. 1981 Reprint. *Sāmayikpatre Bāṃlār samājcitra*. Pt. 5. Calcutta: Papyrus.

Goblet d'Alviella, Eugene Felicien Albert, Comte. 1885. *The Contemporary Evolution of Religious Thought in England, America and India*. Translated by Jacques Moden. London: Williams and Norgate.

Götz, Wolfgang. 1970. "Historismus: Ein Versuch zur Definition des Begriffs." *Zeitschrift des deutschen Vereins für Kunstwissenschaft* 24/1–4: 196–212.

Gupta, Kṣetra. 1967. *Madhusūdan racanāvalī*. Calcutta: Sāhitya Saṃsad.

Habermas, Jürgen. 1982. "The Entwinement of Myth and Enlightenment: Rereading *Dialectic of Enlightenment*." *New German Critique* 26: 13–30.

———. 1983. "Modernity—An Incomplete Project." In Foster 1983.

Hacker, Paul. 1978. "Aspects of Neo-Hinduism as Contrasted with Surviving Traditional Hinduism." In *Kleine Schriften*. Edited by L. Schmithausen. Wiesbaden: Franz Steiner Verlag.

———. 1983. "Inklusivismus." In *Inklusivismus: Eine indische Denkform*. Edited by Gerhard Oberhammer. Vienna: University of Vienna.

Halbfass, Wilhelm. 1988. *India and Europe: An Essay in Understanding*. Albany: State University of New York Press.

Harvey, David. 1989. *The Condition of Postmodernity: An Inquiry into the Origins of Cultural Change*. Malden, Mass.: Basil Blackwell.

Hassan, Ihab. 1985. "The Culture of Postmodernism." *Theory, Culture and Society* 2/3: 119–131.

Hatcher, Brian A. 1994. "'The Cosmos Is One Family' (*vasudhaiva kuṭumbakam*): Problematic Mantra of Hindu Humanism." *Contributions to Indian Sociology* 28/1: 149–162.

———. 1996. *Idioms of Improvement: Vidyāsāgar and Cultural Encounter in Bengal*. Calcutta: Oxford University Press.

Hegel, G. W. F. 1955. *Hegel's Lectures on the History of Philosophy*. 3 vols. Translated by E. S. Haldane and Frances H. Simson. London: Routledge and Kegan Paul.

Heesterman, J. C. 1985. *The Inner Conflict of Tradition*. Chicago: University of Chicago Press.

———. 1991. "Hinduism and Vedic Ritual." *History of Religions* 30/3: 296–305.

———. 1993. *The Broken World of Sacrifice: An Essay in Ancient Indian Ritual*. Chicago: University of Chicago Press.

Hodder, Alan. 1988. "Emerson, Rammohun Roy, and the Unitarians." *Studies in the American Renaissance*. 133–148.

Holzhey, Helmut. 1983. "Philosophie als Eklektik," *Studia Leibnitiana*. 15/1: 19–29.

Horkheimer, Max, and Theodor Adorno. 1972. *The Dialectic of the Enlightenment*. Translated by John Cumming. New York: Seabury Press.

Hume, R. E., trans. 1931. *The Thirteen Principal Upanishads*. 2d rev. ed. New York: Oxford University Press.

Hutchison, William R. 1976. *The Modernist Impulse in American Protestantism*. Cambridge: Harvard University Press.

Huyssen, Andreas. 1984. "Mapping the Postmodern." *New German Critique* 33: 5–52.

Inden, Ronald. 1990. *Imagining India*. Malden, Mass.: Basil Blackwell.

Irving, Robert Grant. 1981. *Indian Summer: Lutyens, Baker and Imperial Delhi*. New Haven: Yale University Press.

James, William. 1961. *The Varieties of Religious Experience*. New York: Collier Books.

Jameson, Frederic. 1983. "Postmodernism and Consumer Society." In Foster 1983.

———. 1984. "Postmodernism, or the Cultural Logic of Late Capitalism." *New Left Review* 146: 53–92.

Jay, Martin. 1984. *Adorno*. Cambridge: Harvard University Press.

Jefferson, Thomas. 1989. *The Jefferson Bible*. Boston: Beacon Press.

Keith, A. B. 1976. Reprint. *The Religion and Philosophy of the Veda and Upanishads*. Delhi: Motilal Banarsidass.

Kidney, Walter C. 1974. *The Architecture of Choice: Eclecticism in America, 1880–1930*. New York: George Braziller.

King, Anthony D. 1984. *The Bungalow: The Production of a Global Culture*. London: Routledge and Kegan Paul.

Kitagawa, J. M. 1990. *Religion in Japanese History*. New York: Columbia University Press.

Klostermaier, Klaus K. 1994. *A Survey of Hinduism*. 2d ed. Albany: State University of New York Press.

Kopf, David. 1969. *British Orientalism and the Bengal Renaissance*. Berkeley: University of California Press.

———. 1979. *The Brahmo Samaj and the Shaping of the Modern Indian Mind*. Princeton: Princeton University Press.

Lattin, Don. 1993. "Religion a la carte." *Grand Rapids Press* (Saturday, July 31).

Levin, Miriam R. 1986. *Republican Art and Ideology in Late-Nineteenth Century France*. Ann Arbor: UMI Research Press.

Lévi-Strauss, Claude. 1966. *The Savage Mind*. Chicago: University of Chicago Press.

Lewis, C. S. 1964. *The Discarded Image: An Introduction to Medieval and Renaissance Literature*. Cambridge: Cambridge University Press.

Lewis, Ivor. 1991. *Sahibs, Nabobs and Boxwallahs: A Dictionary of the Words of Anglo-India*. Bombay: Oxford University Press.

The Life of Swami Vivekananda by His Eastern and Western Disciples. 1989. 2 vols. 6th ed. Calcutta: Advaita Ashrama.

Long, James. 1848. *Hand-book of Bengal Missions*. London: John Farquhar Shaw.

MacAdam, Barbara. 1991. "'Inspired Eclecticism' or 'Post-Modernist Joke'?" *ARTnews* (September): 20.

Madan, T. N. 1987. *Non-Renunciation: Themes and Interpretations of Hindu Culture*. Delhi: Oxford University Press.

Mason, John Hope, ed. 1982. *The Irresistible Diderot*. New York: Quartet Books.

McGowan, John. 1991. *Postmodernism and Its Critics*. Ithaca, N.Y.: Cornell University Press.

Meade, Martin. 1988. "The Anglo-Indian Bungalow." *Puruṣārtha* 11: 133–157.

Michel, Petra. 1984. *Christian Wilhelm Ernst Dietrich (1712–1774) und die Problematik des Eklektizismus*. Munich: Mäander.

Mill, John Stuart. 1963. *The Earlier Letters of John Stuart Mill, 1812–1848*. Edited by Francis E. Mineka. Toronto: University of Toronto Press.

———. 1981. *Autobiography and Literary Essays*. Edited by John M. Robson and Jack Stillinger. Toronto: University of Toronto Press.

Miller, Barbara Stoler, trans. 1986. *The Bhagavad-Gita: Krishna's Counsel in Time of War*. New York: Bantam Books.

Moorhouse, Geoffrey. 1986. Reprint. *Calcutta: The City Revealed*. New York: Penguin.

Nandy, Ashis. 1983. *The Intimate Enemy: Loss and Recovery of Self under Colonialism*. Delhi: Oxford University Press.

Neevel, Walter G. 1976. "The Transformation of Sri Ramakrishna." In *Hinduism: New Essays in the History of Religions*. Edited by Bardwell L. Smith. Leiden: E. J. Brill. 53–97.

Nehamas, Alexander. 1985. *Nietzsche: Life as Literature*. Cambridge, Mass.: Harvard University Press.

Newton, Judith Lowder. 1989. "History as Usual? Feminism and the 'New Historicism.'" In Veeser 1989.

O'Flaherty, Wendy D. 1980. *Women, Androgynes, and Other Mythical Beasts*. Chicago: University of Chicago Press.

———. 1984. *Dreams, Illusion, and Other Realities*. Chicago: University of Chicago Press.

———. 1988. *Other People's Myths: The Cave of Echoes*. New York: Macmillan.

Ondaatje, Michael. 1993. *Running in the Family*. New York: Vintage Books.

Otto, Rudolf. 1934. *Die Urgestalt der Bhagavadgītā*. Tübingen: Mohr.

Panikkar, Raimundo. 1975. "Some Notes on Syncretism and Eclecticism Related to the Growth of Human Consciousness." In *Religious Syncretism in Antiquity: Essays in Conversation with Geo. Widengren*. Edited by Birger A. Pearson. Missoula, Mont.: Scholars Press.

Porphyrios, Demetri. 1982. *Sources of Modern Eclecticism: Studies on Alvar Aalto*. London: Academy Editions.

Portoghesi, Paolo. 1983. *Postmodern: The Architecture of the Postindustrial Society*. New York: Rizzoli.

Prabhavananda, Swami. 1964. *The Sermon on the Mount according to Advaita Vedanta*. London: George Allen and Unwin.

Proust, Marcel. 1982. *Remembrance of Things Past*. Vol. 1: *Swann's Way / Within a Budding Grove*. Translated by C. K. Scott Moncrieff and Terence Kilmartin. New York: Vintage Books.

Radhakrishnan, Sarvepalli. 1970. *Radhakrishnan: Selected Writings on Philosophy, Religion, and Culture*. Edited by Robert A. McDermott. New York: E. P. Dutton.

———. 1988 Reprint. *The Hindu View of Life*. London: Unwin Paperbacks.

Ramakrishna, Sri. 1988. *Śrīśrīrāmkṛṣṇakathāmṛta*. Compiled by Śrī M. Calcutta: A. K. Gupta.

Rambachan, Anantanand. 1991. *Accomplishing the Accomplished: The Vedas as a Source of Valid Knowledge in Śaṅkara*. Honolulu: University of Hawaii Press.

———. 1994. *The Limits of Scripture: Vivekananda's Reinterpretation of the Vedas*. Honolulu: University of Hawaii Press.

Raychaudhuri, Tapan. 1988. *Europe Reconsidered*. New Delhi: Oxford University Press.

Reader, Ian. 1991. *Religion in Contemporary Japan*. Honolulu: University of Hawaii Press.

Richardson, Robert D. 1995. *Emerson: The Mind on Fire*. Berkeley: University of California Press.

Rolland, Romain. 1970. *The Life of Ramakrishna*. Calcutta: Advaita Ashrama.

Rorty, Richard. 1985. "Habermas and Lyotard on Postmodernity." In *Habermas and Modernity*. Edited by Richard J. Bernstein. Cambridge: MIT Press.

———. 1989. *Contingency, Irony, and Solidarity*. New York: Cambridge University Press.

Rose, Margaret A. 1991. "Post-Modern Pastische." *British Journal of Aesthetics* 31/1: 26–38.

Roy, Rammohun. 1906. *The English Works of Raja Rammohun Roy*. Allahabad: Panini Office.

Rushdie, Salman. 1981. *Midnight's Children*. New York: Alfred A. Knopf.

———. 1989. *Satanic Verses*. New York: Viking.

———. 1991. *Imaginary Homelands: Essays and Criticism 1981–1991*. New York: Viking.

Rusk, Ralph L., ed. 1966. *The Letters of Ralph Waldo Emerson*. Vol. 1. New York: Columbia University Press.

Ryan, Judith. 1990. "The Problem of Pastiche: Patrick Suskind's *Das Parfum*." *German Quarterly* 63/3–4: 396–403.

Rydell, Robert. 1984. *All the World's a Fair: Vision of Empire at American International Expositions, 1876–1916*. Chicago: University of Chicago Press.

Said, Edward W. 1978. *Orientalism*. New York: Random House.

Sarkar, Sumit. 1985. "The Complexities of Young Bengal." In *A Critique of Colonial India*. Calcutta: Papyrus. 18–36.

Sastri, Sibnath. 1983. Reprint. *Rāmtanu Lāhiḍī o tatkālīn baṅgasamāj*. Calcutta: New Age Publishers.

Seager, Richard Hughes. 1995. *The World's Parliament of Religions: The East/West Encounter, Chicago, 1893*. Bloomington: Indiana University Press.

Sekida, Katsuki. 1975. *Zen Training: Methods and Philosophy*. Edited by A. V. Grimstone. New York: Weatherhill.

Sen, Keshub Chunder. N.d.. *Jīvan veda*. Calcutta: Navavidhan Publication Committee.

———. 1940. *Life and Works of Brahmananda Keshav*. Compiled by Prem Sundar Basu. 2d ed. Calcutta: Navavidhan Publication Committee.

Sharpe, Eric. 1975. *Comparative Religion: A History*. New York: Scribner's.

Sil, Narasingha P. 1995. "Swami Vivekananda in the West: The Legend Reinterpreted." *South Asia* 18/1: 1–53.

Smith, Brian K. 1989. *Reflections on Resemblance, Ritual, and Religion*. New York: Oxford University Press.

———. 1994. *Classifying the Universe: The Ancient Indian Varna System and the Origins of Caste*. New York: Oxford University Press.

Smith, Jonathan Z., ed. 1995. *The HarperCollins Dictionary of Religion*. San Francisco: HarperSanFrancisco.

Steinfels, Peter. 1993. "World Religions Endorse Common Paths of Peace." *New York Times* (Sunday, September 5).

Stickley, Gustav. 1988. Reprint. *Craftsman Bungalows: 59 Homes from* The Craftsman. Edited and with a new introduction by Alan Weissman. New York: Dover.

Sturrock, John. 1979. *Structuralism and Since: From Lévi-Strauss to Derrida*. New York: Oxford University Press.

Tagore, Debendranath. 1953 Reprint. *Brāhmasamājer pañcaviṃśati vatsarer parīkṣita vṛttānta*. Calcutta: Sādhāraṇ Brāhmo Samāj.

———. 1975. Reprint. *Brāhma Dharmaḥ*. Calcutta: Sādhāraṇ Brāhmo Samāj.

Taylor, Mark C. 1984. *Erring: A Postmodern A/theology*. Chicago: University of Chicago Press.

———. 1992. *Disfiguring: Art, Architecture, Religion*. Chicago: University of Chicago Press.

Thite, Ganesh Umakant. 1975. *Sacrifice in the Brāhmaṇa-Texts*. Poona: University of Poona.

Thomas, M. M. 1969. *The Acknowledged Christ of the Indian Renaissance*. London: SCM Press.

Tillotson, G. H. R. 1989. *The Tradition of Indian Architecture*. New Haven: Yale University Press.

———. 1995. "Architecture and Anxiety: The Problem of Pastiche in Recent Indian Design." *South Asia Research* 15/1: 30–47.

Toolan, David S. 1993. "Chicago's Parliament of the World's Religions." *America* (September 25).

Tuck, Andrew P. 1990. *Comparative Philosophy and the Philosophy of Scholarship: On the Western Interpretation of Nāgārjuna*. New York: Oxford University Press.

Turner, Bryan S. 1990. "Periodization and Politics in the Postmodern." In *Theories of Modernity and Postmodernity*. Edited by Bryan S. Turner. London: Sage.

Vaughn, Philippa, ed. 1997. *The Victoria Memorial Hall: Conceptions, Collections, Conservation*. Mumbai: Marg.

Veeser, H. Aram, ed. 1989. *The New Historicism*. New York: Routledge.

Vivekananda, Swami. 1985. *The Complete Works of Swami Vivekananda*. 8 vols. Calcutta: Advaita Ashrama.

White, Hayden. 1973. *Metahistory: The Historical Imagination in Nineteenth-century Europe*. Baltimore: Johns Hopkins University Press.

Winternitz, Maurice. 1987. Reprint. *A History of Indian Literature*. Vol. 1. Translated by V. Srinivasa Sarma. Delhi: Motilal Banarsidass.

Witzel, Michael. 1987. "On the Origin of the Literary Device of the 'Frame Story' in Old Indian Literature." In *Hinduismus und Buddhismus*. Edited by Harry Falk. Freiburg: Hedwig Falk.

Wolin, Richard. 1985. "Modernism vs. Postmodernism." *Telos* 62: 9–29.

———. 1994. "Antihumanism in the Discourse of French Postwar Theory." *Common Knowledge* 3: 60–90.

Wyschogrod, Edith. 1990. *Saints and Postmodernism: Revisioning Moral Philosophy*. Chicago: University of Chicago Press.

Zeller, Eduard. 1883. *A History of Eclecticism in Greek Philosophy*. Translated by S. F. Alleyne. London: Longmans, Green.

Ziolkowski, Eric J., ed. 1993. *A Museum of Faiths: Histories and Legacies of the 1893 World's Parliament of Religions*. Atlanta: Scholars Press.

Index